C.L.R. JAMES
and the
21ST CENTURY CARIBBEAN

C.L.R. JAMES
and the
21ST CENTURY CARIBBEAN

Tennyson S. D. Joseph

The University of the West Indies Press

Mona • St Augustine • Cave Hill • Global • Five Islands

The University of the West Indies Press
7A Gibraltar Hall Road, Mona
Kingston 7, Jamaica
www.uwipress.com

A catalogue record of this book is available from the National
Library of Jamaica.

ISBN: 978-976-640-940-1 (print)
ISBN: 978-976-640-944-9 (epub)

Cover Image © Neil Paul used with permission of the artist
Cover and text design by Christina Moore Fuller
Printed in the United States of America

DEDICATION

This work is dedicated to the memory of C.L.R. James, Walter Rodney, Bob Marley, Maurice Bishop, George Odlum, George Lamming, Tim Hector, and to all the unnamed martyrs whose blood, sweat and tears have flowed in the struggle for Caribbean freedom. May their sacrifices not be in vain.

CONTENTS

Preface

This work represents the coming to life of a research effort which had remained dormant and hidden from wider circulation for more than two decades. It was written in 1994 in fulfillment of the MPhil degree in Political Science at the University of the West Indies, and since its completion, has been available only to users of that University's libraries. The positive reviews on the work from the small circle of students and colleagues who have read it, have always been a nagging stimulant fueling the drive to make it available to a wider public.

The application here of the "public" pertains, above all else, to persons actively engaged in political activism on behalf of classes and nations suffering marginalization and exploitation in the context of the domination of global capital. Much of James's intellectual effort was spent on picking out the small seeds of liberation possibilities from "what is happening everyday" (James Forrest and Stone 1972), or, in other words, in identifying "the future in the present" (James 1977a). Today, given the far more hegemonic nature of global capitalism and the relatively barren landscape which characterizes revolutionary possibilities, it is even more important that academics continue the Jamesian tradition of allowing their intellectual curiosity to be guided more directly by the needs of revolutionary activists in the field. It is only in this sense that thought truly becomes action.

Given the nearly thirty-year time lag between its completion for certification and its submission for publication, there was need for major updating of the sections pertinent to the politics of the contemporary Caribbean, the global politico-economic environment, the fate of global Marxism and the nature and possibilities for revolution in the twenty-first century. In addition, in the last fifteen years, there has been a large body of publications on and around C.L.R. James, which needed to be engaged as part of the process of clarifying the continuing relevance of his ideas. This process of updating the work has not only helped to demonstrate and confirm the utility and timelessness of James's ideas, but more importantly it has assisted in capturing the critical features of contemporary Caribbean politics insofar as they relate to the potentialities of revolutionary organization in the era of globalization.

This work seeks therefore to make a concrete contribution to Caribbean political thought. Presently, much of the effort at the conscious chronicling of Caribbean thought has been pre-occupied with "making a case" or justifying the existence and validity of such thought, particularly in the face of classic Western notions of what constitutes true philosophy. While such an undertaking is necessary particularly considering the relatively recent nature of this intellectual enterprise (post-1970s) for the Caribbean, the second stage of the process involves the concrete demonstration of the validity of the intellectual output of Caribbean intellectuals to existing political reality. Indeed, the tendency to characterize Caribbean thought as "a series of extended debates over projects of colonial domination" (to use Paget Henry's (2000) troublesome phrase), conveys the impression of permanently locking the Caribbean into the unfortunate posture of a "respondent" to Europe (see Joseph 2015a, 47). The aim of this work therefore, is to move beyond this epistemological debate, and to apply the thought of C.L.R. James, to concrete political contexts. Such an exercise, in my view is equally important in making a case for the validity of the thought, since its validation springs from its demonstrated relevance. Such an effort also adds to the durability of the thought, since it is applied to a new context, and to new situations and challenges, very different from the one for which it was initially conceptualized.

It is a book which I hope will be valuable to all students of Caribbean political thought, all persons curious about C.L.R. James, everyone interested in Marxist thought, and to all intellectuals and activists searching for ideas to assist in the advancement of revolutionary change beyond what was seen as possible in the communist revolutions in the early twentieth century and since the collapse of European Communism in the early 1990s.

Acknowledgements

This work is the result of a collective effort, spread over several years. It was first begun in fulfillment of the requirement of the Master of Philosophy in Political Science at the University of the West Indies between 1992 and 1994. As such, principal thanks first and foremost, must go to UWI whose post-graduate scholarship made this study possible.

While UWI offered the scholarship, I would not have been able to accept the offer had it not been for the support, encouragement and understanding of my late father Peter Joseph and my mother Chriselda Joseph, whose reflexive instincts were always tuned to allowing me to maximize my academic potential. It is not without spiritual significance that my father ended his earthly sojourn in the very year (2009), when I recommitted myself to transforming the MPhil thesis into a book. Like the biblical Moses he took me to the Promised Land but never held the fruits thereof in his hand.

In the production of this work my parents provided financial space and psychological support, but the intellectual spur which "pricked the sides of my intent" was provided by Dr George Belle, former Dean of the Faculty of Social Sciences at UWI, Cave Hill Campus. His inspiring lecture, '*The Collapse of the Soviet System: Implications for the Caribbean Left*' (Belle 1994) provided the cement which glued the loose and unformed elements of my embryonic ideas into a more solid and coherent study. His lecture also brought C.L.R. James to life for me and my miserable "postmodern" generation whose period of political maturation, has been marked above all else by political defeat and reversal and by the death and "demise" of great ideas. His lecture started for me a quest to familiarize myself with the thought of C.LR. James, and its relevance to the Caribbean. Special thanks also to Professor Neville Duncan, who, along with George Belle provided advice and guidance on the work in their capacity as thesis supervisors.

This study of C.L.R. James would not have been possible had I not been afforded the opportunity for formal and informal contact, (some brief and passing, others enduring), with key Caribbean persons involved in the study of Caribbean political thought. Hilary Beckles, Paget Henry, Rupert Lewis, Anthony Bogues, Brian Meeks, Horace Campbell, Hilbourne Watson, Christian Høgsbjerg, Rodney Worrell, Frederick Ochieng-Odhiambo, Aaron Kamugisha, Maziki Thame, Selwyn Cudjoe, Glen Richards, and the recently deceased Charles Mills deserve special thanks for their contributions to my own intellectual development and understanding of the significance of C.L.R. James as a Caribbean thinker.

I owe a debt of gratitude to Dr Ayodele Harper, who, in her earlier capacity as a research assistant in the Department of Government at Cave Hill, was responsible for chasing down precious documents from the C.L.R. James Institute online depository, to the manuscript reviewers for their helpful criticism and to Althea Brown and Christine Randle of the UWI Press for their patience and guidance as we worked through the various stages, from submission of manuscript to final publication.

I also owe respect and gratitude to the department of political science of North Carolina Central University for allowing me to teach a course on the political thought of C.L.R. James to a class of attentive undergraduate students in the Fall term of 2023. Teaching the course has helped to sharpen many of the ideas and claims of this book.

Finally, I must thank my wife, Fiona, and my daughters, Nzingha and Choiselle, for their tolerance.

Acronyms and Abbreviations

ALP	Antigua Labour Party
BLM	Black Lives Matter Movement
BREXIT	British Exit from European Union
BSC	Banana Salvation Committee
CARICOM	Caribbean Community
CPUSA	Communist Party of the USA
DSH	Desert Star Holdings
GM	General Motors Corporation
G7	Group of Seven
IBAR	Institute of Black Atlantic Research
IMF	International Monetary Fund
IMT	International Marxist Tendency
JEWEL	Joint Endeavour for Welfare and Educational Liberation
LKP	Lyannag Kont Pwofitasyon (Alliance Against Profiteering)
MACE	Movement for the Advancement of Community Effort
MAI	Multilateral Agreement on Investments
MAP	Movement for the Assemblies of the People
NATO	North Atlantic Treaty Organization
NBM	New Beginning Movement
NJAC	National Joint Action Coordinating Committee
NJM	New Jewel Movement

OAS	Organization of American States
OECD	Organisation for Economic Cooperation and Development
OWTU	Oilfields Workers' Trade Union
PNC	People's National Congress
PNM	People's National Movement
PNP	People's Nationalist Party
PRG	People's Revolutionary Government
PPP	People's Progressive Party
PPP	People's Political Party (St Vincent and the Grenadines)
SLBGA	Saint Lucia Banana Growers' Association
SLP	Saint Lucia Labour Party
SVLP	Saint Vincent Labour Party
UCLAN	University of Central Lancashire
UNIA	Universal Negro Improvement Association
USSR	Union of Soviet Socialist Republics (Soviet Union)
UWI	The University of the West Indies
WFP	Workers and Farmers Party
WPJ	Workers Party of Jamaica

1.
Introduction

The whole world today lives in the shadow of state power. This state power is an ever-present self-perpetuating body over and above society. It transforms the human personality into a mass of economic needs to be satisfied by decimal points of economic progress. It robs everyone of initiative and clogs the free development of society. This state power, by whatever name it is called, One-Party State or Welfare State, destroys all pretense of government **by** the people, **of** the people. All that remains is government **for** the people. Against this monster, people all over the world, and particularly ordinary working people in factories, mines, fields and offices, are rebelling every day in ways of their own invention. Sometimes their struggles are on a small political scale. More effectively, they are actions of groups, formal or informal, but always unofficial, organized around their work and their place of work. Always the aim is to regain control over their own conditions of life and their relations with one another. Their strivings, their struggles, their methods have few chroniclers. They themselves are constantly attempting various forms of organization, uncertain of where the struggle is going to end. Nevertheless, they are imbued with one fundamental certainty, that they have to destroy the continuously mounting bureaucratic mass or be themselves destroyed by it.

C.L.R. James, Grace Lee and Pierre Chaulieu – *Facing Reality*

The Intellectual and Political Context for a Study of C.L.R. James in the 21st Century

This work proposes a contemporary (twenty-first century) treatment and application of the political ideas of Caribbean Marxist and Pan-Africanist intellectual, C.L.R. James to the politics of the Caribbean. Its main aim is to examine the applicability of his central ideas on the nature of revolutionary activity beyond Leninism and Stalinism to the politics of the twenty-first century world in which the Caribbean is immersed. As such, the work seeks to move beyond a mere description and discussion of the main ideas of C.L.R. James and seeks to apply his ideas to contemporary global and Caribbean political developments.

There have been significant transformations in Caribbean political life since James's most impactful political ideas were formulated in the 1950s and since his passing in 1989. In the mid-1990s, the formative conditions of globalization and neo-liberalism which now dominate the politics of the Caribbean were still processes in early formation. At that time, the capitalist world was freshly abuzz with the euphoria of the collapse of the Soviet Union, and Western intellectuals had made a virtual industry of writing the epitaphs of Marxism. A coherent, intellectually sound, radical counterargument to the dominant Western analyses of these events was slow in emerging, and the mood was bleak for Marxist intellectuals. In this context, Francis Fukuyama's triumphant "end of history" gloat was both reflective of the general mood and contributory to it (Fukuyama 1992). At that time too, the intellectual assumptions of global neo-liberalism as the ideological handmaiden to the objective realities of globalization were on the ascendancy, and politicians and their technocrats were busy adjusting their domestic spaces to reflect these new realities.

In the Caribbean, these developments assisted in frustrating the possibilities of independence and sovereignty that had been pursued in the 1950s, 1960s, and 1970s. Having in effect witnessed the retreat of the Caribbean left following the collapse of the Grenada revolution, the road was open for the unbridled adoption of neo-liberal adjustment. With the end of the Cold War, the Caribbean region suffered a "downgrading" of its strategic importance to US and North-Atlantic capital and the immediate result was a loss of economic support for the region's development objectives. In Europe, the emphasis on adjustment for global competition had meant that the post-colonial protectionist regimes for primary products like sugar and bananas were being dismantled, as the region's principal colonial power Britain, formalized its inclusion in the European Union. The common cry at the time, from the historically dependent cadre of Caribbean leaders, was that for the first time since independence, the Caribbean was truly on its own.

Given C.L.R. James's concerns with the rethinking of analytical categories, and with the creative application of the Marxist dialectic to contemporary issues faced by each new generation, his ideas remain undoubtedly critical particularly in a context where the old modes of thinking and organizing by the left, have come into question.

The main concern of this book therefore, is to utilize James's thought as an analytical tool to account for the major features of Caribbean political developments in the first three decades of the twenty-first century, specifically Caribbean anti-systemic activity, in their relation to the wider global setting. My focus is on the implications of James's ideas for Marxist thought, Caribbean anti-colonial thought, and for the organizational tactics of radical, anti-capitalist movements in the twenty-first century. It is worth highlighting that most of James's major works (1937, 1980a, 1986b; and James, Lee and Chaulieu [1958] 1974), were concerned with transformations occurring in the advanced capitalist countries in the middle of the twentieth century. This has led to a general claim that James's Marxist theories are more applicable to the advanced capitalist countries than to the Caribbean, and that James, for example, did not believe the schisms within Marxism "(not even his own New Left perspectives) to be relevant to the needs of Trinidad in the 1950s and early 1960s, except in a very indirect manner" (Lai 1992, 179). This work in contrast, presents a wholly different view on the question of the applicability of James's major Marxist theoretical works to the Caribbean. It deliberately shows how twenty-first century developments in the Caribbean, fit within the perspectives that James was presenting on the general movement of the workers' movement from vanguardism to self-activity, which in themselves, were linked to wider changes within capitalism.

Paul Buhle (1988, 172) writing in the late 1980s noted that "a Jamesian politics, for the end of the twentieth century and beginning of a new millennium, would surely begin with the wholesale changes wrought in world politics and the world economy since James effected his fullest theoretical 'system' roughly forty years ago". It is such a framework which animates this present study. There have been unprecedented levels of technological, political, and economic transformation in the world since the late 1990s. There is thus a need to examine and discuss the applicability of James's ideas to the developing countries of the Caribbean in light of these transformations. One of my major assumptions is that whereas the thought of James was expressed at the level of the *Idea* in the mid-twentieth century, the period of the late twentieth and early twenty-first centuries represents the stage of *Actuality* of James's thought (James 1980a). Thus, I argue that James's insistence that Leninist and particularly Stalinist modes of organization would be transcended and replaced by greater levels of autonomous and self-directed proletarian activity, can be seen concretely in the emergence of mass popular movements like Occupy Wall Street, the *gilets jaunes* in France, the Fees Must Fall movement among South African students and the Me Too and Black Lives Matter movements, and in related Caribbean expressions of similar-type movements. By studying the actual and concrete expressions of radical activity in the early twenty-first century, thirty to forty years after the collapse of European

Marxism, the relevance of James's thought to the analysis of contemporary Caribbean and global political developments, can be made concrete. In short, the current work is undertaken in support of the assertion that "the story of C.L.R. James will look different, more complete and more understandable from the mid twenty-first century than from today's perspective" (Hector 2000, 127).

One of the more valuable aspects of James's thought was his insistence on the need to dialectically alter analytical categories to correspond with material changes in phenomenon being studied (James 1980a). Indeed, James's thought, leaning heavily on Hegel, is a brilliant exposition and demonstration of how such shifts in analytical categories can be undertaken. A major premise of this study therefore, is that the world, since the 1990s, has been experiencing a state of qualitative transformation at the material level of technological production of quantum leap proportions rendering the old categories of analysis largely in need of rethinking and fresh application (Toffler 1981, [1970] 1990, 1991; Boggs 1968; Thomas 1989; Watson 1990a). James's active analysis roughly ends with the crisis of the 1970s and the end of welfare state capitalism in the West. It is necessary therefore to apply his analytical method to the post-1990 modes of existence and internal contradictions of capitalism, inclusive of its advances and reversals, and its state-capitalist expressions as seen in the case of China. Equally important, is the need to apply the Jamesian analysis to capitalism under the ideology and practice of neo-liberalism and globalization.

Indeed, the reversals in the ideological smugness and self-confidence of global neo-liberalism with the onset of the "great recession" of 2008/2009, coupled with internal crisis associated with the COVID-19 shut-down of global capitalism in 2020/21, and the rise of right-wing fascism in the USA, compounded by the Black Lives Matter and related social revolts, suggest a potential collapse of capitalism mirroring the impact which these global shifts had on European communism in the late twentieth century.

In this context of collapse and reversal of erstwhile dominant ideologies and perspectives, not only the "what" and "why" of James, but also his example in transforming analytical categories, both in theory and in practice, become critically important. By identifying how James developed and applied his method, and by explaining and clarifying that method itself, I hope to show how James's ideas assisted in advancing anti-systemic thought and action.

This work is nevertheless *not* a study of James's life. It is a study of his political ideas, his method of analysis and its relevance to the twenty-first century Caribbean. More specifically, it is a study of the application of James's ideas to radical political organization and revolutionary, anti-capitalist activity in the twenty-first century. However, in identifying, explaining, and clarifying James's thought, it will be necessary to locate these ideas in specific historical moments and lived experiences in which James was engaged, which might have impacted upon his thinking.

The application of the ideas of C.L.R. James to the politics of the twenty-first century Caribbean, cannot be undertaken without a thorough understanding of the philosophical basis which underpins his thought, and the way he built on the philosophical outlook which he inherited. Relatedly, in the study of James's thought and its application to the Caribbean, it is also necessary to defend the validity of his analytical method, which was primarily a modified form of the Hegelian-Marxist dialectic. This latter consideration is of extreme importance given the close association of the dialectical method with the crisis of actually-existing socialism. Thus, understanding the specific way James used and applied the dialectical method to the issues of the mid-to-late twentieth century, is of critical importance in clarifying the relevance of his thought to the questions of the twenty-first century Caribbean. It is also necessary as well in rescuing Marxism from its post-USSR trauma, particularly the brand which was wedded to the Russian experience and which remained largely oblivious to alternative Marxist schools, such as those with which James himself was associated.

While studying the applicability of James's perspective to radical politics in the twenty-first century, his contribution to Marxist theory must be understood. This contribution was shaped firstly through his conscious and deliberate attempt to "fine tune" Marxism to enhance its utility as a tool for analysis, accounting for transformations occurring in the capitalist world economy and providing useful guidelines and signposts for identifying new and emerging contradictions. In doing so, James sought to rescue Marxism from the sterile dogmatism to which it had been brought by "official Marxism" (Robinson 1983, 395). The value of James's thought to the rethinking process, and to the twenty-first century Caribbean lies specifically in its ability to address the failures from within the Marxist perspective itself. James's work confronts simultaneously, the errors and disillusionment of the left and the hostile skepticism of the neo-liberal right. James's critique of early twentieth century Russian Marxism is therefore critical in advancing the process of rethinking. The viewpoint offered in this work therefore holds that the utility of James's thought is further appreciated if the "crisis" within Marxism is partly understood as arising from the weaknesses in the application (or non-application) of the dialectical method to concrete social and political developments. This is of critical importance in a period of rapid change associated with globalization, as evidenced in the collapse of communism and the crisis of early twenty-first century capitalism, where new contradictions have emerged beyond the concerns of Marx in the nineteenth century and Marxism of the twentieth.

Another Work on James? Rationale and Justification

Writing in 2012, Anthony Maingot observed that "in the years since his death in 1989, there have been at least three dozen scholarly books including five biographies as well as the appearance of a *C.L.R. James Journal*. There is now a C.L.R. James institute[1] but there have long been C.L.R. James Centres" (Maingot 2011, 292).

Maingot surmises that this wide production on the work of James, may be attributed variously, to James's "'plasticity', i.e. one steady in identity but constantly shifting identifications strategically", or to his "bold political maneuverings and capacity to adjust and prosper intellectually" (291), or to the fact that "James wrote on so many topics, was involved in so many political groupings without ever being personally or ideologically subservient to any, that his appeal has remained broadly humanistic in a universal sense" (291). However, Maingot quite correctly observes that one of the dangers of the wide and flexible nature of James's intellectual interests and political activities is that everyone is left with the freedom of "discovering one's own C.L.R. James".

A survey of recent publications on the life and work of C.L.R. James justifies Maingot's concerns. Amongst the most notable of recent works include Høgsbjerg's historical work on the C.L.R. James in Imperial Britain (2014), David Austin's work on C.L.R. James in Canada (2009; 2018), works on James's reflections on cricket (Featherstone et al. 2018), and other works related to specific interests with which James was associated. These include works addressing James's reflections on Pan-Africanism and anti-colonialism Høgsbjerg (2014); cricket (Renton 2007) specific aspects of his Marxism (McLemee and LeBlanc 1994); the works relating to post-colonial studies and socio-cultural concerns (Gair 2006; King 2001); and general works on James combining all of his thematic concerns (Rosengarten 2008; Nielsen 1997; Farred 1996). There are also several works on aspects of James's life by persons who were fortunate to have been close to James and his associates, and who have written books of a biographical nature with varying degrees of analytical value (Cripps 1997; Dhondy 2001; Rennie 2017).

Further complicating the landscape of James-related works is the wide number of special productions which have emerged to celebrate specific anniversaries associated with James and some of his major works. Thus, the anniversaries of the *Black Jacobins* and *Beyond A Boundary* typically saw the production of celebratory works assessing the impact and relevance of these works for the contemporary period (see for example Douglas 2019). Similarly, the hundredth anniversary of the Russian Revolution saw the organization of a number of conferences on themes around which the work of James would be relevant. One such conference, for example, was organised by the Institute for Black Atlantic Research (IBAR) of the University of Lancashire (UCLAN), entitled *The Red and the Black* in October 2017, devoted to discussing the link between black radicals and radicalism and the Russian Revolution, a theme central to the life and work of C.L.R. James, and out of which has emerged yet further publications pertinent to CLR James (see Featherstone, Høgsbjerg and Rice 2022). The plethora of conferences which are often organised to mark such anniversaries have no doubt accounted for the several "special issues" on James, inclusive of a journal named in his honour, the *C.L.R. James Journal*, all of which add to the sense of "overstatement" in the treatment of James. In addition to these anniversary and conference publications should be added the rich editor introductions and reviews which accompany any new re-issue of James's original works such as Christian Høgsbjerg's contribution to the recent re-publication of James's *World Revolution* (see James [1937] 2017). Another similar type, and important work on James, is the *Black Jacobins Reader*, edited by Charles Forsdick and Christian Høgsbjerg (2017) and with a foreword by Robert Hill. Among the chapters in that work which are of critical relevance to understanding James's method and how it may be potentially applied to the Caribbean is the chapter by Mathew Quest concerned with 'rethinking direct democracy and nationalism' (Quest 2017b).

In addition to the above cited publications, are those books which have been written by persons who had, in many cases, been in contact with James during his lifetime. These works, due to the close association of the writers with their subject, had tended to deal with James in a largely biographical manner (Buhle 1986a, 1988; Grimshaw 1992; Grimshaw and Hart 1991).[2]

Buhle's treatment of James in *The Artist as Revolutionary* (1988), for example, is explicitly biographical, though the closing pages are dedicated to an analysis of the anticipated tendencies in world politics which would serve to validate James's work and thought (Buhle 1988, 172–73). In Buhle's other major work, an edited volume, *C.L.R. James - His Life and Work* (1986a), there is an attempt to move beyond the purely autobiographical and there is a more conscious concern with applying the thought of James to the analysis of concrete situations. This is clearly borne out in three of the chapters, notably Walter Rodney's *The African Revolution*, Paul Buhle's *Marxism in the U.S.A.* and Basil Wilson's *The Caribbean Revolution* (Rodney 1986; Buhle 1986b; Wilson 1986). Much of the book however, deals with a discussion of C.L.R. James's *life* with his *work* being relegated to a position of secondary importance.

Of similar biographical leaning is the work of Anna Grimshaw and Keith Hart (Grimshaw 1991; Grimshaw and Hart 1991), though their work demonstrates clear evidence of an attempt to interpret and analyse the thought of James. Thus, in *C.L.R. James and the Struggle for Happiness* for example, Grimshaw and Hart (1991, 16–17) attempt to address such issues in James's thought as the role of intellectuals in modern political life and their relationship to the working-class movement, and the Jamesian conception of democracy (Grimshaw and Hart 1991, 22). They also seek to provide an analysis of James's contribution to an understanding of state-capitalism (Grimshaw and Hart 1991, 40–41). While there is an emphasis on the biographical in the major existing writings on James, this should not be taken to mean that these works are of no value in contributing to an understanding of his political thought. Indeed, several of the biographical works, including and especially the efforts by Buhle, serve as rich sources of information and insight into the thought of James.[3]

Moreover, there are several works which attempt to deal specifically with the political thought of James. However, many of these works have tended to focus on specific aspects of James's thought, such as the question of race (Martin 1984;

Singham 1970; Robinson 1983); Marxism in the United States of America (Buhle 1986b; Richards 1992; Worcester 1983); his socialist thought (Glaberman 1992); or the relation of his political thought to Trinidadian or Caribbean politics (Oxaal 1982; La Guerre 1968; Harvey 1974; Henry and Buhle 1992; Rennie 2017); or the importance of his work for intellectual history and the understanding of the West Indian intellectual (Cudjoe 1992, 1997; La Guerre 1968; Campbell 1992). More recently, the above-mentioned work of Høgsbjerg (2014) has sought to focus on C.L.R. James in imperial Britain and has been concerned with tracing the origins of a pan-African consciousness and practice in James, while the work of Joseph (2015b) has sought to apply the thought of James to understanding the experience of the Grenada Revolution, and Henry (2000) has focused on the place of C.L.R. James in contributing to the development of Caribbean political philosophy. This current effort however differs from previous studies in its specific focus on applying the thought of James to understanding the political and economic transformations impacting on the Caribbean from the late twentieth to the early twenty-first century.

Further, many of the existing works on James tend to be oriented towards providing a historical exposition of James's political activity in specific historical and geographical contexts rather than analysing and applying his thought as an analytical framework for understanding and explaining the developments occurring in the various settings being studied. Thus, for example, Oxaal's work *Black Intellectuals Come to Power* (1968) deals with the period of the transition to independence in Trinidad and Tobago and analyses the roles, contributions and struggles of the intellectuals and political activists in the country in establishing the early foundations of the independent state of Trinidad and Tobago. The work is extremely useful as a narrative of political developments in Trinidad and Tobago in which the experiences of James in the politics of nationalism can be gleaned.

Similarly, there are several works which address James's life *in* the Caribbean, but very few which apply his thought *to* the

Caribbean. Many of the works which have been produced on James in the Caribbean pertain, not surprisingly, to his early life in colonial Trinidad and to his later period of association with the PNM and his dalliance with electoral politics in the 1958–62 period. These works are important for showing how the early intellectual and political influences on James in Trinidad shaped and influenced his later political views and particularly how they might have contributed to his early anti-colonial perspectives. Such works engage largely in illuminating aspects of James's Trinidad experience which account for the later evolution of his political thought and practice, and also place in context James's specifically 'Caribbean' works such as *The Case for West Indian Self-Government* first published in 1933, the *Life and Times of Arthur Cipriani* first published in 1932 (see James 2014) and to a lesser extent, *Beyond A Boundary,* first published in 1962 (James 1993).

The work by Høgsbjerg (2021) is a useful example of the kind of effort concerned with showing how James's Caribbean experiences helped to shape his early Caribbean writings, particularly, the work on Arthur Cipriani. Other writers who have made significant contributions to understanding C.L.R. James's early life in Trinidad, include Selwyn Cudjoe and Walton Look Lai.

Selwyn Cudjoe's works on James's early years (Cudjoe 1992; 1997) are largely historical in orientation and are valuable to students interested in intellectual history. Cudjoe's work is important in showing how James's Caribbean-island upbringing might have contributed to his 'global citizen' and global actor consciousness. Fully aware of the hotly debated question of James's Anglophilism (see Joseph 2022), Cudjoe's work was concerned with showing the cultural and intellectual influences from Trinidad and Tobago which impacted on the later James. According to Cudjoe (1992, 42–43), while James "may have learned a lot through English periodicals... a vibrant culture was taking place on the island as society asserted its specificity and people spoke of the need to control their affairs" and "although James chose not to mention the impact of such cultural influences, the entirety of his contribution suggests that he understood this culture's impact upon the shaping of his adult response to the world".

Cudjoe was also interested in showing how the very physical smallness of James's immediate island home contributed to shaping a consciousness which transcended island-ness and which fostered an understanding of the Caribbean in its global connectedness (Cudjoe 1992, 51). In Cudjoe's view, it is on this basis that intellectuals like "Sylvester Williams, usually described as the father of Pan Africanism, George Padmore (author of *Pan Africanism or Communism*, among other titles, but another prominent member of the activists in Pan Africanism), Eugene Chen, twice minister for foreign affairs of the Nationalist government of China under Sun Yat-sen, Eric Williams, prime minister of Trinidad and Tobago from 1962 to 1981 and author of *Capitalism and Slavery*, Oliver Cromwell Cox, author of *Caste, Class and Race*, C.L.R. James and others" had been produced by Trinidad and Tobago in the first half of the twentieth century (Cudjoe 1997, 5). According to Cudjoe, James and others like him, demonstrate an 'audaciousness' in the way they assume global prominence that transcends their island origins. In his view "this 'boldfacedness' (perhaps audacious) would characterize the behaviour of other Trinidadian intellectuals as they worked their way across the world stage and contributed to world understanding" (Cudjoe 1992, 46).

A similar focus on C.L.R. James in Trinidad can be seen in the work of Walton Look Lai (1992, 175) which focussed on James's political activities upon his return to his homeland to participate in the nationalist politics between 1958 and 1962. Just as Cudjoe's work showed the intellectual and political context in which James's early Caribbean writings were undertaken, then similarly was Lai's work concerned with showing how the political environment into which James returned in the late 1950s influenced his writing of *Party Politics in the West Indies* (Lai 1992, 179). Like Cudjoe, as well, Lai addresses the unavoidable theme of reconciling James's insistence on a "Western source of strength of West Indian people" against an understanding of the place of Africa in Caribbean development (181). While Cudjoe addresses this by showing the presence of a Caribbean context (though unacknowledged by James himself), Lai argues instead that James himself "saw no contradiction" since his "points about Westernization were made with emphasis on Caribbean creativity, especially folk creativity" (Lai 1992, 181). Similarly, Worcester's political biography of C.L.R James, particular the chapter on "parties and politics in the West Indies", offers useful historical insights into James's political life in the Caribbean in the 1950s to 1960s period which are important for framing his political ideas and their broader meanings for understanding Caribbean politics, beyond the period of James's activism (Worcester 1996,147–71).

These works make useful contributions to understanding the intellectual and political context of early-to-mid twentieth century Trinidad in which James existed and in highlighting the environment which shaped James's ideas. However, these works, even while highlighting the Caribbean influence on James, continue to enlarge the view of a separation of the 'global Marxist James' from the 'Caribbean James', since according to Lai (1992, 179), "James himself had his own unique view of Trinidad and its requirements, a view that was far removed from the vision of a deterministic Marxist mind or 'knee jerk radical'". Once the view of a global James separated from a Caribbean James becomes the operative framework, it then becomes difficult to apply James to understand the Caribbean. It is my emphasis on applying James's most advanced theoretical positions as an explanatory tool for understanding Caribbean politics in the twenty-first century which distinguishes this book from other nevertheless valuable studies on James.

C.L.R. James, writing to Jamaican Prime Minister Michael Manley in 1982, in response to news of Manley's support for the communists against the Solidarity Movement in Poland, issued the following urgent plea, which assists in clarifying my own understanding of the inextricable link between the global James and the Caribbean James:

> Someone sent me a statement that you made in the Nation of April 3rd 1982, on Solidarity and the Communists. Let me be as plain as possible. It may be that your political position compels you to side with the communists against Solidarity. If so that would be a disaster but one about which nothing can be done... In any case please let me know if you have read my recent books: *Notes on Dialectics* and *Spheres of Existence*. They give as complete a case as possible to show that Solidarity is an inevitable development forecast years ago and a definite stage on the future collapse of the Russian regime (James to Manley, May 10, 1982)

The year was 1982. Within one decade the Soviet Union had collapsed, and global communism entered a deep crisis.

This exchange between James, the most globally prominent Caribbean Marxist and Michael Manley, the leading political figurehead of Caribbean social-democracy in the post-independence period, in many ways problematises the perspectives which suggest that James's European-applied Marxism may be inapplicable or of limited relevance to the contemporary Caribbean. As seen from James's letter to Manley, it is clear that James maintained deeply-rooted connections with Caribbean political figures and with Caribbean life in general. However, what is also clearly revealed is the fact that James's principal interests were too closely tied to the shifting fortunes of global capital, and to the political development of the workers' movement at their most advanced centres to make the Caribbean and Caribbean politics the central empirical field from which his observations were grounded.

The view of the Caribbean as not being at the centre of James's analysis is a commonly held perspective which appears to have caused unease in many close followers of James. Indeed, a work which devotes itself to James on the Caribbean (Henry and Buhle 1992, vii) opens with the admission that while James's writings "have brought him worldwide recognition, even celebrity, among a multitude of different audiences, particularly in Britain and the United States... because many of his best-known texts focus on the advanced countries, recognition came without adequate understanding of his work as a whole and of its firm roots in his native Caribbean."

Another writer, Basil Wilson (1986) commenting on James's criticism of Eric Williams's PNM in *Party Politics in the West Indies*, appeared unable to reconcile James's most advanced theoretical works on the international workers' movement with his later decision to become involved in Trinidadian electoral politics. Central to such a perspective is a tendency to effect a separation between an "international" James and a "Caribbean" James, in which little theoretical and practical continuity can be seen between James's theory and its application to the Caribbean. According to Wilson (1986, 122):

> When James returned to the Caribbean, he did so without any romantic illusions about establishing a revolutionary society. He returned to the Caribbean willing to abandon temporarily his own revolutionary activities and to work sacrificially for the building of the Peoples National Movement into a mass force. Here, one has to pause, catch a few gasps, and ponder awhile. Convinced that was where the mass movement in Trinidad was at its historical juncture, C. L. R. James buried his revolutionary Marxist position, not to lead the nationalist struggle but to edit the PNM paper and to do the nitty-gritty, unglamorous, organizational tasks most theoreticians simply shun.

Putting aside the writers' attempt to confer 'sacrificial lamb' status on James, the critical issue which is captured here is again the view that the politics of the Caribbean was not a field where James's most advanced ideas were expected to be actualised.

A similar notion of the assumed disconnect between the 'international James' and the 'Caribbean James' is echoed by James Milette (1995) who in an article on C.L.R. James and the politics of Trinidad, argues that,

> for all his adult and politically active life, James lived and worked outside of the region. He had left Trinidad in 1932 and did not return for more than twenty-five years. In the interim, he had acquired a towering reputation as a Marxist scholar and politician and as an

anti-colonial activist. But in none of these, as well as in his other literary and philosophical capacities, did he ever directly relate to the West Indies. His Marxist political life was lived in Great Britain, France, Mexico and the United States of America. His anti-colonial activity was conducted in the main from London... (Millette 1995, 328).

Those who advance the thesis of the limited applicability of James to the Caribbean point to his major Caribbean work, *The Black Jacobins*, as confirmation, rather than as refutation of their perspective. In their view, James focused on the Haitian revolution because slavery and the Caribbean plantation system represented the earliest stages in the evolution of global capitalism – a thesis which would be more fully developed in Eric Williams's *Capitalism and Slavery* (Williams 1966). According to this perspective it was the centrality of the slave system to the global economy which compelled the 'global' James to bring the Caribbean to the centre of his analysis. This was similarly achieved in other analyses such as his *Making of the Caribbean Peoples* (James 1966a). In these works, James presents the thesis that the Caribbean slave and sugar economy represented the beginning of the modern global capitalist economy, and by extension, the enslaved Caribbean persons, represented the most advanced sections of the global proletariat based on their objective location in the global production process. The revolts of the enslaved, and the success of the Haitian revolution, are understood in such a context. When taken to its logical conclusion, as this explanation goes, James's focus on Haiti, was precisely because of Haiti's location at the centre of the world economy at the time of Atlantic slavery. In contrast, the post-slavery peripheral status which the Caribbean has since occupied in the world-economy has meant that the region and its political activities were not central to James's analysis once his attention turned to the politics of mature capitalism and proletarian struggles in the mid twentieth century.

The main perspective offered by this book, which demarcates it from previous studies on James, is my insistence on erasing the artificial line that separates the Caribbean James from the global

James and to show how James's most advanced reflections on post-vanguardism, proletarian worker-council type democracies, Pan-Africanism and post-colonial development and transformation are applicable and relevant to the politics, and in particular the anti-systemic activity of the Caribbean in the twenty-first century. While this will be shown more clearly in each of the later chapters, the example of James's commentary in *Party Politics in the West Indies* and his proposal of the 'mass party', which has often been treated as a "politically disappointed" James responding to his marginalisation by Eric Williams's PNM, will be shown to be consistent with James's critique of vanguardism and his reflections on post-bureaucratic politics in Europe.

In a large measure therefore, it is the persistent perception of James's most advanced works being of little relevance to the Caribbean, which has resulted in a situation in which, while there are several works on James in general, and while there have been a few works on James in the Caribbean, there are very few books, if any, that have sought to apply James's most advanced ideas to particular moments in the Caribbean. Such works, therefore, while very useful for enhancing understanding of who C.L.R. James was, his main ideas, and the concrete activities and theatres in which he was engaged, are less useful for offering insights into the relevance of his reflections outside of the context in which he engaged and more specifically, for understanding twenty-first century developments in the Caribbean.

This observation points to an additional factor which further underscores the necessity of this current work. Since James's intellectual activity was not confined to political theorising and included historical works as well as literary criticism and fiction writing, there is a large body of work which focuses upon James as a historian, cricket writer and a literary critic. As a result of this, it is very common to find works dealing with James's political thought which rely very heavily on his non-political writing. Thus, for example, Cedric Robinson in an article entitled *C.L.R. James and the World System* (1992) which attempts to analyse

C.L.R. James's contribution to world system analysis, relies heavily on James's *Mariners Renegades and Castaways* (1953), an interpretation of Herman Melville's *Moby Dick*, to demonstrate James's understanding of World System analytical thought. Robinson (1992, 66), argues that "Melville did not have to imagine this international division of labour under the embryonic hegemony of American capital and management. In the middle of the nineteenth century, in New England's shipping industries and the social insurrections concomitant to the same region's factory system, he could observe it". Elsewhere, Robinson would observe that "the bureaucrats whom James helped to vilify in *State Capitalism and World Revolution* would reappear in his study of Melville and totalitarianism with a vengeance" (Robinson 1992, 64).

It is clear therefore, that there is a single unifying thread running through James's philosophical, political, historical and literary works and major elements of his political thought can be gleaned from an investigation of such works, negating the very concept of a 'non-political' Jamesian work. However, for the political scientist there is the need for a more rigorous mode of analysis and as a result, the analyses and conclusions of this work are based upon a more rigid, empirical, and historical basis than can be achieved from the reliance on works in which literary criticism was James's primary focus. In contrast to the more overtly historical works which deal with James's life and personal experiences, this study attempts to pay less attention to a historical, narrative exposition than to an interpretation, analysis and application of his political thought to twenty-first century events.

Among the efforts which have addressed directly the political thought of C.L.R. James, have been an edited work by Selwyn Cudjoe and William Cain (1995) entitled *C.L.R. James: His Intellectual Legacies* and another by Anthony Bogues (1997), *Caliban's Freedom: The Early Political Thought of C.L.R James*. The significance of both these works is that they represent a definite shift towards a more overt treatment of the political thought of

C.L.R. James, and, in this regard, their concerns mirror one of the aims of this book.

Bogues's work however, like that of Henry (2000) is more directly concerned with using the thought of James to advance the project of "making a case" for Caribbean political thought. His work is located in the need to "rethink our perspectives on political thought with reference to the experiences of the black struggle for freedom" (Bogues 1997, xii). Specifically, while Bogues's work is on the political thought of C.L.R. James, and he locates James within a stream of Marxism, his principal concern is to demonstrate that "it was the black radical tradition which was the source of his radicalism" (Bogues 1997, xii). Bogues's work was therefore written in response to the fact that "western political thought in its homogenising universality has not yet recognised a black intellectual tradition" (3). As such therefore, Bogues, is concerned mainly with the significance of James's thought as a species of black, anti-colonial thought. His main thematic concern is the need to demonstrate the validity of the black radical tradition as an independent body of ideas, free of the homogenising and universalising assumptions, particularly of European Enlightenment thought. In this sense therefore, Bogues's thematic pre-occupation is with defending the validity of Caribbean political thought in the face of Western denial, a concern which has long occupied Caribbean academics.[4]

The work by Cudjoe and Cain (1995), as indicated earlier, is another production, which seeks to address the political thought of C.L.R. James. Given its concern with capturing the intellectual legacies of C.L.R. James, the work, like earlier edited collections, offers a wide range of perspectives on James that address issues well outside his political thought per se, including his literary and sociological concerns. Significantly though, the sections which deal with the political dimension (163–90), philosophical dimension (193–211) and theoretical dimension (277–313) contain important insights into James's political thought, including useful discussions on his philosophical method (Roderick 1995, 205–11).

Given Maingot's (2012) concerns about the dangers arising from the tendency of everyone discovering their own C.L.R. James, it is important to clarify how James is applied in this work, and what distinguishes this book from existing productions on James. In clarifying this question, it is useful to reflect on what Maingot proposes as the core and essential James, which escapes individual interpretation. According to Maingot (2012, 296), the drum to which C.L.R. James marched "had two fundamental tenets which no amount of historical rewriting, juggling and vulgar hagiography can erase: James was categorically opposed to any form of state capitalism and opposed also to the idea that the revolutionary masses had necessarily to be led by a Stalinist-like 'vanguard' party, in short he was a Marxist for the ages not just the one we opportunistically find convenient for one's present agenda".

While existing texts on James make useful contributions to deepening the understanding of James's political thought, they differ from this book in that its main concern is, above all else, to *apply* James's perspectives as explanations for, and as a guide to the expressions of radical politics in the Caribbean in the twenty-first century. Similarly, this book serves less to 'discover' or re-interpret the ideas of James, but more to respect and retain the essential core of his ideas and to apply them to new conditions in the Caribbean. One writer who perhaps has been most consciously 'applying' James's method in his work is Matthew Quest, though his 'application' has been less concerned with the politics of the Caribbean in the twenty-first century and more towards utilising James's method for capturing how the underclass in the Caribbean have thought about political and economic problems and the kinds of solutions which they have offered to these problems. This can be seen in Matthew Quest's edited work of the political ideas of the Jamaican working class intellectual Joseph Edwards, who himself was influenced by James, but equally importantly, in the manner in which Quest has privileged the voice of Edwards himself in offering political assessments of the Jamaican situation in the 1960s and 1970s (see Plys 2015).

This book, in contrast, is largely concerned with applying James's method and ideas to understanding the politics of the Caribbean in the twenty-first century. The work seeks to provide a comprehensive analysis of C.L.R. James's political thought, to clarify, explain and justify his method, and to apply his ideas to concrete political developments occurring in the twenty-first century Caribbean in its interconnection with the rest of the world. The work offers a unique treatment of James in three distinctive ways: first, in its scope and specific focus on the application of the thought of James to the post-Soviet Union, post-Cold War era of Caribbean politics; secondly in relation to discussing the possibilities for radical, anti-systemic possibilities in the Caribbean in the early twenty-first century; and thirdly, in the employment of James's thought and method as an explanatory tool for understanding those contemporary issues.

Finally, it is necessary to outline the normative perspective guiding this work, and more specifically my normative stance towards James's socialist proposals. Much of my academic life has been spent thinking about the implications of the economic challenges of globalization and the hegemony of neo-liberalism for the Caribbean's post-colonial, self-determination and development project. My work has largely sought to identify the meaning and implications for sovereignty and national self-determination in a context where the options and ideas which had sustained the Caribbean post-colonial development project have been undermined by global transformations. Many of these issues were addressed in my study on the independence experience of St. Lucia (Joseph 2011). However, while this and related works point to the broader global politico-economic forces impacting on the Caribbean, they offer little in terms of the ways in which the internal politics of resistance of Caribbean populations can mediate and transform the impact of external economic forces (one hesitates to say imperatives) on Caribbean life. While in my regular newspaper column in the *Daily Nation* of Barbados (some articles of which have been published as *Defending Caribbean*

Freedom (Joseph 2020)) I have attempted to offer normative responses to some of the major ongoing challenges confronting the Caribbean working class specifically, these interventions have not been undergirded by clear theoretical scaffolding to make the interventions anything more than an 'alternative' approach to that taken by mainstream politicians and the Caribbean economic elite.

It is there that James's normative prescriptions for a socialist alternative to capitalism in the Caribbean emerge as useful prescriptive formulae for overcoming the challenges facing the Caribbean in the era of neo-liberalism. What makes James particularly useful is not only his perspicacity in anticipating the crisis of state-capitalism and other forms of authoritarian, anti-democratic rule, but equally important has been his prescriptive call for various forms of worker and grass-roots self-organisation and free creative activity as both the expression of and as the route to the post-capitalist alternative for which generations of Caribbean people have yearned.

This work is therefore normatively Jamesian. It is hoped therefore that the reader will find, running through the pages of this book, not only descriptive analyses of dominant features of Caribbean contemporary life that confirm the Jamesian viewpoint, but normative prescriptions of 'what is to be done' using the Jamesian tools of mass mobilisation, self-organisation, direct democracy and spontaneous 'free creative activity' as responses to the many deep, persistent, but not insurmountable challenges confronting the Caribbean.

Chapter Outline

The structure of this work aims to capture the dual aims of presenting the thought of James, while simultaneously applying his thought to the political developments in the early twenty-first century Caribbean.

Chapter two explains the Jamesian method. This is necessary since in order to fully understand the implications of James's political thought for the contemporary issues in Caribbean politics, it is important first to grasp the analytical method and philosophical assumptions that underpinned his thought. While an emphasis on method is important for understanding any thinker, it is particularly critical in the case of James, given the fact that he expended a significant amount of intellectual effort in exploring, clarifying the Marxist-Hegelian dialectical method and his application of that method to his own political concerns in the mid-twentieth century. In much the same way that James applied his method to understanding the nature of radical politics in the mid-to-late twentieth century, the task of this work will be to apply that method to the new developments in radical politics in the early twenty-first century. Chapter two will therefore highlight the critical elements of the philosophical tradition which James inherited, explain and clarify how he used and applied his method to the questions of his day, and demonstrate the practical utility of his method as an aid to understanding Caribbean political issues in the twenty-first century.

Chapters three, four and five, present the thought of James under the headings of Socialism, Democracy, Race and Pan-Africanism respectively. In each of these chapters the thought of James on these questions (how he understood Socialism, Democracy, Race and Pan-Africanism) will be presented, following which, the application of his ideas to the twenty-first century Caribbean will be undertaken. The main approach of the chapters will be to highlight contemporary political developments which show how these concerns are manifesting themselves, both in their local and global settings. Given that a significant aspect of the Jamesian approach was to highlight the "future in the present", particularly in terms of the possibilities for self-organisation for liberation by the underclass, each chapter will seek to trace the potential possibilities for advancing human freedom in the existing tendencies being identified.

The work concludes with chapter six, which seeks to address the gaps between the issues which might have occupied James's concerns and framed his perspectives in the twentieth century and the new contemporary reality of the third decade of the twenty-first century. This is important because the rise of identity questions around topics of gender, sexuality, and the framing of epoch-shifting developments like climate change and global pandemics like COVID-19, have presented new challenges which were not present during James's lifetime. The book will therefore close by discussing the Caribbean and the world in the twenty-first century and applying James's thought to the new developments. The aim, throughout, will be to highlight the possibilities for proletarian liberation, that can be gleaned from the existing features of Caribbean society, economy and polity, in their location in the global environment.

2.

The Jamesian Method: Foundations and Applicability

The death agony of socialist hope in the world opens up an immeasurable ideological crisis. It will be the part of the epigones of a powerless generation to make out the balance sheet of national Bolshevism, of international communism and of traditional socialism, and to draw from it some useful lessons. And this should logically lead them to examine what is alive and what is dead in the parent doctrine, Marxism.

Boris Souvarine

There are people who think that Marxism is a kind of magic truth with which one can cure any disease. We should tell them that dogmas are more useless than cow dung. Dung can be used as fertilizer.

Mao Tse Tung

The Dialectical Method

Understanding the dialectical method is critically important for understanding the political thought of C.L.R. James and, by extension, for understanding how he applied it to discussing the prospects for the radical, anti-capitalist projects of his lifetime. It is necessary therefore, to study James's specific application of Marx's dialectical method, in order to apply the method, as James would have used it, to understand the radical projects which have emerged in the period after James, in the twenty-first century Caribbean.

A basic assumption of the dialectical method is that change and transformation is the normal, and most significant characteristic of any phenomenon. To study a phenomenon without taking into consideration the fact that it had a definite beginning and, once formed, would be experiencing external and internal transformations leading to its eventual dissolution, would be to distort and misunderstand the nature of the thing being studied. Such an approach would render false any findings and conclusions reached by a researcher. The clear distinction between the way a non-dialectician and dialectician examines the world, is most famously expressed by Friedrich Engels when he claims that,

> the world is not to be comprehended as a complex of ready-made things ... but as a complex of processes, in which things apparently stable ... go through an un-interrupted change of coming into being and passing away (in Krapivin 1985, 146).

Similarly, Maurice Cornforth (1971, 1:41) stresses that what is of interest to the dialectician is not so much the "thing" in itself, but the "process" of the creation and destruction of that thing.

This emphasis on the process of the "coming into being and passing away" of things, does not mean that the dialectician is not involved in the study of "things", that is of phenomena or objects in themselves. In fact, quite the opposite is true; for certainly, if the researcher is to investigate how a thing is created and how that thing changes, then it is necessary to possess a thorough knowledge of the internal structure and working of that thing. This incidentally, was what Marx's *Capital* was concerned with - how capitalism came into being, what constituted the essential internal dynamic structure and working and operationalisation of capitalism, what were the forces which sustained it, and what were the internal contradictions which would eventually result in its withering away, in a particular external environment. To achieve his goal, Marx had to study the "thing", capitalism, in its most intricate detail. However, the dialectician maintains that an intricate study of capitalism, like the study of any other phenomenon, can only be achieved by understanding and studying the process of its formation and eventual destruction.

The dialectician, therefore, is principally concerned with change. It is this emphasis on change, transformation, adaptation and eventual destruction which differentiates the methodology of the dialectician from other competing analytical methods. C.L.R. James (1980a, 55) informs us that,

> dialectical logic is the science of tracing by what laws in what way, notions, our concept of things, change, to know that they change, to know how they change, constantly to examine these changes. Scientific method is the examination of an object in its changes, and the examination of our concepts of that object, watching how both change, doing it consciously, clearly, with knowledge and understanding.

A major clue to the significance of the contribution that James makes to Marxism, lies in his claim that the scientific method consists not only in the examination of an object but in the "examination of our concepts of that object". This observation admits to a realisation that our conscious awareness of an object is as liable to change as the object itself. It is James's awareness of the need to change analytical concepts and to demonstrate how and why they change which marks one of his most significant contributions to Marxist political thought.[1]

Another important feature of the dialectical method is the recognition that the essential nature of a thing or a phenomenon cannot be grasped in isolation from the environment in which it is immersed. In other words, an entity should always be studied in its interconnectedness and relation to other phenomena to which it is joined as part of a whole or which constitute sub-elements in its structure. To study the phenomenon in isolation from its conditions of existence (Cornforth 1971, 1:46; Engels 1978) as it actually exists, serves to distort both the phenomenon being studied and the conclusions and results of one's investigations.

Cornforth (1971, 1:46-47) illustrates the dangers of un-dialectically separating phenomena from their environments when he writes that,

> nothing exists or can exist in splendid isolation, separate from its conditions of existence, independent of its relationships with other things... The very nature of a thing is modified and transformed by its relationship with other things. When things enter into such relationships that they become parts of a whole, the whole cannot be regarded as nothing more than the sum total of the parts. But the mutual relations which the parts enter into in constituting the whole modify their own properties, so that while it may be said that the whole is determined by the parts it may be equally said that the parts are determined by the whole.

The entire emphasis of the dialectician, therefore, in keeping with the highest traditions and basic principles of the scientific method, is to study things as they really are, that is, as they actually exist. It is because the dialectical method takes these factors into consideration that it serves as such a useful analytical tool for the study of society. Unlike the study of natural phenomena, the environments in which social phenomena are studied cannot be artificially created (or in cases where they can be, this cannot be done without seriously affecting the outcomes of one's investigations, or without violating ethical or moral standards).

Not only does the dialectical method assist in demonstrating that change and movement are integral to all things, it also assists with offering explanations as to why specific changes occur. This compels the dialectician to investigate the internal contradictions within all phenomena, as well as to identify, as will be discussed later, antagonistic and non-antagonistic contradictions, as variables which explain outcomes. 'Contradictions' here refer to the struggle between those forces which tend towards stability on the one hand, and disequilibrium on the other, or those forces which seek to preserve a structure and those which result in its transformation. It is this internal struggle which results in movement and transformation. All 'equilibrium' is therefore seen as temporary. Indeed, what is referred to as 'stability' is maintained through transformation, change and adjustment and therefore cannot be considered as 'stability' in the strict sense of permanent stasis and unchangeability. This is why V.I. Lenin claims that "the unity of opposites ... is conditional, temporary, transitory, relative. The struggle of opposites is absolute" (in Cornforth 1971, 1:98). Cornforth (1971, 1:98) therefore shares Lenin's perspective that, "whatever the domination relationship in the unity of opposites may be, it is always apt to change, as a result of which the former unity of opposites will be dissolved and a new unity of opposites takes its place".

In the application of the dialectical method therefore, there is a need to correctly identify, and to study the *internal* contradictions within a given entity, for it is the internal dynamics more than anything else which will determine the nature of the new "unity of opposites" that will emerge out of the struggle within the old. It is C.L.R. James's grasp of this element of the dialectic, and his deliberate attempt at identifying the critical contradictions of the post-Lenin Soviet era, which makes his worldview of critical importance to the study of radical political possibilities in the early twenty-first century.

James's main focus when applying the dialectic, is on the internal forces struggling and operating within the entity he was studying. It is only with such an emphasis that the objective movement and development of the entity being studied can be discerned. According to James, Lee, and Chaulieu[2] ([1958] 1974, 105),

    a. all development takes place as a result of self-movement, not organisation or direction by external forces.

    b. self-movement springs from and is the overcoming of antagonisms within an organism, not the struggle against external foes.

It is this internal struggle within an organism that shapes its internal development and determines the nature of the end product (albeit temporary) which emerges out of this internal struggle.

Perhaps the best summary of the main principles and ideas governing the dialectic is provided by Lenin (1977, 1:23):

> A development that repeats, as it were, stages that have already been passed, but repeats them in a different way, on a higher basis, ("the negation of negation") a development, so to speak, that proceeds by leaps, catastrophes, and revolutions, "breaks in continuity", the transformation of quantity into quality; inner impulses towards development, imparted by the contradiction and conflict of the various forces and tendencies acting on a given body or within a given phenomenon, or within a given society; the interdependence and closest and indissoluble connection between all aspects of any phenomenon (history constantly revealing ever new aspects), a connection that provides a uniform, and universal process of motion, one that follows definite laws - these are some of the features of dialectics as a doctrine of development that is richer than the conventional one.

A Defence of the Dialectic Against Old and New Challenges

Lenin (1977, 1:49) reminds us of a saying which holds that if geometrical principles could affect human relations, then a more vigorous effort would be made to refute them. Indeed, much of the criticism which has been levelled at the dialectical method has arisen precisely because of its implications for human social relations. A world view which is concerned primarily with change, showing how such change occurs by identifying the major antagonisms within a society, will inevitably be anathema to those with a vested interest in preserving the existing social system. Given the wide array of enemies against which the dialectical method has had to contend, it is necessary to offer a response to clarify the utility of the method, before identifying and discussing its specific application by James.

In this regard, two main sets of challenges can be identified. The first is the anti-science claims against the method by Karl Popper and the second is the more recent post-modernist rejections of the scientism and so-called structuralist tendencies of Marxism. It should be noted here, that while there are many enemies of 'Marxism' to be found in the everyday liberal and 'free-market' alternative world views, the task here is to focus on the more philosophical positions which have emerged in direct and deliberate opposition to the dialectical method, and not to the general opposition to Marxism in general. It is for these reasons that focus is being placed here on the earlier critique by Popper, on one hand, and the more recent perspectives of the post-modernists, on the other.

The work of Karl Popper is among one of the most comprehensive and widely celebrated philosophical critiques of the dialectical method and of Marxism (Popper 1960; 1962, vol. 2). Popper essentially characterises the Marxian dialectic as being unscientific. He does so for a number of reasons.[3] Popper accuses the dialectical method of what he calls 'historicism' which he defines as,

> an approach to the social sciences which assumes that historical *prediction* is their principal aim, and which assumes that this aim is attainable by discerning the 'rhythms' or the 'patterns', the 'laws' or the 'trends' that underlie the evolution of history (Popper 1960, 3).

To Popper, what he calls historical prediction has no place in social science since *exact* and *detailed* scientific social predictions are impossible (Popper 1960,14).

Popper maintains that for a study to be considered scientific, it must be subject to repetition. The investigator must outline clearly his procedures, stating clearly the conditions under which the experiment was carried out, providing exact details of the results, findings and conclusions of the investigation. This is in keeping with his emphasis that falsifiability is the hallmark of scientific investigation. The difficulty with 'historicism' Popper maintains, is that it "denies the possibility of repeating large-scale social experiments in precisely similar conditions" (Popper 1960, 9). For this reason, Popper insists that the historical materialist method does not fall within the purview of science. Popper (1962, 2:93) maintains that, the arguments underlying Marx's historical prophecy are invalid. His ingenious attempt to draw prophetic conclusions from observations of contemporary economic tendencies failed. The reason for this failure does not lie in any insufficiency of the empirical basis of the argument... The reason for his failure as a prophet lies entirely in the poverty of historicism as such, in the simple fact that even if we observe today what appears to be a historical tendency or trend, we cannot know whether it will have the same appearance tomorrow.

The second major flaw which Popper sees in the dialectical method is what he refers to as its inherent essentialism. Popper (1960, 28) holds that essentialism was founded by "Aristotle, who taught that scientific research must penetrate to the essence of things in order to explain them". Though Popper (1960, 30–34) sees the validity of such an emphasis in certain areas of study, he feels that essentialism, when applied to the social sciences results ultimately in the very historicism which he unequivocally denounces. Popper also accuses the dialectical method of "reinforced dogmatism", since the dialectician constantly transforms his analytical categories as new conditions emerge, rendering the old categories obsolete (Cornforth 1968, 21–22). As such, he sees the method as always escaping the charge of being wrong.

However, while the work of Popper is widely touted as representing the ultimate refutation of Marxism and the dialectical method (Magee 1975, 96), his arguments have been soundly rebutted. Cornforth (1968) maintains that Popper makes assumptions about Marxism, which Marxism does not make for itself. Firstly, contrary to Popper's claims, Marxism makes no claim to making 'exact and detailed' social predictions. Cornforth (1968, 137) points out that, instead, the Marxist studies,

> the past sequence of events in order to try to discover explanatory *generalisations* about how later events issue from earlier ones. Marx's discovery was that to explain the historical sequence we must always, first, examine how people acted socially in order to adapt their production relations, and their institutions and ideas, to their forces of production (emphasis added).

The emphasis is on a generalisation, a relationship which in a past historical setting has largely manifested itself. This relationship is examined in a new context in an attempt to discern further generalisations about the way in which the adaptation to the means of production will affect social relations. No attempt is made to give an 'exact' account of how the adaptation of the social relations and mode of production will be enacted or a 'precise' prediction of what the outcomes of those adaptations will be (Bluhm 1978, 420).

Popper's charge of "reinforced dogmatism" also reflects a lack of appreciation of the Marxian method. This accusation stemmed directly from Popper's emphasis on falsifiability as being the major criterion of science. It is this emphasis on falsifiability which allows Popper to maintain, quite correctly, "that every good scientific theory is a prohibition: it forbids certain things to happen" (Cornforth 1968, 20). However, Popper's criticism appears to deny Marxism of the normal practice of science to adjust explanations when new empirical data emerges. Indeed, it is this very feature of the dialectical approach, that is, its alterations of its generalisations to suit changing conditions, which shows the method to be scientific and not dogmatic, for it is dogmatism alone which remains unchanged in total oblivion to conditions which emerge to refute them. As Cornforth (1968,18) claims,

> Marxism stands or falls entirely on whether it can or cannot justify its scientific claims. But if it is, as is claimed, scientific, then it must be allowed to share the generally recognized character of scientific theories and views - namely, that it stakes no claim to finality or completeness but keeps on adding to, modifying, reformulating and rearranging its generalisations and recommendations as new experiences and new problems are presented... Yet when Marxists try to press forward the scientific development of Marxism - and that includes not only expansion and elaboration but correction - our critics tell us: stop! Marxism is unscientific and is not allowed to develop like that.

Further, Marxism adheres very tightly to Popper's criterion of scientific theory as prohibition. Marxism does forbid certain things from happening which, if they occur would certainly mean the end to Marxism, as a scientific theory. Marxism insists that, "there must always be a certain kind of correspondence between forces of production and relations of production. This allows all manner of things to be done within the bounds of such correspondence, but denies the possibility of going outside these bounds" (Cornforth 1968, 20–21). Thus, it is simply not possible for a monarchical feudal structure to be imposed upon a society in an advanced stage of industrialisation, nor is it possible to identify a hunter-gathering, pre-agricultural society which lives by elaborate principles of "the rights of man" or one which has a political structure based on complex representative systems (Cornforth 1968; Toffler 1981). As a final, Caribbean specific example, it is simply not possible for an economy constructed on the social relations of slavery, to have laws which prohibit the possession of human beings as property.

In addition to these early criticisms of the Marxist method offered by Popper, a more recent intellectual adversary of Marxism, which like Popper's criticism has been widely celebrated as a 'definitive' overthrow of Marxism, is post-modernism. Unlike Popper's criticism which came at a time when actually-existing Marxist projects were still enjoying global respectability, the post-modernist challenge has gained ascendency in the period following the collapse of the Soviet Union and in a moment of intellectual crisis for Marxism.

On close examination, many of the claims of post-modernism appear to be based on similar assumptions as Popper's, but with a deeper and more all-encompassing attack on Marxism. This is because the timing of the post-modernist assault has coincided with a moment when the global material, economic, political, and ideological conditions have been more favourable to alternatives to the Marxist world view. While post-modernism has been levelled as an attack on the assumptions of the "age of modernity" in general, the main arrows of the post-modernist world-view have been aimed directly at the heart of the Marxist worldview. In some cases, much of the anti-Marxist positions by post-modernists arise from their own personal disappointments with Marxism, and therefore, their turn to post-modernist theorising cannot be divorced from an ongoing quarrel with Marxism. In this regard, for example, Lyotard's post-modernist turn cannot be separated from his active involvement in the Marxist collective *Socialisme ou Babarie* following his admission into the group in 1954 (See Chrome and Williams 2006, 4; see also Breckman 1998) during which incidentally, he had a close association with C.L.R. James's associate Cornelius Castoriadis, who co-wrote *Facing Reality* with James, under the pseudonym Pierre Chalieu (see Castoriadis 1995).

Lane (2009, 10) highlights Baudrillard's interest in countering Hegel, and argues that "without doubt, the main reason for the interest in Hegel was the fact that his philosophy, and especially the notion of the dialectic, had heavily influenced Marxism, which was one of the dominant political movements in post-war France". Further, much of the internal motivation of post-modernism was to counter the Hegelian dialectic for the sake of countering, rather than arising out of any inherent weaknesses with the method. This viewpoint by Lane (2009, 12–13) is worth deep examination for a full appreciation of why post-modernism has advanced consciously as an anti-Marxist perspective:

> Hegel's dialectic is a voracious thing: it is all-encompassing, all-consuming… [O]ur intellectual problems are made apparent to us, through, or because of, the workings of the dialectic (another way of putting this is that the dialectic means we can think in the first place)… Put this way, it has an uncanny knack of preceding and answering all intellectual movements and ideas… [T]he dialectic does not somehow end or finish with the above outcome. Instead, we move on to the next stage in human existence, where the dialectical process starts all over again (we could say: the dialectic never rests). *This is where, for thinkers such as Bataille and Baudrillard, the bigger problems begin. How are we to think 'outside' the dialectic? If it is a process which never ends, you could say there is no outside. How are we to counter such an imposing, all-consuming philosophical system? Perhaps the question might be: "If it is such a*

successful system, why might we want to counter it?" A quick answer would suggest that thinkers such as Bataille and Baudrillard are suspicious of totalizing systems of thought – they argue that there are experiences in the world that cannot be subsumed by the dialectic and somehow operate at its limits, working (potentially) to fracture the entire system, just a small crack in a large bell can ultimately destroy the entire structure (Emphasis added).

This direct confrontation with Marxism becomes immediately clear in the work *Symbolic Exchange and Death* by Jean Baudrillard, which takes direct aim at the main arguments in Marx's critique of political economy. According to Baudrillard (1996, 441–42),

> The critique of political economy begins with social production of the mode of production as its reference. The concept of production alone allows us, by means of an analysis of that unique commodity called labour power, to extract a surplus (a surplus value) which controls the rational dynamics of capital as well as its beyond, the revolution. Today everything has changed again. Production, the commodity form, labour power, equivalence and surplus value, which together formed the outline of a qualitative, material and measurable configuration, are now things of the past.

Beyond this early tentative criticism of Marxism, is Jean Baudrillard's related claim that signs and sign systems, expressed in terms of various degrees of "simulation" offer reliable alternatives to reality. A central claim by Baudrillard is that the world of technology and virtual reality and television has blurred the lines between the real and unreal, and to a large extent, may even serve as a reliable substitute for the real, or become the real itself. His famous description of Disneyland, illustrates this tendency: "Disneyland is there to conceal the fact that it is the "real" country, all of "real" America which is Disneyland... Disneyland is presented as imaginary in order to make us believe that the rest is real, when in fact all of Los Angeles and the America surrounding it are no longer real, but of the order of the hyperreal" (in Lane 2009, 87).

This immediately highlights a key issue which separates the Marxist perspective from the post-modernist. While post-modernists elevate subjective reality (individual perceptions of things) to the realm of reality, Marxists, owing to their insistence on identifying the conditions which make for true freedom and unfreedom, are careful to classify as real, only those outcomes which are grounded in the material plane. It is for this reason that Marxists classify perceptions, feelings and beliefs based on non-material factors as "false consciousness". Indeed, religion, mores, morals, and values are themselves products of man's material environment and man's economic relations, as seen for example, in the use of religion to justify slavery.

Notions of "true or false consciousness", "idealism vs realism" and "subjectivity vs objectivity" which are central to the Marxist worldview, are rejected by post-modernists as simplistic reductionism. Instead, the post-modernist viewpoint recognises a spectrum of reality. It rejects what it sees as simplistic dualisms like bourgeois/proletariat, advanced/backward, and free/unfree. At the centre of notions like Baudrillard's signs and symbolism substituting for reality, is the blurring of lines which makes it difficult to measure concrete stages in human relations. It delegitimises struggles aimed at achieving shifts in social relations and it denies the acknowledgement of progress. The implications for Marxism's promise of measurable stages of progress towards a definitive point of transformation, become immediately apparent.

Closely related to Baudrillard's elevation of signs and symbols as reliable substitutes to concrete reality, is Jacques Derrida's positing of the need for 'deconstruction' of reality, in which the idea of common-sense is rejected. A central notion of deconstruction is the subjectivity of experience and the denial of the objectivity of structure. Derrida's deconstruction therefore partly springs from the assumption that "experience contains the possibility that my experience is unique to myself" (Stocker 2006, 183). The meaning of meaning is itself questioned. In a typical post-modernist assertion, although resembling very much the Marxist notion of the 'negation of the negation', Derrida asserts that,

> Deconstruction cannot limit itself or proceed immediately to neutralisation: it must by means of a double gesture, a double

science, a double writing, practice an overturning of the classical opposition and a general displacement of the system... *Deconstruction does not consist in passing from one concept to another, but in overturning and displacing a conceptual order, as well as the conceptual order with which the conceptual order is articulated* (in Stocker 2006, 189) (Emphasis added).

Given the primacy of empiricism, objectivity and the relationship between economic infrastructure (means of production and relations of production) as the broad structural framework within which other aspects of human relations are mediated and explained within the Marxist perspective, Derrida's notion of deconstruction overturns a central aspect of Marxian methodology. Further, deconstruction, by de-emphasising the link between structural cause and social effect, undermines the validity of any radical politics aimed at societal transformation. Thus, major concepts in the Marxian framework around which some degree of political action can be undertaken, are potentially upended by Derrida's emphasis on deconstruction.

Similar negative implications for Marxist theory can be seen in the ideas of Jean Francois Lyotard, who is perhaps best known for his arguments against grand, meta-narratives. Indeed, Lyotard's (1996, 482) definition of postmodernism and his attack on science, centres the "grand narrative" as the main culprit in his overturning of "science" and the modern. He uses the word modern "to designate any science that legitimates itself with reference to a metadiscourse... making an explicit appeal to some grand narrative, such as the dialectics of Spirit... the emancipation of the rational or working subject, or the creation of wealth". In contrast he defines postmodernism as "incredulity toward metanarratives. This incredulity is undoubtedly a product of progress in the sciences: but that progress in turn presupposes it". Given Marxism's claims to scientism as distinct from "utopianism" and given Marxism's overt dependence of structuralist explanations, Lyotard's approach automatically problematizes Marxism as an analytical method, a socio-political theory and a political practice.

Finally, in the examination of post-modernism's attack on the central assumptions of Marxism, is the work of Michel Foucault. Foucault's work, like the related efforts at deconstruction, takes aim at some key assumptions of knowledge construction which has framed the Marxist world-view. According to Merquior (1991, 15), the main aim of all of Foucault's major works has been finding the "conceptual underpinnings of some key practices in modern culture" and "placing them in historical perspective". It is worth noting, that the works of Marx have a similar purpose, although with major differences in explanatory emphasis and normative political outcomes. It is perhaps the differences in explanatory emphasis, and methodological outlook which separates Foucault from the Marxists.

A central contention of Foucault is that power is exercised in a diffused, diverse and dispersed way at various levels through "discourses". When adopting Foucault's outlook, emphasis is placed on the discontinuities and the disruptions in structures and patterns. Thus, in Foucault's reading of the understanding of power, individual agency assumes a greater level of significance than the assumed impact of economic structural and class forces as advanced in the Marxist perspective. The manner in which Foucault advances his argument in a critique of the historical method, reveals the spaces it opens up for a non, or even anti-Marxist perspective. According to Foucault (2002, 4),

> The old questions of the traditional analysis (What link should be made between disparate events? How can a causal succession be established between them? What continuity or overall significance do they possess? Is it possible to define a totality, or must one be content with reconstituting connexions?) are now being replaced by questions of another type: which strata should be isolated from others? What types of series should be established? What criteria of periodization should be adopted for each of them? What system of relations (hierarchy, dominance, stratification, univocal determination, circular causality) may be established between them? What series of series may be established? And in what large-scale chronological table may distinct series of events be determined?

In answer to these questions Foucault proposes that, instead of searching for "continuities of thought" and "solid homogenous manifestations of a single mind or collective mentality" researchers should now try to "detect the incidence of interruption...whose status and nature vary considerably" and which "direct historical analysis away from the search for silent beginnings, and the never-ending tracing-back to the original precursors, towards the search for a new type of rationality and its various effects" (4–5).

This insistence on the relative accidental or arbitrary nature of the rationality of science, is made even more explicit by Foucault in the opening pages of his work *The Order of Things* (2005), in which he sought to show the "naturalness" of an arbitrary list of categories of animals, taken, not surprisingly, from a work of fiction, which Foucault (2005, xvi) openly admits was the source of the inspiration for some of his claims:

> This book first arose out of a passage in Borges, out of the laughter that shattered, as I read the passage, all the familiar landmarks of my thought – our thought, the thought that bears the stamp of our age and our geography – breaking up all the ordered surfaces and all the planes with which we are accustomed to tame the wild profusion of existing things, and continuing long afterwards to disturb and threaten with collapse our age-old distinction between the Same and the Other. This passage quotes a 'certain Chinese encyclopaedia' in which it is written that 'animals are divided into: (a) belonging to the Emperor, (b) embalmed, (c) tame, (d) sucking pigs, (e) sirens, (f) fabulous, (g) stray dogs, (h) included in the present classification, (i) frenzied, (j) innumerable, (k) drawn with a very fine camelhair brush, (l) et cetera, (m) having just broken the water pitcher, (n) that from a long way off look like flies'. In the wonderment of this taxonomy, the thing we apprehend in one great leap, the thing that, by means of the fable, is demonstrated as the exotic charm of another system of thought, is the limitation of our own, the stark impossibility of thinking that. But what is it impossible to think, and what kind of impossibility are we faced with here? Each of these strange categories can be assigned a precise meaning and a demonstrable content...

What is striking is not only the arbitrary nature of the categories of 'animals' but the willingness of Foucault to make a case for their validity. It is this posing of an alternative epistemological foundation to the rationality and scientism of the Enlightenment which is the essence of the challenge to Marxism. The notion of the arbitrary nature of categories, the absence of identifiable and coherent explanatory variables and the valorization of a world view which facilitates conceptual anarchy, is deliberately aimed at overturning both the explanatory as well as the remedial counter-hegemonic perspectives of Marxism. At the same time, post-modernism's own claims to outward anti-hegemonic status, in capturing radical options largely down-played by Marxism, places the world-view in the status of an alternative to the Marxist perspective.

Not surprisingly, the deep impact of postmodernist thought on post-1990 political thought and practice, particularly in the wake of the collapse of actually-existing socialist projects in Europe, has reflected itself in attempts at revising Caribbean Marxism (Lindahl 2001, Meeks 1994). Significantly, the most notable instance of Caribbean attempts to apply post-modernist revision to Marxism, frontally addressed the work of C.L.R. James (Meeks 1994) and it is useful to examine both the arguments which sought to implicate James in post-modern revisionism as well as the Marxist rebuttal.

The main writer who has deployed the postmodernist argument in the attack on Caribbean Marxism has been Folke Lindahl (2001). In a work entitled, *Caribbean Diversity and Ideological Conformism: The Crisis of Marxism in the English-Speaking Caribbean*, Lindahl provided a distillation of all the main implications of postmodernist ideas, and marshalled them against key assumptions, though somewhat caricatured, against Caribbean Marxism. Echoing standard post-modernist claims, Lindahl argues that present-day disenchantment with Marxism "is best understood as a growing scepticism vis-à-vis the grand promises of Marxism and the unpersuasive categories with which it makes its utopian claims" (311). Lindahl proposes that a "critical and deconstructive attitude towards the Marxist 'language game' or 'master code' might prove to be the most fruitful and promising approach" (311). Interestingly, much of Lindahl's attack on Marxism is aimed at specific policy flaws of actually-existing Marxist experiments. Similar to Popper, Lindahl rails against the fact that failed Marxist projects are viewed, not as a "possible flaw inherent in the policy but as a failure only in the implementation stage" (312). Writing specifically in response to C.Y. Thomas's work *The Poor and the Powerless* (1988), in which Thomas offers a reflection on the possibilities for Caribbean socialist democratisation Lindahl, offers the standard post-modern critique against Thomas's assumptions:

> First of all, once we recognize individual liberties, we also recognize conflicts, dissent, factions, and most importantly, limits to power and government. Second, we cannot have both a planned society and completely democratized governmental structure (whatever that means)... Third, although appealing in its rhetoric, and persuasive in terms of its empirical reality of most Caribbean societies, the assertion about basic needs of the masses does not hold up to scrutiny... [T]here are no clearly definable 'basic needs', and there are no homogenous 'masses'... 'The masses' - if the concept means anything – are of course both heterogeneous and pluralistic, and their needs are not to be assumed prior to politics but *through* politics, hopefully a somewhat democratic and representative politics... I take this latter assumption of knowing what people want, as emblematic of Marxist ideology, whether it appeals to 'the masses', 'the people', or 'the proletariat'. Democracy is only embraced as an afterthought since the theory has already spelled out what the outcome is and should be (Lindahl 2001, 312-313).

While acknowledging that Marxism has made and will continue to make a significant contribution to Caribbean intellectual life, Lindahl argues that Marxism has been a "two-edged sword: on the one hand providing illuminating insights with important practical political consequences and, on the other, displaying areas of blindness and, to put it mildly, less impressive politics" (2001, 310). In essence therefore, Lindahl's post-modernist lens, facilitates an outright rejection of the key analytical categories of Marxism.

Of more direct significance to the specific purposes of this work, have been the attempts to apply the post-modernist outlook to the work of C.L.R. James. In such efforts, James is claimed as a post-modernist while denied as a Marxist. While acknowledging that James had made indelible contributions to Marxist theorising, Lindahl (2001, 310), in his postmodernist revision makes the claim that individuals like James, "received their intellectual prominence due to their brilliance and talents as original writers and critics rather than as Marxist theorists or Marxist political analysis".

This post-modernist re-reading of James is undertaken even more directly in Meeks's post-modernist reading of C.L.R. James's *Black Jacobins*. In a 1994 work entitled, "Re-reading the Black Jacobins: James, The Dialectic and the Revolutionary Conjuncture", Meeks argues that James's methodology, although "in form and stated intent is clearly Marxist, nevertheless follows its own peculiar trajectory" (1994, 77). Meeks, thus proposes to answer: "what is the Jamesian method? How does it differ from other contemporary Marxist schools? How does this affect his conclusions? And how can we better understand his overall intellectual direction from this?"

In answering this question, Meeks (1994, 77) includes the work of James alongside other Marxist thinkers like E.P. Thompson, Antonio Gramsci and Louis Althusser who have all, "in response to lacunae detected in classical Marxism...broken from the Marxist canon and proceeded to elaborate frameworks of interpretation with only tentative connections to core conclusions of historical materialism". He suggests that the central issue in these re-interpretations, has revolved around "the relative importance to be placed in historical determination on 'superstructural' elements, including race, religion, political factors, and, most critically, human agency" (78). Describing this debate between agency and productive forces as "the central field of combat", Meeks (1994, 81) argues that the "relationship between the two, is not to be restricted to some arcane debate between historians or political scientists, but extends into the very core notions of democracy and the relevance of Marxism, not just as a tool for analysis, but for human emancipation".

Meeks's re-reading of James's *Black Jacobins* therefore, involves the re-examination of instances in which, James, on reflecting on the role of Toussaint L'Ouverture in the conduct of the Haitian Revolution, analyses the relative weight which should be given to objective material forces (the supposedly classical Marxist position) on one hand, and the subjective field of individual human agency (the more avowedly post-modernist position) on the other. Relying on a passage which he claims, from the perspective of method is perhaps "the most important passage of the book", Meeks seeks to demonstrate the tension between the two positions in James's work:

> The revolution had made him; but it would be a vulgar error to suppose that the creation of a disciplined army, the defeat of the English and the Spaniards, the defeat of Rigaud, the establishment of a strong government all over the island, the growing harmony between the races, the enlightened aims of the administration – it would be a crude error to believe that all these were inevitable. At a certain stage, the middle of 1794, the potentialities in the chaos began to be shaped and soldered by his powerful personality, and then henceforth, it is impossible to say where the social forces end and the impress of personality begins. It is sufficient that, but for him, this history would be something entirely different (Meeks 1994, 99).

On weighing the relative weights which James gives to the two positions, and in assessing their implications for his Marxism, Meeks's main conclusion is that James adheres "formally to a Marxist position, but his honest reading of the San Domingo revolution, his own sensitivity to the colonial and, critically, racial questions, carry him to the verge of severance with the Marxist canon" (Meeks 1994, 81). He claims that "in the end James remains a Marxist, but in order to do so, he elevates the individual and agency to levels unprecedented in classical Marxism" (81).

It is important to note however that the relationship between agency structure and the role of the individual in making of revolution had been addressed by Trotsky in his *The History of the Revolution*. An important question occupying Trotsky's mind was how to assess the personal role of Lenin in contributing to the success of the Bolshevik revolution. In Trotsky's view, this was "no unimportant question, although easier to ask than answer":

> How would the revolution have developed if Lenin had not reached Russia in April 1917? If our exposition demonstrates and proves anything at all, we hope it proves that Lenin was not a demiurge of the revolutionary process, that he merely entered into a chain of objective historic forces. But he was a great link in that chain... Until his arrival, not one of the Bolshevik leaders dared to make a diagnosis of the revolution... Inner struggle in the Bolshevik Party was absolutely unavoidable. Lenin's arrival merely hastened the process. His personal influence shortened the crisis (Trotsky [1932] 1965, 343).

Trotsky (ibid.) then asks the very agency vs structure question, occupying C.L.R. James and Brian Meeks, and now over-determined by the post-modernists:

> Is it possible, however, to say confidently that the party without him would have found its road? The factor of time is decisive here, and it is difficult in retrospect to tell time historically. Dialectical materialism at any rate has nothing to do with fatalism. Without Lenin the crisis, which the opportunist leadership was inevitably bound to produce, would have assumed an extraordinary sharp and protracted character... The role of personality arises before us here on a truly gigantic scale. It is necessary only to understand that role correctly, taking personality as a link in the historic chain.

Significantly, long before Trotsky had arrived at his reflections on Lenin's personality and the revolution, he had offered a similar analysis of the role of the personality of the Russian Czar in causing the revolution to occur, and reached similar conclusions to the ones he reached for Lenin. According to Trotsky ([1932] 1965, 73), "foremost in our field of vision will stand the great, moving forces of history which are super-personal in character. Monarchy is one of them". In Trotsky's view, "monarchy is by its very principle bound up with the personal. This in itself justifies an interest in the personality of that monarch whom the process of social development brought face to face with a revolution. Moreover, we hope to show... just where in a personality the strictly personal ends – often much sooner than we think – and how frequently the 'distinguishing traits' of a person are merely individual scratches made by a higher law of development" (ibid.). In short, merely reflecting on the relationship between personality and structure is insufficient to transform a Marxist into a post-modernist, and Marxism was never oblivious of the relationship between agency and structure.

This then, provides an indication of the broad challenges to Marxist methodology from post-modernism and how James has been implicated in this post-modern revisionism. Given the aim of this current work to offer a case for the relevance of Marxism to the challenges of the twenty-first century, and more importantly, given James's application of the Marxist dialectic and methodology in the latter half of the twentieth century, it is necessary to offer a defence of Marxism and of Jamesian Marxism in the face of the post-modernist counter-thesis.

The most direct response to the post-modern challenge to Marxism in the Caribbean has come from Caribbean Marxist scholar, Hilbourne Watson (2001). Watson surmises that the haste with which Meeks appeared to be abandoning Marxism for the embrace of post-modernism, might have itself been a consequence of Meeks's own flirtation, at an earlier juncture, with the Workers Party of Jamaica (WPJ), which "had embraced a pro-Soviet outlook that was equated with Marxism". This would have made Meeks less sensitive to the richer and longer tradition of original non-dogmatic creative application of Marxist methodology (of which James was a key contributor) and render him less capable of resolving tensions within Marxism after the fall of the Soviet Union (Watson 2001, 356). Critically, because of this, Watson argues that Meeks "settles for a reductionist concept of Marxism" (356), and indeed "a close reading of *Struggle*, the ideological organ of the former WPJ, tends to show a closer affinity between the WPJ and Sovietism than with Marx's Marxism"

(370). Watson challenges Meeks to demonstrate "outside of commonplace liberal excess, that there is a dichotomy in any serious reading of Marx with respect to 'determination by agency or productive forces'" (360). Watson (2001, 357) also argues that Meeks "simply attributes to Marxism all the problems he has with *The Black Jacobins,* without referencing any degree to which James might have modified his position at any subsequent point".

Most critically however, Watson rejects the claim made for the autonomous, individual, so critical to the post-modernist worldview and so central to Meeks's re-reading of James. Watson insists that "theories of the primacy of the individual must account for how individuals enter and participate in social systems, since it is impossible for thinking to be independent of socially heterogenous processes" (Watson 2001, 365). As a broad concluding rejection of the post-modernist denials of grand narratives and essentialising concepts, Watson argues (2001, 372) that "it is impossible to escape essentialising concepts. Marxist materialists would essentialise in strategic, contingent ways; Cartesian modernists would essentialise as absolute necessity; postmodernists would deny that they essentialise because they deconstruct and leave debris strewn across the intellectual landscape."

It should be noted however, that Meeks, in a response to Watson, has denied any rejection of Marxism on his part, as any wholesale embrace of post-modernism (Meeks 2001). Indeed, Meeks suggested that his goal was, "not to abandon the powerful analytical tools elaborated by Marx, but to seek to use them better" (154). Instead, Meeks suggests that his goal was to rethink Marxism beyond its limits of actually-existing socialism of the twentieth century, not dissimilar to James's own motivations. According to Meeks (2001, 154–55), his

> underlying argument was that the theoretical failure of the Caribbean Left of the Seventies, was to assume that history was on its way, already 'overdetermined' by the course of accumulated events, by the 'world balance of forces' and the strength of 'really

existing socialism'. At the level of local politics, this implied that the need to convince people, in the broadest sense of that term, was subordinate to the imperative to take power... The purpose of my re-reading, then, was to open the door on an examination of human agency as neither simply a subset of economic forces, nor necessarily a minor element in a complex and vaguely understood 'overdetermination', but as a consideration, sui generis, in modern history, particularly at those rare moments of revolutionary boil.

In addition to the theoretical differences between post-modernism and Marxism, far more critical for the application of the thought of James to the politics of the twenty-first century, are the questions which are raised for the practical unfolding of anti-capitalist revolutionary projects in the era of globalization and neo-liberal capitalist hegemony. Despite claiming a space for itself as a 'radical' critique of the present order, post-modernism has not eclipsed the insight of Marxism as a theoretical and practical rejection of the dominant capitalist system. As Watson declares, while "it is not difficult to generate criticism of Marxism that announce the irrelevance or death of Marxism in politically correct ways... [t]here remains the serious matter of how to get over the historical necessity capitalism has imposed under the mantle of the national state" (Watson 2001, 373). In Watson's view, the class dimensions of ongoing social struggles globally, make it impossible to abandon Marxism. He agrees with Callari and Ruccio that there are no "intelligent grounds on which to make a case for a complete break between modernity and postmodernity, unless one wants to posit the 'conditions for an uncontested restoration of bourgeois modernism'" (in Watson 2001, 373).

In short, post-modernism has not assisted with advancing concrete anti-capitalist struggles. This inherently politically debilitating feature of post-modernism is seen in the now popular tendency by activists to downplay the relevance of class, while elevating "identity issues" to the centre. The negative implications for concrete struggle of these tendencies have been captured in a theoretical denunciation of post-modernism by a prominent Marxist collective, the International Marxist Tendency (IMT), in a paper entitled, 'Marxist Theory and the Struggle Against Alien Ideas' (later published as 'Marxism vs Identity Politics') (IMT 2018). While acknowledging that "oppression takes many forms... among the most universally painful being the "oppression of women in a male-dominated world", the IMT insisted that "the central contradiction in society remains the antagonism between wage labour and capital" and it insisted that the rebellion of women against all forms of gender oppression "cannot be attained without the full participation of women in the fight against capitalism".

However, it is the specifically anti-revolutionary nature of the post-modernist outlook which forms the crux of the paper's denunciation. Central to the IMT's rebuff of the post-modernist worldview is its "rejection of revolution in favour of 'small deeds' (like pettifogging arguments over words and 'narratives'), a retreat into subjectivity, a denial of the class struggle, elevating 'my' particular oppression over 'yours', which in turn leads to an increasing compartmentalization, and ultimately atomization of the movement". A specific problem arising out of post-modernism's tendencies towards compartmentalization is the absence of organizational unity against all forms of oppression and the tendency to focus on "particular forms of oppression", while tending to "ignore or play down the real basis of oppression, *which is class society itself*". The IMT's position paper also condemns the post-modernists for breaking down the struggle into its smallest component parts: "pitting black women against black men, black disabled women against black able-bodied women", and of inviting "every separate segment... to assert *our* rights against *your* rights" (IMT 2018). As a result of this, "the movement thus is broken into smaller and smaller parts", and as a consequence, diverts "*attention from the main issues and pitting different groups of the oppressed against each other*" (Emphasis in original) (IMT 2018).

It is clear therefore that there are real and concrete political consequences of the post-modernist turn, specifically as they relate to the blunting of revolutionary activity. It is also clear that despite the best attempts of contemporary revisionists to 'discover their own C.L.R. James' and to deny the Marxism in C.L.R. James, the true essence of his contribution to Caribbean and Marxist thought, resides in his application of the Marxist method to understanding the possibilities for radical responses to capitalist-based oppression since the late twentieth century. Instead of denying the Marxism in James, it is therefore more intellectually useful to explore his specific application of the Marxist dialectical method as a tool for understanding the transformations in global capitalism and the possibilities for anti-capitalist revolt. How James marshals the dialectic to explain the contradictions in Stalinism, and to anticipate the future directions in anti-capitalist struggles, provides the clearest basis for grasping his relevance for understanding the potential transformation of global capitalism in the twenty-first century.

James's Dialectic and the Post-USSR Era

A full appreciation of the relevance of the political thought of C.L.R. James to understanding the potentialities of revolutionary, anti-capitalist revolt can be gleaned from James's reformulations of the generalisations which he inherited from a preceding period, and his corresponding application of the dialectical method to his own observations and lived reality of capitalism in the twentieth century. Specifically, it is how James applied the method to understand the internal crisis of Marxism, following the deviations in the Soviet Union and the split in the movement under Stalin, which makes a study and application of his thought of critical importance to contemporary, twenty-first century Marxism.

The crisis which pervaded Marxism in the middle of the twentieth century emerged over the nature of the Soviet Union under Stalin, how it should be categorised and what sort of theoretical and tactical position should be adopted towards it. To many, the distortions created by Stalin represented an inherent flaw in Marxism itself, and many committed Marxists became its most bitter critics. Indeed, Popper's critique of Marxism, which was examined earlier, was heavily influenced by such an attitude (Magee 1975, 10–12).

While others saw Stalinism as being evidence of the failure of the inherent state-centrism of socialism, James in contrast saw the Stalinist state as being part of the development of global capitalism. He saw Stalinism as representing the objective movement of the proletariat; a movement which had developed to the point where private appropriation had been superseded, but where social proletarian ownership and control had not been achieved (James 1986b; Worcester 1983, 25). He defined the Soviet Union as *state-capitalist*, while Trotsky, remaining wedded to the Leninist categories, saw state ownership as being synonymous with socialism and defined Russia as a 'degenerated workers' state' (James 1980a). This use of dialectical thought, to continually rethink analytical categories, while remaining fixed on his universal of a free proletariat is the key which makes James particularly relevant to the present concerns of twenty-first century Marxism.

However, the external tensions and internal contradictions which manifested themselves in the eventual failure of the Soviet Union and which gave rise to notions of a crisis of Marxism, cannot be spuriously brushed aside or ignored. Indeed, the lessons of the failure of the Soviet Union have been the concrete material for the analysis of the possibilities of the creation of a more advanced post-capitalist socialist and democratic future. Indeed, as the head of the South African Communist Party, Joe Slovo (1990, 25) noted at the time of the internal revolts against Russian and Eastern European communism, these were "popular revolts against unpopular regimes" and "if socialists are unable to come to terms with this reality, the future of socialism is indeed bleak".

While these Eastern European communist regimes represented the highest concrete and material expression of socialist possibilities at the time, in terms of actual practice, it is also true that they were highly undemocratic, providing their citizens with little scope for participation in the political process. They were characterized by severe restrictions on travel and access to information. Although private ownership of the means of production had been abolished, and basic needs of most citizens had been met, there remained significant limitations in production, distribution and consumption under state ownership. The absence of a more democratic basis for deciding economic priorities resulted in a heavy statist bias. The emphasis was on heavy industry while basic consumer items were a virtual scarcity (Gorbachev 1988) or were the preserve of the *nomenklatura*.

It is these internal weaknesses in the Soviet Union and twentieth century Marxism which makes the Jamesian application of the dialectic necessary not only against hostile critics coming from outside the Marxist perspective, but in light of misconceptions and distortions that have arisen from within the Marxist school itself. Such distortions were partly the result of official Stalinist interpretations of Marxism, forcefully and opportunistically applied to the political needs of the regime as the situation demanded, but also lazily copied and adopted to regions outside the Soviet Union. It was these distortions which had been addressed by the wide array of Marxist (re)thinkers such as C.L.R. James and Antonio Gramsci (Joll 1977; Finocchiaro 1988), and by Michael Albert and Robin Hahnel, in *Unorthodox Marxism* (1978).

Gramsci was specifically critical of the positivist interpretation of the Marxist infrastructure/superstructure relationship (Joll 1977, 82–83; Finochiaro 1988, 164–65). His analysis of this question was heavily influenced by Marx's 1859 preface to the *Critique of Political Economy*, in which he outlined the classic relationship between technology and social change: "no social order ever perishes before all the productive forces for which there is room in it have developed; and new, higher relations of production never appear before the material conditions for their existence have matured in the womb of the old society" (Joll 1977,

84).[4] Gramsci's concept of hegemony was based on the view that elements of the superstructure such as culture, values and the realm of ideas can impact upon the development of human society (Joll 1977, 85), and he also emphasised the view that the transition to a qualitatively different mode of existence can be a long, drawn-out process. Gramsci also reinforced the notion that no form of prediction can be established through the dialectic since all the possible forms of social relations that can be established upon future modes of production remain unknown, since they can only be determined by concrete reality. Similarly, it has been noted by Trotman (1993, 46) that "both James and Gramsci moved from an orthodox Marxism to a new and higher praxis in which material forces were thought to be reciprocally linked with form, thus dramatically transforming the notion of social change".

It is the assumption that the method is a tool of prediction (an error shared both by positivist Marxists and the enemies of Marxism) which lures the orthodox Marxist into thinking that the dialectical method provides one with an *apriori* solution to the puzzle of history. Indeed, as Bertell Ollman (1986, 42) explains,

> the dialectic as such explains nothing, proves nothing, predicts nothing, and causes nothing to happen. Rather, dialectics is a way of thinking which brings into focus the full range of changes and interactions that occur in the world. It includes how to organise a reality viewed in this manner for purposes of study, and how to present to others, most of whom do not think dialectically, the results of what one finds.

It is on such a basis that the contribution of C.L.R. James to Marxist thought, and in particular, his contribution to understanding the possibilities of revolutionary politics since the latter half of the twentieth century can be understood.

James's Marxism is marked by strong intellectual understanding of the capacity of bottom-up, grass roots activity by working people to undertake the organisation of the new social relations that would replace capitalism. His vision of the post-capitalist society is one in which free reign is given to the creative instincts of ordinary people. James's insistence on the dialectical alteration of analytical categories makes his work of prime importance in serving as a critique of orthodox Marxism, and in overcoming the extended period of post-USSR mourning, defeatism and hopelessness. This insistence on the dialectical alteration of analytical categories, is an attack on all orthodoxy, for it is in the nature of orthodoxy to remain fixed in unmoving categories and, as a result, to develop into dogmatism. James's perspective on the race question, for example, demonstrates his willingness to move beyond the orthodox interpretations of historical and materialist dialectics. To James, the race issue held a central place in his analysis rather than being relegated to a subordinate position as was the case within the orthodox Marxist interpretation (James 1992f, 1989; Richards 1992; Robinson 1983). Albert and Hahnel (1978, 63) maintain that the "orthodox Marxist misses the fact that people arrive at revolutionary consciousness via different routes due not only to class, but to racial and sexual differences as well", and this appears to be the basis upon which James utilized and advanced the dialectical method.

To speak of a Jamesian dialectic, therefore, is to acknowledge the original, deeply insightful and profound manner in which James applied the dialectical method to political developments occurring in the middle of the twentieth century in general, and more importantly to the development of the labour movement in particular. It is also reflective of his conscious and deliberate use of the dialectical method to formulate a Marxism for the middle of the twentieth century.

C.L.R. James's dialectic was informed just as heavily by Hegel as it was by Marx (see Cambridge 1992: 1, 176). This does not mean that James was guilty of idealism. What it means is that James, like Marx, was aware of the analytical value of the Hegelian dialectic, but grounded it firmly in the analysis of society. However, whereas Marx's dialectic focuses primarily on the study of capitalism as a productive and social system, James's dialectic is applied to the study of the movement of the proletariat; the movement of the class seeking to overcome capitalism. James's unique contribution to Marxism therefore, lies in his application of dialectical analysis to the labour movement.

To James, the most important thing for a dialectician, both in thought and in action, was to alter his analytical categories in line with changing material conditions. This stemmed from his appreciation of two of Hegel's philosophical categories, *Understanding* and *Essence* and their significance for understanding the transitions in the labour movement. James understood Hegel to be saying that *understanding* is a category of thought which is based upon fixed, limited and finite classifications. It does not realise that categories of thought should change as the conditions which gave birth to their emergence change as well. Hegel suggests that "understanding makes determinations and maintains them" (James 1980a, 16).

James found Hegel's definition of *understanding* to be expressed clearly in Hegel's critique of the Kantian mode of thought. According to James, in Hegel's view, Kant,

> did not look to see where his categories came from, he just took them over from the old logic. He did not see that the categories developed out of one another, in a consistent movement, of opposition and resolution of opposition, and were all connected. He did not see that at critical moments, a new category appeared because the old categories could no longer contain the new content (James 1980a, 17).

It is clear therefore that *understanding* lies in stark contrast to dialectical logic, but as James points out, it is a necessary stage in the development of thought. This is why James insists that the dialectician must fully appreciate the way *understanding* works. James (1980a, 105) maintains that the main aim of Hegel's logic was,

> how to keep out of fixed, limited, finite categories. That is all. But what an all! To get out of the clutching hands of fixed categories. It isn't easy. Precisely because we have to get them fixed and precise before we can do anything. We can remain fixed in them when they are grabbed on to by people who are objectively satisfied to remain there. Worse still,

we can remain fixed in them when they no longer exist. The result is complete frustration and blindness to reality.

The other Hegelian category of significance to James's application to the labour movement is *Essence*. According to James, Hegel informs us that,

> Becoming in essence - its reflective movement - is the movement from Nothing to Nothing and through Nothing back to itself. The transition or Becoming transcends itself in its transition : that Other which arises in the course of this transition is not the Not-Being of a Being, but the Nothing of a Nothing - which constitutes Being - Being exists only as the movement of Nothing to Nothing and this is Essence; and Essence does not contain this movement in itself but is this movement, an absolute show and pure negativity, which has nothing without it that could negate it, but negates only its own negativity, which is in this negation (James 1980a, 75).

This definition stresses the fact that *essence* is a movement. *Understanding* does not appreciate that *essence* is a movement. *Understanding* can only relate to the *Being* that *essence* creates throughout its movement. The *Being* that essence creates is in fact a 'nothing' since it is negated by essence in its movement towards the universal, which is the ultimate thing that essence is trying to become.

James's conclusions are of direct significance to the present-day Caribbean and global workers' movement. He maintains that all previous forms assumed by the workers' movement were *Nothings*, which the movement temporarily adopted in its movement towards the *Universal* which is a free proletariat, one that has overcome the limitations of capitalism. James (1980a, 77) claims that,

> these forms show the labour movement going somewhere. But the 1948 revolutions, they came and went, the commune came and went [one may add to this list the Grenada revolution and the USSR]... But ... the proletarian movement continues. They have an external being, and these vanish, then new external forms appear.

Thus, despite the fact that various historical external forms and creations of the proletarian movement have appeared and have been negated, their experiences contribute to the development of the movement in general, and the new movement incorporates into itself the experiences of the old. As a result, the new expression of the proletarian movement is qualitatively richer than the past experience. This is why James defines essence as a "movement of stored up Being" (James 1980a, 77). The important thing, James warns, is not to mistake the *Being* for the *Essence*, that is, not to take the *Particular* for the *Universal* (James 1980a). This, to James, was Trotsky's error in his struggle with Stalin. It is this error which led to his insistence that the Soviet Union under Stalin was socialist. This is because Trotsky remained wedded to the categories which saw nationalised property as representing socialism. According to James (1980a, 52) "the Universal of socialism is not nationalised property and plan". He insisted that the "Marxist movement did not say this until about 1929", and he proposed instead that "the Universal of socialism is the free proletariat" and that "any socialist determination must contain this 'in principle'".

It is a similar persistence in focusing too heavily on the *Particular* of twentieth century Russian Communism which has resulted in the over-determined claims of a crisis of Marxism, and in the widely held interpretation of the fall of the Soviet Union as representing the 'death of Socialism'. The USSR, like the Paris Commune, was merely a *Particular* (a *Nothing*) that the proletarian movement created and as James had argued, would negate in its eventual movement given its internal contradictions (Belle 1994, 99). The fall of the Soviet Union has not meant that the labour movement itself has ceased, for as Miliband (1991a, 26) has argued, "what renders such proclamations absurd is the existence of capitalism itself". Indeed, the period of euphoria of triumphant capitalism following the fall of the Soviet Union in 1990, was very brief. It was interrupted by the crisis of global capitalism of 2008/2009. The period since 2008 has witnessed the gradual retreat from bellicose neo-liberal assumptions, an increasing level of scepticism towards its theoretical claims, and an about-turn to an increasing level of state intervention as a practical response to the crisis. In addition, further crises in global capitalism arising out of the global pandemic associated with COVID-19, have deepened the material conditions which have brought neo-liberal capitalist assumptions into question.

Therefore, the most significant value of James to twenty-first century political realities, lies in his attempt to outline what, in his view, represented the new determinant features in the development of the labour movement, and more specifically, the broader social movement in the world and in the Caribbean, incorporated in which are activities of working people and those resisting or 'responding' to the exigences of capital. It is in the expressions of broad social movements in the twenty-first century and in the Caribbean, and in the interpretation and understanding of how these activities impact on the future existence of capital and point to the possibilities of a post-capitalist future, that the value of James for the twenty-first Caribbean is appreciated.[5] James felt that the new antagonism within the labour movement was that between organisations of the proletariat such as the party and the trade union and the desire for 'free creative activity' on the part of the proletariat, which involves freedom from direction and guidance from above. According to James (1980a, 61–62),

> the conflict of the proletariat is between itself as object and itself as consciousness, its party. The party has a dialectical development of its own. The solution of the conflict is the fundamental abolition of this division ... The revolutionary party of this epoch will be organised labour itself and the revolutionary petty bourgeoisie. The abolition of capital and the abolition of the distinction between the proletariat as object and the proletariat as consciousness will be one and the same process. That is our new notion and it is with these eyes that we examine what the proletariat is in actuality.

This position of James grew out of his historical analysis of the labour movement. James felt that in every instance of working class activity, the spontaneous action of the mass movement proved to be far more revolutionary than the middle class leadership. James (1980a, 119–20) argues that historically, when the working class movement bursts into action, the middle class leadership "as a rule bitterly oppose this new and unexpected expression of the very class they have supported". This focus on the spontaneous activity of the working class finds a similar emphasis in the work of Rosa Luxemburg. James's critique of the role of leadership in revolutionary situations is echoed by Luxemburg (1961, 93) where she claims that,

> the unconsciousness comes before the conscious. The logic of the historic process comes before the subjective logic of the human beings who participate in the historic process. The tendency is for the directing organs of the socialist party to play a conservative role. Experience shows that every time the labour movement wins new terrain these organs work it to the utmost. They transform it at the same time into a kind of bastion, which holds up advance on a wider scale.[6]

This feature of stagnation and inertia on the part of the working-class leadership and its organisations led James to some significant conclusions about the future of revolutionary organisations, which are now manifesting themselves more fully in the age of the internet, and post-Soviet Union reality. James felt that while at an earlier stage in the development of the labour movement the formation of revolutionary parties and workers' trade unions represented an advancement in the consciousness and activity of the proletarian movement, in the present context, where a more sophisticated and experienced labour movement exists, the role of the organs of representation of the working class has tended to inhibit and stifle this movement. This is why James advocated that for the working class movement to find itself it had to abolish organisation (James 1980a). It is only in this way that a more complete democracy and genuine socialism would be acheived. James's notion of the development of the labour movement, and his emphasis on the need to alter analytical categories to correspond with the development of this movement forces him to conclude that Lenin's vanguard party, an organisational type which heavily influenced the development of the workers' movement in the Caribbean (Mills 1991, 14–16), had now become a fetter on the further development of the working class. According to James, Lee and Chaulieu ([1958] 1974, 87), the Leninist vanguard party "was a particular theory, designed to suit a specific stage of development of society and a specific stage of working-class development". They argued however, that "that stage of society is now past", and that the "theory and the practice that went with it, if persisted in, lead to one form or another of the counter-revolution". This view was advanced not only in relation to Lenin's vanguard party but to all organisations of the working class which were established upon the principle of representation. According to James, it is only the direct action of the working class itself, a working class which has abolished the distinction between the 'proletariat as being' and the 'proletariat as consciousness' which can ensure the continued advancement of the working class movement.

A Jamesian Political Thought for the Caribbean?

The above exposition, then, offers a broad summary of the essence of the Jamesian Marxist outlook and method. Why then, is James relevant to the twenty-first century Caribbean?

Of direct relevance to the Caribbean is the fact that, to James, socialist advancement meant advancement of democracy beyond the limits imposed upon it by a bourgeois, capitalist order. In James's view, socialism and participatory democracy were inextricably intertwined. As will be seen in the chapter on Jamesian democracy (chapter four), this re-examination of the link between socialism and democracy is particularly important for the Caribbean for several reasons.

First, despite its claims to the adherence to formal democratic norms, the Caribbean has not advanced democracy beyond the mere holding of formal elections. There are substantive areas of democratic culture such as the recognition of minority rights, and other more formal aspects of democratic behaviour such as recall mechanisms and term limits which are yet to take form in Caribbean democratic practice. Secondly, despite new technological developments which allow for more direct forms of democratic participation, the Caribbean remains wedded to narrow forms of representative practice that effectively militate against newer and further democratic advancement. Finally, the Caribbean has been wedded to Cold War interpretations of socialism, which deny the possibilities for greater levels of democratic participation, related to forms of economic distribution and enfranchisement. An opportunity thus exists, as will be shown in chapter four, to apply James's framework of socialist democracy to Caribbean politics, and this opens new vistas of democratic practice, yet untapped in the Caribbean.

James was particularly critical of a form of socialism which was based on a sharp distinction between the leaders and the led. Significantly, this criticism was levelled with equal force at modern systems of democracy which, in James's perspective, all suffered from the limits of representation.[7] Indeed, to James, the representative principle serves as a barrier to, or a negation of, the direct participation or self-government of the working class. It is this view which makes Jean-Jacques Rousseau the most significant of all the social contract theorists to James. James did not see Rousseau as being the father of modern totalitarianism as held by some theorists. Instead, he saw Rousseau as a most uncompromising advocate of direct democracy and popular sovereignty. James, in his public library lecture series given in Trinidad in 1960, held that although other writers had written about the social contract,

> they had made the contract in regard to not only the association of men but a contract in regard to government. Rousseau says the contract is between us, as people to form a society; but we have no contract with any government; the contract is strictly between us, and the whole trend of this thought is that any time a government does not do what is satisfactory, we are finished with it; the contract is broken; we have to start all over again. That is a doctrine of profound revolutionary implications (James 1960, 19).

James explains further that in Rousseau's view, representative government was a complete farce. Representative government was no guarantee that the interests of people would be served. Instead, it served to ensure that the government had a free hand in pursuing its own interests (James 1960, 20). Parliaments, political parties and trade unions represented "all sorts of private or special interest" while totally ignoring the interests of society which they claim to represent (James 1960, 20). Relatedly, James's insistence that the development of society was heading towards participatory democracy, explains his attraction to ancient Athenian democracy. What fascinated James most about the ancient Greek city state was the highly democratic relationship which it reputedly established between citizen and government. James (1960, 21–22) insists that,

> much of our study of modern politics is going to be concerned with this tremendous battle to find a form of government which reproduces on a more highly developed economic level, the relationship between the individual and the community, that was established so wonderfully in the Greek city state.[8]

James's preoccupation with Greek democracy should not be viewed as a nostalgic, idealist fixation on a once tenable, but now outdated, system of government. In fact, quite the contrary is the case. His interest in the modern application of a Greek-type democracy was based on a materialist analysis of the objective development of society. He was of the firm conviction that the development of the forces of production had created new forms of communication and participation which made possible the transcendence of limited representative democracy. Indeed, the work of several writers, such as Alvin Toffler (1981) and Benjamin Barber (1984), have largely moved towards confirming James's early insights. Many such writers conclude that modern day advances in communications technology, increases in the levels of education, as well as increasingly more complex and varied, personal and private political issues, point to a situation in which a return to a democracy akin to that of the Greek city state is feasible.

Another element of James's thought which makes it of specific relevance to the Caribbean, is his preoccupation with the 'race question', its implications for the establishment of socialism and democracy, and its relation to anti-colonialism and anti-imperialism. The fact of James's blackness made it difficult for him merely to accept European Marxism passively, with all its inherent assumptions about European superiority (Singham 1970, 84) and its emphasis on class struggle while downplaying other antagonisms such as those associated with race and gender (Mills 1991). It is this awareness of the black radical tradition impacting on the thought of James, which has been isolated for deeper analysis by Anthony Bogues (1997) and Christian Høgsbjerg (2014). The race question therefore forms a crucial pillar of James's ideas, and his Marxism cannot be understood without an appreciation of the manner in which it colours his otherwise transparent Marxist lens. James's contribution to the race/class debate within the Marxist paradigm makes his work one of critical importance to any study of Caribbean politics for, as has been pointed out, 'racial oppression can uncontroversially be categorised as the salient oppression of the region' (Mills 1991, 24).

It can be readily admitted that James's views have been shaped more overtly by his Marxism which emphasises the primacy of class antagonism rather than by his blackness. However, James never ignored the 'race question', and it influenced and permeated all his political writings, growing in significance and emphasis as his political thought matured. The place of the 'race question' in James's thought has been best encapsulated in the (perhaps over worn and mis-understood) comment in *The Black Jacobins* where James had sought to resolve the race/class dilemma in his account of the Haitian Revolution:

> the race question is subsidiary to the class question in politics, and to think of imperialism in terms of race is disastrous. But to neglect the racial factor as merely incidental is an error only less grave than to make it fundamental (James 1989, 283).

The basis of the mis-understanding of the above statement has arisen from the assumption that, in James, the "race question" was always treated as being "subsidiary" to the class question in theory and in practice. Indeed, James's views on self-government, free creative activity and spontaneity made a 'race first' outlook and a movement on the basis of race perfectly consistent within the entire Jamesian framework. This is not to deny the centrality of race in James's analysis, but his advancement of the notion of worker self-activity allowed his Marxism to be perfectly consistent with modes of black self-organisation (see Joseph 2022). This is clearly borne out in James's (1992f) work on the race question in the United States and in his activities as a pan-Africanist in collaboration with George Padmore, T. Ras Makonen, Kwame Nkrumah and others. In works such as *The Revolutionary Answer to the Negro problem in the U.S.A.* and in his 1939 meeting with Trotsky in Mexico, James advocates that the Negro struggle was a struggle independent of the socialist movement and should not be repressed but should be given whole-hearted support by the socialist parties. Tony Martin (1984, 173), writing on this feature of James's thought, notes that the "lines of thought - that black people should unite with white workers, and that black people should capitalise on the contradictions within white society", usually flow from the same analysis in James's thought and he "does not normally consider them opposed but complementary".

Given the centrality of the race question in Caribbean political life and political thought, coupled with the rise of newly emergent questions around reparations for slavery and genocide as well as the growing awareness of the need for a renewed pan-Africanist vision to shape the relations between Africa and the Caribbean, the exploration of James's view of race to contemporary questions of Caribbean political life becomes critically important. Chapter Five will address more frontally the relevance of James's views on race to the contemporary race discourse in Caribbean political life.

Finally, and in the broadest sense, the utility of James's thought to the politics of the twenty-first century Caribbean, can be seen in his specific use of the dialectic as a key which allows for the alteration of analytical categories in the face of 'disnormative' transformation. The usefulness of James therefore resides in his ability to demonstrate how qualitative transformation in the entire global political economy has impacted upon the possibilities of radical transformation, and in the guidelines which he presents for the application of radical alternatives in the midst of these transformations.

James's focus on the objective movement of social and political forces makes his work of critical importance to the Caribbean. His deliberate focus on the need to alter analytical categories lends itself as a tool to be applied to the analysis of present-day transformations and their attendant consequences. The transformations of the twenty-first century, rooted as they are in a qualitatively and rapidly altering economic mode of production, has implications for the entire superstructure, inclusive of the political system. The impact of these global developments on Caribbean politics was seen particularly in the late 1980s when the framework under which Caribbean sovereignty had been fought and won, was beginning to be eroded. By the early 1990s, the overarching global framework of trade preferences, political alliances, global geo-political relations and underlying economic and political ideologies which had sustained the decolonisation movement in the Caribbean, and which had legitimated its aspirations to sovereign statehood were being overturned. These developments eroded the space for the kinds of development that had defined the post-colonial period.

All of these issues hold critical questions for the state and level of development of the Caribbean working class in the twenty-first century. The full implications of the impact of these transformations on the nature of working-class activity, modes of organisation and expression, the issues around which mobilisation occurs, and their connection to global developments, remain to be explored. Each of the following three chapters, therefore, is organised around isolating specific areas around which Jamesian political practice and theorising had been undertaken (socialism, democracy and race) and in each instance, providing an analysis and description of Caribbean working-class activity and organisation around each of these themes. The emphasis, therefore, is to use the work of James as an explanatory model for understanding twenty-first century transformations in Caribbean politics, and as a lens through which working class political organisation and activity can be understood.

3.

C.L.R. James's Socialist Thought and the 21st Century Caribbean

Proletarian revolutions ... criticize themselves constantly, interrupt themselves continually in their own course, come back to the apparently accomplished in order to begin it afresh, deride with unmerciful thoroughness the inadequacies, weaknesses and paltriness of their first attempts, seem to throw down their adversary only in order that he may draw new strength from the earth and rise again, more gigantic, before them, recoil ever and anon from the indefinite prodigiousness of their own aims until a situation is created which makes all turning back impossible...

Karl Marx – The Eighteenth Brumaire of Louis Bonaparte

The State and Socialism

One of the critical areas germane to the rethinking of Marxism in light of the twentieth century experience of the collapse of the European/Russian Soviet model, is the question of the role of the state in the establishment of socialism. This question has been the focus of much disagreement among revolutionary forces from the very inception of Marxist political theorizing and, indeed, many of the errors which have occurred in actually-existing socialism have been the consequence of 'fetishizing the state and state power' in the construction of socialism. An examination of C.L.R. James's perspectives on the role of the state in the construction of socialism is important therefore, for understanding the possibilities of socialist state or 'post state' formations in the post-Soviet Union period.

A central idea that unites Marxist thinkers is that the capitalist state is "nothing but a committee for managing the common affairs of the whole bourgeoisie" (Marx and Engels 1968, 5). The capitalist state is seen, not as a neutral arbiter among contending interests, but as an instrument whose essence lies in the safeguarding and enhancement of the interests of the economically dominant class. One major area of disagreement, however, has been over the method or mechanism through which this class character of the capitalist state can be overcome in the establishment of socialist society. This question has remained a major source of debate amongst Marxists.

One of the first major Marxist debates around the question of how to overcome the bourgeois-class character of the state took place within the party founded by Marx himself, the International Workingmen's Association, and has been generally referred to as the Anarchist-Marxist debate. This debate gave rise to what has been descried by (Eckhardt 2016) as the "first socialist schism". It occurred in the earliest days of the formation of the International Workingmen's Association, and essentially revolved around the role and nature of the state in a post-capitalist order. While the anarchist camp led by Bakunin called for the immediate dissolution of the state, the Marxist camp, led by Marx, advocated the proletarian seizure of state power as a necessary prelude to its withering away (Engels 1978, 339–40).

A later, and equally important debate in which the question of the deployment of state power in a socialist revolution was a central concern, was the Marxist-Revisionist debate. This debate, occurring in the decades leading up to the Russian revolution saw the militaristic and revolutionary formulations of Vladimir Lenin for the overthrow of the bourgeois state, pitted against the gradualism of reformists like Eduard Bernstein. Bernstein had advocated a longer-term accommodation to the capitalist state form, and had posited that "the Social Democratic movement had been transformed from a revolutionary class struggle into a political and social reform movement" (Korsch 1937).

Despite Miliband's claim that Lenin's main concern in *State and Revolution*, "is to attack and reject any concept of revolution which does not take literally Marx's view that the bourgeois state must be smashed" rather than to argue against reformism per se (Miliband 1983, 155), there is no escaping the fact that the Marxist-Revisionist debate was as equally concerned with the question of the seizure of state power. Indeed, the Marxist-Revisionist debate foreshadowed the future to which concrete Marxist projects were headed. While the Anarchist-Marxist debate involved a question of the withering away of the state, the Marxist-Revisionist debate was concerned primarily with how state power would be seized. That debate, however, never fully addressed the question of the implications of the existence of the state, after the revolution, and its potential impact on the establishment of socialism (Wallerstein 1984, 51).[1]

Much of the later crises which beset Marxism in the late twentieth century, was as a result of a too heavy emphasis being placed on the need to seize, consolidate, defend and maintain state power, and the insufficient theoretical attention given to the question of the post-capitalist forms which would facilitate the emergence of socialism. This reality has pointed to an inconsistency between the theory of the dominant Marxist view which anticipates the withering away of the state once the proletariat has seized political power (Engels 1978, 339–40), and what actually obtains in practice (Wallerstein 1984; Miliband 1983; Luard 1979). Evan Luard (1979, 20) writing in *Socialism Without the State* has noted that, "far from achieving the withering away of the state, socialism brought about the establishment of a state more powerful, more totalitarian, more ubiquitous in its influence and control than any the world had yet seen", a view which James had made forcefully in *World Revolution* in the 1930s ([1937] 2017, 222–34) as indeed Trotsky himself in The Revolution

Betrayed ([1937] 1972, 248–56), despite the fact that they offered different theoretical and tactical responses to the expansion of state power.

This enlargement in the role and power of the state in post-revolutionary situations cannot be attributed to individual or particular weaknesses. Instead, it can best be understood as an objective, structural consequence of the establishment of an 'autonomous' singular socialist state structure, within a capitalist world economy (Wallerstein 1984) dominated by an industrial mode of production (Toffler 1981). Wallerstein (1984, 52) in underscoring this development, argues that "what we have discovered is that the soviet experience – the anti-systemic movement coming to power and strengthening markedly the state machinery – is not an aberration but the result of deep structural forces operating on the social movements themselves". Not only is this growth in state power an inauspicious development from the point of view of Marxist theory, but from a practical, tactical perspective it raises fundamental questions about the effectiveness of the acquisition of state power as a route to socialism. As Luard (1979, 2) has noted, the twentieth century socialist experience had failed "to increase equality, failed to abolish alienation, failed to provide any genuine sense of control for the worker over his destiny or, for the citizen over the decisions which affect him".

These historical experiences of the failure of the socialist and communist states to achieve more tangible forms of human freedom beyond the experience of capitalism, have led to a number of theoretical reflections on the limits of socialist transformation within the confines of the capitalist world economy.

One such formulation is Immanuel Wallerstein's world-system theory. It has provided a useful analytical framework for understanding why Marxist projects suffered exhaustion in the twentieth century. Wallerstein's (1984, 144) argument is that, "the state is not the framework within which social action occurs but merely one of the institutions created to sustain and promote the interest of the various actors in the world-economy". Based on these observations, he downplays the ability of the socialist states to achieve qualitative and revolutionary transformation, preferring instead to describe these moments as "anti-systemic" rather than as concrete negations of capitalism. In his view, "the acquisition of state power by an anti-systemic movement can therefore only be what the acquisition of state power by anyone else is, an instrument with which to maneuver in the political arena of the world economy. It is not the only such instrument. And like all instruments, it is only useful when placed within a continuing global strategy" (144). Given these realities, Wallerstein goes further to suggest that the acquisition of state power may, in some instances, act as a fetter on the further advancement of socialism (Wallerstein 1984, 94–95). One of the potential drawbacks which the holding of state power may pose is that revolutionaries "put themselves in a position where they fear revolutionary upheavals" (Wallerstein 1984, 95).[2]

It is this detailed focus on the question of the state in the context of socialist revolution which makes the work of C.L.R. James of critical importance to the rethinking and re-application of Marxist theory to the politics of the twenty-first century. Perhaps the most salient aspect of C.L.R. James's socialist thought is his total disillusionment with the state as a mechanism through which socialist development can be initiated. In James's work it is the "withering away of the state", rather than the seizure of state power which receives critical attention. Despite the fact that James's conceptualization of worker-council led forms of organization was open to the possibility of some form of 'worker's state', this anti-statist orientation, particularly as it relates to the hierarchical and exploitative features of power relations seen in capitalist and pre-capitalist forms, remains a central feature of the Jamesian perspective.

James was insistent that a state system which was characterized by the alienation of the majority from the decision-making process, the absence of avenues for democratic expression, and the existence of standing armies and para-military units standing over and above society, could never be considered socialist. To James, socialism can only be said to have been realized after the bourgeois state, both in its structure and in its functions, had ceased to exist and had been replaced by organs which facilitate proletarian participation, ownership and control. In outlining the differences between Stalinist politics and that of a new revolutionary international, James (1992b, 199) argues that while the "Stalinists seek to establish themselves in the place of the rival bureaucracy" a genuinely socialist alternative, "must not seek to substitute itself in the place of these, not after, not during nor before the conquest of power". Instead, it must recognize "the necessity that the bureaucracy as such must be overthrown". James views all states – "the Stalinist state, the Nazi state and, in their varying degrees, all states today" – as denials of socialist possibility, since they are all "based upon property and privilege" and are "the negation of the complete democracy of the people". According to James, "it is this state which is to be destroyed, that is to say, it is this state which is to be negated by the proletarian revolution" (James 1980b, 79–80).

What is profound about James's insistence on the "withering away" of the state, is its analytical proximity to the assumptions of Wallerstein's world-system perspective which gained prominence decades after James's anti-Stalinist formulations. Like Wallerstein, James was aware that socialism could not be truly achieved in one country existing within a global capitalist economy (Robinson 1992), nor did he feel that it could be built on a mode of production which had not qualitatively superseded the technological foundations of industrial society. James (1992b, 198) felt that "although completely centralised capital 'in a given country' can plan, it cannot plan away the contradictions of capitalist production". He built upon those arguments in *State Capitalism and World Revolution* (1986b, 38–39) arguing that,

> the whole tendency of the Stalinist theory is to build up theoretical barriers between the Russian economy and the economy of the rest of the world. The task of the revolutionary movement, beginning

in theory and ... reaching to all aspects of political strategy, is to break down this separation. The development of Russia is to be explained by the development of world capitalism and specifically capitalist production in its most advanced stage in the United States.

James, like Wallerstein, rejected the claims to socialism in these states, given the futility of their attempts at erecting economic barriers between themselves and the rest of the capitalist world. In addition, James's litmus test for determining the socialist content of a new social formation was based on factors such as the existence of avenues for direct participation and control over every aspect of decision making and implementation, the abolition of worker alienation and powerlessness, and the emergence of a new mode of production which represented a qualitative leap from the capitalist mode of production. In his view a qualitatively different state structure, which ensures wider participation and which dispenses with the division of labour in all spheres of life, can only be erected upon a qualitatively different material base.[3] James (1986b, 115–16) therefore saw Stalinism as a form of capitalism distinguished by its greater capacity to exploit workers:

> the philosophy of planned economy and one-party state is distinguishable from that of the bourgeoisie only by its more complete rationalism. The labour bureaucracy in power or out of it sees the solution to the crisis of production in scientific progress, greater output. It consciously seeks to plan and organize the division of labour as the means to further accumulation of capital.

To James, to deny that the Stalinist division of labour needs to be overcome would mean that "workers' control of production is an empty phrase" (James 1992b, 191–92).

It is on this basis that James categorized the political and economic systems of such countries as state-capitalist (James 1986b; Worchester 1983; Grimshaw 1991). Significantly, James identifies state-capitalism as a necessary stage in the development of capital. He points to US President Franklyn D. Roosevelt's "New Deal" which had seen a general expansion in the role of government, as an example of state capitalism in the most advanced capitalist economy. James saw this as a response to the fact that anarchy in production and an unfettered free market could no longer withstand the demand of the mass of the working people for more direction and control of the production process. In James's view, this mass pressure coupled with the 'crisis in production' was forcing the labour bureaucracy to "consciously seek to plan and organize the division of labour as the means to further accumulation of capital" (James 1986b, 116). James argued that this bureaucracy developed out of the working class, and was,

> a product of the modern mass movement, created by the centralization of capital, and holds its position only because of this movement. At the same time, it cannot conceive the necessity for abolishing the division of labour in production, the only solution to the crisis in production. By a remorseless logic, therefore, representation of the proletariat turns into its opposite, administration over the proletariat" (338).

Critics, however, may point to the fact that far from moving towards greater levels of state capitalism as James had anticipated, the world has appeared to move in the opposition direction. Since the 1990s notions of "minimal government" and the "free market" are upheld as the bases upon which societal production and distribution decisions should be established. In the years immediately following the collapse of Eastern European Communism, governments which sought to play active roles in the economy and society were increasingly pressured by the World Bank and the International Monetary Fund (IMF) to dispense with such functions. This question of the 'rolling back' of the state held major implications for Caribbean states whose independence projects had meant the provision of health, housing, education and social welfare services as legitimate and necessary functions of government, in stark contrast to the colonial states which were concerned only with the subjugation of the labor force and the extraction of resources to enrich the metropolis (Thomas 1988, 174).

The claim however that a rolling back of the state is the new normal, is contradicted by the heightened role of the coercive arm of the state in maintaining private capital relations, even when more production, ownership and management functions appear to be undertaken by the private sector. It is noteworthy, therefore, that the new thrust which advocates less ambitious government still sees the need for the role of government in retaining standing armies and police forces as deterrents against industrial agitation and social unrest, and as being even more critical to the survival of capitalism in the present moment. It is clear therefore that what is sought is not the termination of the role of government, but greater selectivity in the functions of the state, and in the extent to which government becomes involved in the economy. James's observations on state-capitalism as being a response to the growing unsustainability of free-market capitalism, therefore, have not been invalidated. Indeed, James had foreseen that the state would wither away "by expanding to such a degree that it is transformed into its opposite" (James 1980a, 176).

In summary therefore, the Jamesian concept of state capitalism unequivocally rejects any claim that nationalization of the means of production in a given territory is an indication of the construction of socialism. State ownership is not synonymous with worker participation in production and management decisions. James's perspective on state capitalism resonates with the observations of none less than Engels (1978, 338) who posits that,

> the modern state, no matter what its form, is essentially a capitalist machine, the state of the capitalists, the ideal personification of the total national capital. The more it proceeds to the taking over of productive forces, the more does it actually become the national capitalist, the more citizens does it exploit. The workers remain wage workers - proletarians. The capitalist relation is not done away with. It is rather brought to a head. But, brought to a head, it topples over. State ownership of the productive forces is not the solution of the conflict, but concealed within it are the technical conditions that form the elements of that solution.

The Party and Socialism

James's skepticism towards the state as an organ of revolutionary transformation was matched by his rejection of the political party, and this is also important in rethinking the nature of socialist revolution in the post-USSR twentieth century, and for examining its implications for the Caribbean. If it is agreed that genuine socialism can be achieved only after the state has been abolished, and more importantly, that socialism cannot be achieved through the acquisition and retention of state power, then logically this problematizes the political party as the mechanism through which working class empowerment can be achieved.

Firstly, the main aim of all political parties is, through one means or the other, the seizure of state power (Harvey 1974, 39). Secondly, all political parties – from the Leninist vanguard party to the "bourgeois" variety – are based on the principle of representation, a cornerstone of rationalist philosophy, which stands as the main barrier to direct worker participation in government. In other words, the political party, is the antithesis of socialist democracy (Miliband 1982, 22).

The contradiction surrounding the political party is two-fold. Firstly, as suggested by Toffler (1981, 61) the principle of representation upon which the political party is based is a product of the division of labour shaped by the industrial-capitalist infrastructure. The very Taylorite system which the socialist party seeks to overthrow is incorporated into the structure of the party itself. A similar point is made in *Notes on Dialectics* where (James 1980a, 172) stresses that the once beneficial separation between the "proletariat as being" and the "proletariat as knowing" which the party symbolizes was no longer necessary, and thus the party should now be abolished (Harvey 1974). It is on this basis that James and his inner circle in the Johnson-Forrest Tendency and other micro-groupings were often critical of Lenin's vanguard party:

> the Bolshevik party of Lenin was the greatest political party the modern world has known... But even this party in the last analysis

was a type of parliament with representatives of the workers divided into debating factions, increasingly removed from the actual conditions of social and particularly proletarian life. Today a party on that model in an advanced country can be nothing else but an instrument of oppression, tyranny and acute failure (James, Lee and Chaulieu [1958] 1974,94).

Similarly, Franklyn Harvey, a Jamesian scholar, has noted that since an important function of the party is the political education of its members through their own self-activity, then the logical conclusion would be for the whole working class to achieve 'intellectual knowing' and experience and as a result to become the party as a whole. He notes however, that such an ideal development, "has never taken place in history and in all likelihood will never take place" (Harvey 1974, 39). Instead, he notes that it is often the case that after seizing political power, the middle class uses both the state and political party against the masses. It is for these reasons that the working class will normatively abandon party politics altogether and build an organized revolutionary social movement of the whole class to liberate itself (39). It is in such a manner, and for the very reasons outlined by Harvey, that James advocates the supersession of the party, and its organic replacement by new organs of proletarian power beyond the models which reached their peak, and suffered exhaustion, in the twentieth century revolutions.

In addition to these concerns, James was also ambivalent about the capacity of the party to facilitate revolutionary transformation, given the preoccupation of the party with the acquisition of state power. James felt that the political party, because of this fixation on the control of state power, often served as a barrier to the spontaneously created worker organizations which were far superior to the state as organs of working-class representation and as instruments for the enhancement of socialist democracy. Thus, he felt that popular social formations like the Paris commune (1871), the Russian soviets (1905 and 1917) and the Hungarian workers' councils (1956) have always been crushed by 'revolutionary' governments bent on strengthening state power, and who often fail to understand the revolutionary nature of the new social formations which are emerging (Arendt 1963, 250-251; Albert and Hahnel 1978, 329; James 1966b; James, Lee and Chaulieu [1958] 1974). James was very much in agreement with Hannah Arendt (1963, 252–53) who had sought to outline the revolutionary nature of these new social formations, and who had argued that,

> each time they appeared they sprang up as the spontaneous organs of the people, not only outside of all revolutionary parties but entirely unexpected by them and their leaders...[T]hey were utterly neglected by statesmen, historians, political theorists and most important, by the revolutionary tradition itself... [T]hey failed to understand to what an extent the council system confronted them with an entirely new form of government, with a new public space for a new freedom which was constituted and organized during the course of the revolution itself.

In Arendt's understanding, the very existence of parties suggests the presence of ready-made formulas against which Rosa Luxemburg had warned, which had to be imposed upon the people and whose directives demanded not action but execution and had "to be carried out energetically in practice" (Arendt 1963, 267).

It should however be noted that the short-lived experiences of these soviets and workers' councils are far more complex and fraught with internal weaknesses than the unidimensional conclusion that they were destroyed by 'counter-revolutionary' yet nominally revolutionary forces. Indeed, the experiences of soviets and workers' council have been too fleeting to fully assess the extent to which they could exist as genuine alternatives to organs of state power in a sustained manner. Often, the soviets were dominated by reformists and indeed they could not have succeeded in their political aims without the role of key members of the Bolshevik party. Indeed, the susceptibility of the Paris Commune to dissolution by the organized French army, and the vulnerability of the soviets to the many counter-revolutionary armies and groups involved in the Russian civil war, as well as the crushing of the Hungarian Soviet by the Stalinist army in 1956, show clearly the weaknesses of workers' councils in sustaining themselves and in pursuing their revolutionary aims.

Despite these weaknesses, the argument of writers like James and Arendt in insisting that these councils represent in embryonic form, an alternative organizational form capable of replacing the organized power of the bourgeois state power with worker power cannot be dismissed. James had always insisted that the existence of such organs of working-class democracy pointed to a future in which the party became theoretically unnecessary since they performed all the political functions of the party, and went much further in that they performed the executive functions of government as well (Lenin 1943, 40–42; Albert and Hahnel 1978, 329). Significantly however, in all periods of revolutionary struggle, where such councils existed, they have been met with hostility by the party,[4] due, according to Arendt, to the largely statist orientation of the party. Arendt (1963, 260) notes that the party being, "firmly anchored in the tradition of the nation-state... conceived of revolution as a means to seize power". She notes however that in actual revolutionary situations, what was often witnessed was a "swift disintegration of the old power, the sudden loss of control over the means of violence, and, at the same time, the amazing formation of a new power structure which owed its existence to nothing but the organizational impulses of the people themselves". As a result, she argues that instead of seizing state power, revolutionary parties often found that at the moment of revolution, "there was no power left to seize" and "revolutionists found themselves before the rather uncomfortable alternative of either putting their own pre-revolutionary 'power', that is, the organization of the party apparatus, into the vacated power center of the defunct government, or simply joining the new revolutionary power centers which had sprung up without their help" (260).

It is for these reasons that James advocated the transcendence of the bourgeois political party. He was aware that the party under western capitalism, liberal representative democracy and its Eastern European post-revolutionary offshoot[5], by its structure and function was an inherently anti-proletarian organization, and that existing within the party, was a contradiction between the party as government and the party as mass mobilization.[6] These two functions are mutually incompatible and though they may manifest themselves independently as functions of the party, would come into conflict when both functions are pursued simultaneously. While the "government did not give any power to the party" and it is the "party that gave power to the government", the two exist in constant conflict because the government, being placed "in the middle of the battle" needs to make concessions, compromises and retreats at the expense of the party's principles and membership (James 1977b, 176). This conflict between the party as government and the party as mass mobilization is best expressed by Hannah Arendt, who argues that while the party is an "institution to provide parliamentary government with the required support of the people", it is "always understood that the people... did the supporting, while action remained the prerogative of government". She argues that once parties step out of this prescribed role and "step actively into the domain of political action they violate their own principle" and they become "subversive... regardless of their doctrines and ideologies" (Arendt 1963, 275).

Despite their shared hostility to totalitarianism, and although they "agreed on much about the significance of the Hungarian Revolution" (King 2006, 121), it should be noted however that C.L.R James and Hannah Arendt, owing largely to her anti-Marxist intellectual outlook and her non-Marxist methodology, differed strongly in their understanding of the political possibilities of the Workers' Councils. In addition, Arendt's "attitude towards revolutionary upheaval in the non-European world was always ambivalent and her views on it ambiguous" and her "depiction of sub-Saharan African cultures in The Origins of Totalitarianism has proven an embarrassment to even her most convinced admirers"

(King 2011, 30–31). According to King (2006, 122), "in contrast to James, who saw the workplace as the privileged site of self-government, and who emphasized the overlapping nature of the economic, social and political spheres, Arendt drew a distinction between the political and economic spheres", since the "gap between 'citizen' and 'worker' in Arendt's thought was too wide to bridge".

In contrast, James was far more optimistic in the capacity of workers' councils to resolve the economic and political marginalization of working people and to simultaneously address the tensions which exist between the party as 'government' and the party as 'mass mobilisation'. To James, these contradictions could be resolved only through the withering away of the party and the spontaneous creation of worker organizations which mirror, in terms of structure and function, the commune, soviets and workers' councils which had manifested themselves in previous revolutionary situations. In all these instances no distinction was made between the "party as party" and the "party as government". In such situations, the withering away of the state and the withering away of the party occurred as a single process of revolutionary transformation. According to James (1980a, 176):

> the party as we have known it must disappear. It will disappear. It is disappearing. It will disappear as the state will disappear. The whole labouring population becomes the state. That is the disappearance of the state. It can have no other meaning. It withers away by expanding to such a degree that it is transformed into its opposite. And the party does the same. The state withers away and the party withers away. But for the proletariat the most important, the primary thing is the withering away of the party. *For if the Party does not wither away the state never will.* [Emphasis added]

James has often been accused of idealism for his rejection of the party and his advocacy of 'free creative activity'. These criticisms have generally echoed Lenin's critique of spontaneity (Lenin 1969, 29–44), which were at the time aimed at Rosa Luxemburg's (1961,

1971) notion of the role of the social-democratic revolutionary party in revolutionary situations. However, what is often ignored is that the debate between Lenin on one hand and James and Luxemburg on the other, was that the criticism of Lenin revolved around the role of the party in the seizure of state power, and the limitations it would place on the emergence of genuine mass social-democratic post-capitalist forms. In this regard, it can be argued that the global collapse of the Eastern European Communist model and their related failure to develop new democratic institutions, have largely vindicated the James and Luxemburg perspective.

However, far from being idealistic (in the sense of not being grounded in material reality), James's perspective points attention to the limits to which the party can serve as a vehicle for social transformation. This concern is echoed in Rosa Luxemburg's notable distinction between the genuine social-democratic revolutionary movement and the 'Blanquist' approach of seizing state power as an end in itself (Luxemburg 1971, 191–93). She clarifies that from the Marxist dialectical perspective "the role of political power in revolutionary times is that of an agent which simply puts into practice the results of the inner development of society and finds its political expression in the class struggle". In contrast, she argues that "Blanquism is a recipe for the making of revolution under any conditions at any time" and is "a universal strategy which could be applied to all countries with the same degree of success" (193).

In other words, the nature of the revolutionary institution is an organic reflection of the inner development of the revolutionary class, and of the state of development of the revolution itself. In Luxemburg's view, the major political progamme of a revolutionary party "*can be neither that of the overthrow nor that of the establishment of states*" (emphasis added), but "must be the winning and widening of the political rights which are absolutely necessary for the organization of the masses within the bourgeois states in which they are active" (Luxemburg 1971, 182). In a similar vein, C.L.R. James points out in his article *Walter Rodney and the Question of Power* that,

> it is good to have a party. But even if you do not have a party, [the] point is to get to the basic objective social and political circumstances that are the inevitable bases to work on the art of insurrection. But you organize by all means, and the more you organize, the better. *But do not link the question of organization to the seizure of power* (James 1982, 143) (Emphasis added).

This then is the essential crux of the Jamesian understanding of the role of the party in its relation to socialist transformation. This holds significant implications for the question of the advancement of socialist revolution in the twentieth century, and opens the door to the question of what was the Jamesian vision of the post-Leninist and post-representative type democratic party. It is this element of the Jamesian vision which allows for his thought to be applied to understanding the nature of socialist revolution in the twenty-first century and to assess its applicability to the concrete anti-systemic politics of the Caribbean.

Free Creative Activity – Working Class Organization

In outlining his post-Leninist vison, James was adamant that the "theory and practice of the vanguard party, of the one-party state" as outlined in V.I. Lenin's writings in *What is to be Done?*, is not "and never was" the central doctrine of Leninism (James 1964, 3). Similarly, Miliband (1983, 159) sees it as an "extraordinary fact" that "the political element which otherwise occupies so crucial a place in his thought, the party, receives such scant attention in *State and Revolution*". Belle (1994, 100–01) argues similarly, that it is misleading to "ossify Lenin's category of the vanguard party and make it a fetish and fail to appreciate that it was his mastery of dialectical negation" which "preserves Lenin's outstanding historical role in and contribution to the labor movement", and he argues that "Lenin should be appreciated in the '*Why? he introduced the vanguard*' not in the vanguard itself" (101) [Emphasis in original].

Having argued against the vanguard party, James, instead, advocated unfettered mass activity as the only guarantee that the bourgeois state would not only be seized, but overthrown and replaced by new socialist structures. As discussed earlier, he was insistent that the historical significance of the Paris commune, the Russian soviets and the Hungarian workers' councils resided in the fact that they were concrete alternatives, and were far superior as organs of working-class democracy, when compared to the state and political party. James, writing on the Hungarian revolution observes that its leading characteristic was that "political parties and trade unions had nothing whatever to do with it" and that it "was established by workers' councils in every department of national life" (James 1960, 90). Writing in *Facing Reality*, James, Lee and Chaulieu ([1958] 1974,7) emphasize that what was crucially significant about the Hungarian soviets is that "from the very start the workers demonstrated such conscious mastery of the needs, processes and interrelations of production, that they did not have to exercise any domination over people". They note that this mastery is "the very essence of any government which is to be based upon general consent and not on force".

In arriving at his position on the democratic and revolutionary nature of the workers' councils, James had relied on Lenin's approach to the soviets during the Russian revolution. James argues that it was the reappearance of the soviets in the heat of the revolutionary struggle of 1917, after they had burst on the scene in 1905, that convinced Lenin that Russia was ready for socialism. In this regard, James would argue that Lenin was never shy about insisting that the state bureaucratic apparatus should give way to the workers' soviets and peasant collectives as the highest governing body of the land:

> the soviets are a new state apparatus, which...provide an armed force of workers and peasants; and this force is not divorced from the people as was the old standing army, but is fused with the people in the closest possible fashion... [T]his apparatus by virtue of the fact that it is elected and subject to recall at the

will of the people without any bureaucratic formalities, is far more democratic than any previous apparatus. [I]t provides the possibilities of combining the advantages of parliamentarianism with the advantages of immediate and direct democracy, that is of uniting in the persons of the elected representatives of the people both legislative and executive functions. Compared with bourgeois parliamentarianism, this represents an advance in the development of democracy which is of historical and world-wide importance (in James 1986b, ix–x).

Similarly, Arendt (1963, 269) like James, recognizes Lenin's acknowledgement of the revolutionary features of the soviets, but she is less assured than James, of Lenin's willingness to concede power to the soviets. She argues that "without Lenin's slogan 'All power to the soviets' there would never have been an October Revolution", but she asserts that "whether or not Lenin was sincere in proclaiming the soviet republic... his slogan was in continuous contradiction to the openly proclaimed goals of the Bolshevik party to 'seize power'". She suggests that "had Lenin really wanted to give all power to the soviets, he would have condemned the Bolshevik party... to impotence".

James was firmly of the view that independent working-class activity was more effective in achieving a more thorough, complete and radical break with the capitalist mode of production, and in achieving genuine socialist democracy, than the activity of any other class. He insisted that in all periods of momentous change, it was always the underclasses which took the most decisive steps towards dismantling the old order (James 1977b, 105), and that the working classes were, more often than not, more farsighted and revolutionary than any other revolting class (James, Lee and Chaulieu [1958] 1974, 92–93). This is why to James the establishment of socialism can only be the work of the working class itself, rather than surrogates acting on behalf of the working class.

In contrast, the middle and petty bourgeois classes usually, in revolutionary situations, tend to play a conservative and counter-revolutionary role. Indeed, the classic operationalization of this phenomenon can be seen in the Caribbean independence movements of the 1930s, where the petty bourgeois class, through its formation of political parties and trade unions stifled the Caribbean revolutionary movement and assisted the British Colonial Office in frustrating the emergence of more complete forms of Caribbean independence (Gittens 1983; Lindsay 1975; Beckles 1992; Belle 1988; James 1984c). James felt that he was vindicated by history and always insisted that it is the "working class alone which is able to produce the organization, the forms, and the ideas which this emancipation demands" (James, Lee and Chaulieu [1958] 1974, 91). While it may be true to argue that in the 1930s the Caribbean nationalist parties and trade unions were relatively weak and still at the stage of their early formation and that a mature revolutionary situation was not on the cards in the 1930s Caribbean, it is however equally true that the underdevelopment of political forces in the Caribbean did result in greater accommodation to British colonialism and neo-colonialism and global capitalism. When Lenin's notion of 'economism' is applied to understand the underdeveloped nature of Caribbean trade unions and their associated nationalist parties, and when the underdeveloped levels of political consciousness of the leadership of the Caribbean labour movement which tilted them towards reformism rather than revolution is considered, it becomes clear that the potential for more radical internal changes which were offered by the mass strikes of the 1930s, were never fully tapped. Such arguments have been fully presented and defended by Caribbean scholars of the 1930s labour rebellions such as Ken Post (1978), Richard Hart (1989) and others.

James's Perspective and Caribbean Socialism: Realities and Critique

James's socialist thought, when used as an analytical framework and applied to the attempts at socialist transformation as experienced in the Caribbean, can serve as a useful model in determining the extent to which these experiments were, theoretically and practically, the correct mechanisms through which socialist transformation could be effected. His ideas can also serve as a useful guide to how twenty-first century attempts at socialist transformation might be understood and implemented, in light of previous twentieth century experiences. It can also allow for the undertaking of a specifically Jamesian critique of the historical experience of Caribbean socialism, thus far.

The 'Non-Capitalist Path Experience'

A cursory examination of the historical record would suggest that a huge gulf exists between James's prognosis and socialism as actually experienced in the Caribbean in the late twentieth century, particularly in the dominant Caribbean socialist 'non-capitalist path' model.

The theoretical rationale governing the non-capitalist path was based on a number of premises from classical Marxism. It was felt that the Caribbean, being situated on the periphery of the world capitalist system, lacked the necessary technological base upon which a truly socialist society could be established. This understanding of the Caribbean as materially and technologically underdeveloped meant, by extension, that these societies were devoid of a developed bourgeoisie and proletariat, the two significant classes of capitalist society whose struggle was seen as being a necessary precondition for the emergence of socialist society. The implementation of the non-capitalist path of development in the Caribbean, was therefore seen to be not the work of the proletariat, but that of the revolutionary petty bourgeoisie (Emmanuel 1983, 202; Ohiorhenuan 1979, 407).

A major assumption of the theory of the non-capitalist path was that certain stages in Marx's formulaic 'modes of production' schema (primitive communism – slavery – feudalism – capitalism – communism) could be by-passed (Gonsalves 1980; Ulyanovsky 1974; Ohiorhenuan 1979). Pointing to the fact that the Caribbean had never experienced a classic feudal mode of production and exchange after the slave mode of production had been superseded, it was argued that in a similar way, the capitalist stage of development could be by-passed and a period of transition to socialism be embarked upon. Non-capitalist development was seen, therefore, as a preparatory stage for the development of socialism in the Caribbean, a stage in which the necessary material and social base for socialism could be built. The emphasis, it was felt, would be on socialist, and not on capitalist development.

The anticipated success of the non-capitalist road was founded on the premise that the objective movement in global politics was towards the consolidation of socialist states. Given the empirical reality of socialist construction in other parts of the world, it was felt that Caribbean socialism would be a continuation of this global movement, and would also be facilitated by the presence of other non-capitalist countries in the world system (Gonsalves 1980; Ulyanovsky 1974). Jacobs and Jacobs (1979, 83) for example, in pointing to this "historical factor" and its influence on Grenada's socialist experience, referenced as cases in point not only the Russian Revolution of 1917 but the fact that "other European nations were to join this move to scientific socialism". They also noted that "the example of Cuba was critical in pointing the way to an ideological alternative that provided the basis for fundamental transformation and socio-economic development". The writers therefore cited the cases of Guyana's Peoples' Progressive Party (PPP) and Burnham's Peoples' National Congress (PNC) in embarking upon the non-capitalist path, as well as Jamaica's democratic socialism under Manley as influencing Grenada's decision to embark upon the socialist road. Given the fact that that the non-capitalist path was anchored on the expectation of a permissive global environment, it was not accidental that one of the defining features of the model was a foreign policy which was intensely third world in orientation and which sought to establish links with other territories which had embarked upon a similar path of development.

Despite the importance of the non-capitalist perspective in allowing newly independent Caribbean states to pursue independence projects which deviated from the inherited colonial-dependent model, there were several features of the non-capitalist path which remained trapped in the kinds of vanguardist perspectives and orientations which C.L.R. James was seeking to transcend.

One such weakness is the fact that the theory makes the backwardness of the proletariat the basis for its necessity. As such, the theory is a species of unveiled petty-bourgeois intellectual chauvinism, and stands in direct contradistinction to James's optimism in the self-emancipating revolutionary potential of the working class. The non-capitalist path theory is based on a subjective view of the revolutionary nature of the Caribbean working class and ignores the objective weaknesses of the petty bourgeoisie. Indeed, it overtly places the responsibility for revolution in the hands of the petty bourgeoisie (Emmanuel 1983, 202), the very class, which James had warned, in all revolutionary situations, tended to betray the working class.

In contrast to this view of a backward Caribbean working class incapable of socialist revolution, one notable Jamesian scholar, Darcus Howe, noted instead that it was the "the complete state of insurrection" of the Caribbean working people "since the late 1960s in Jamaica, Trinidad, Guyana and Grenada" which informed the decisions by the social-democratic leaders in these countries to embark on the non-capitalist path. Howe argues that it was the 1960s insurrection that "pushed Manley from a right-wing trade unionist to what he calls democratic socialism" and which caused Jamaican leaders of all political stripes to become preoccupied "with how to contain this insurrection and how to use this energy and force for the full development of the middle classes" (in Lawrence 1981, 71).

A second major weakness of the theory of the non-capitalist path was the assumption that the material and economic infrastructure suitable to socialism did not exist in the Caribbean, and, as such, its adjustments to capitalism, could not rightfully be called socialist – hence the need for the label 'non-capitalist' path. However, the very recognition of the absence of a socialist economic base is the most salient indictment of the theory and practice of the non-capitalist path from the point of view of the Jamesian perspective. It is the objective absence of a material base sufficient for socialism that makes the subjective need for the role of the petty bourgeoisie and alliances with the bourgeoisie such a fundamental aspect of the theory. This weakness has been adequately expounded upon by C.Y. Thomas (1978, 18), who argues that the "non-capitalist thesis is not altogether very clear about the nature of social relations of production during the non-capitalist phase". He therefore suggests that,

> It would seem reasonable to conclude that the non-capitalist path does not involve any qualitative shift in these. Certain characteristics of social relations may change, for example, the rise of state property, but whether these are built on the foundations of capitalist or socialist relations can only be determined after the study of the position of the various social classes. In so far, however, as the working class is not dominant and so cannot direct social development, changes in social relations can only be confined to the elimination of feudal and pre-capitalist survivals along with the restriction of foreign property. There can be no qualitative change in the indigenous capitalist relations themselves. (Thomas 1978, 18).

In short, from whichever angle the question is examined, the problems of the non-capitalist path revolve around the specifically Jamesian litmus test, as raised here by Thomas, of whether or not the working class plays the politically dominant role in directing social development. This shortcoming in the theory of the non-capitalist path approximates very closely the problem identified by Luxemburg (1971, 191–93) in her criticism of Lenin's vanguard party model and specifically in her description of Leninism as a species of Blanquism, that is, as "a recipe for the making of revolution under any conditions and at any time [ignoring] all concrete historical-social conditions".

It is the objective backwardness of the material base of Caribbean society which has resulted in the persistence and enlargement of the state in the process of non-capitalist development. This enlargement of the state on behalf of, or at the expense of autonomous working-class organizations, presents a third weakness of the non-capitalist path from a Jamesian perspective. All the major attempts at pursuing the non-capitalist path in the Caribbean, and all theoretical arguments for it, envisaged an enlarged role for the state in the transition to socialism. This heavy emphasis on the use of state power frustrated the enhancement of democracy from the bourgeois type to the socialist type. In contrast, in practice, the tendency was generally towards a contraction of democracy rather than on its expansion - an elimination of 'bourgeois' democracy without the corresponding creation of structures of socialist democracy to fill the vacuum.

Nowhere was this development seen more clearly than in the Grenada revolution, under the Peoples' Revolutionary Government (PRG), where it was admitted in a reflection by Trevor Munroe that "the tendency towards absolute negation of liberal democracy helped destroy the Grenada revolution and is in need of re-examination as well as amendment" (Munroe 1990, 18). The increased role and significance of state power meant that direct worker participation in decision-making and implementation, the development of autonomous worker institutions and organizations, and independent working-class activity were viewed with hostility and met with repression on the part of those who controlled state power. The emphasis on state power and the opposition to independent working-class activity, meant also that the 'revolutionary' political party was seen as the only legitimate organ through which working class activity could take place.

This growth in state power during the non-capitalist experiments in the Caribbean, was characterized by a more active role played by the state in the economy as well as an expansion in the repressive and coercive organs of the state. In the case of Guyana, there was a drive to take over the main sectors of the Guyanese economy and by the mid-1970s the PNC had nationalized the bauxite industry and commercial, manufacturing, communications, transport and agricultural companies (Latin American Bureau 1984, 51). Alongside the nationalization policies, Guyana, also witnessed a swelling in the size and role of the coercive arm of the Guyanese state. The need for a large military was rationalized based on the threat posed by Venezuela, Suriname and Brazil with which the country had had long-standing territorial disputes. The level of militarization of the Guyanese state, however, far outweighed the regional threats to its territory, with an estimated one out of every thirty-five Guyanese serving in the Guyanese armed forces in the mid-1980s (Thomas 1983, 42–43; Latin American Bureau 1984).

When the racial imbalance in the composition of the Guyanese armed forces and the exaggerated claims to the country's vulnerability to external attack are taken into consideration, it becomes clear that the principal role of the military in Guyana was to maintain the existing social and economic relations and to frustrate further advancements to workers' economic, social and political transformation. In the view of C.Y. Thomas (1983, 33), one of the major shortcomings of the non-capitalist path was that the "theorists of the radicalization of the state did not see radicalization as being premised on the increased access of the working class and peasantry to the development of their own forms of democratic organization through which their power could be exercised". Indeed, Thomas saw the increased radicalization of the state as being "consistent with the reduction of the limited access of the masses of the working people" to democratic rights and he concluded that "radicalisation and democratic development were in real opposition" (33). His broad conclusion therefore was that the experience of the non-capitalist path in the Caribbean, "ignored the internal class struggle" and it ignored the role of the state in the context of an under-developed bourgeoisie and working class, as the "the principal instrument for the long-run consolidation of one or other class as the dominant class" (33).

This criticism can be similarly applied to the economic sphere. From a Jamesian perspective, without worker participation in every stage of the productive and distributive process, nationalization of private property, cannot by itself be taken as proof of worker economic empowerment. As James has argued in the context of the Stalinist state, nationalization can often result in new forms of alienation and exploitation.

Relatedly, the criticism of state power which had been raised within the framework of the world-system perspective, applies with equal force to the question of nationalization and the creation of state property. Like the seizure of state power, nationalization is merely one tactic of proletarian struggle, and can be useful in one instance and detrimental in another. The danger comes from making it a fetish, and transforming the tactic into a principle, that is, transforming a particular into a universal. The historical experience of state ownership in the Caribbean showed little evidence that nationalization by the state had provided an opportunity for direct ownership and control by the working class on a collective basis, at either the community, credit union, co-operative society or civic group level.

This then, has been the experience of Caribbean socialism in its "non-capitalist path" expression. The attainment of socialism was frustrated by the theory's own recognition of the underdevelopment of the productive infrastructure and the corresponding social superstructure of Caribbean societies. There is very little about the theory and practice of the non-capitalist path that approximated the kinds of direct worker economic control and democratic decision-making at the workplace, free from the oversight of a centralized vanguard, envisaged within the Jamesian framework. From the Jamesian perspective the greatest flaw of the non-capitalist experience, was its denial of the necessity or even the possibility of independent working-class activity.

The Grenada Revolution Experience

Beyond the non-capitalist path, the other major experience of Caribbean socialism was the Grenada revolution, and it has presented a useful case for studying the struggle between the socialist perspective of C.L.R. James and that of more "orthodox" Marxism in the Caribbean. Indeed, it serves as one of the clearest historical examples of the struggle between James's notion of free creative activity on one hand, and the party-state perspective on the other (Marable 1987). This question however has been widely studied, and has been given full treatment in Joseph 2015b, and for the purposes of this work, the main arguments developed there, will be re-presented in summary form.

Despite Bernard Coard's dismissal of the analyses which explain the demise of the Grenada revolution as a conflict between Leninist vanguardism and social-democratic populism as too simplistic (Grenade 2010, 152–53; see also Joseph 2014, 609), much of the surrounding narrative of the events, including those offered by Coard himself, seem to confirm such a thesis (see Coard in Grenade 2015, 63–64). What is striking however, is that despite the fact that James was a leading global Marxist, there is little evidence of any direct engagement by the Grenadian revolution with Jamesianism or with James himself (see Joseph 2015b, 164–65). Indeed, Coard's dismissal of James as a "neo-Trotskyist" has been well documented by Marable (1987) (see Joseph 2015a, 161). It is notable however, that in his more recent reflections on the Grenada revolution, Coard (2018, 134) has identified the "emergence of zonal and parish councils throughout the country" as the "single most remarkable achievement of the 199-83 Grenada Revolution". In Coard's view:

> In a revolutionary process overflowing with projects, programmes, and new developments of all sorts, the Zonal and Parish Councils were unique in that they were the only development which caught us in the leadership of the NJM and the PRG completely by surprise; reacting, not initiating; embracing, but not leading what ordinary Grenadians had started independently (2018, 134).

It can be seen clearly from this, that the Jamesian thesis of the tensions between vanguardist centralism on one hand, and creative, popular democratic autonomy on the other – James's "free creative activity" – were at play during the Grenada revolution.

In light of the tensions, Joseph (2015b, 159) argues that "a Jamesian analysis of the Grenada Revolution should begin, not in 1979 when the state apparatus was seized by the Peoples' Revolutionary Government (PRG), but from the early 1970s when a very conscious and deliberate process was set in motion which had as its main aim the supersession of the old state structures and their replacement by structures of popular democracy, as witnessed in the programmes and activities of the early movements of resistance to Gairyism such as the Movement for the Advancement of Community Effort (MACE), the Movement for the Assemblies of the People (MAP), and the Joint Endeavour for Welfare and Educational Liberation (JEWEL)". He argues, that during this period, it can be seen that "the activities of MACE, MAP and JEWEL, and later the New Jewel Movement (NJM), were consciously geared towards an enlargement of democracy in Grenada, the political education of the Grenadian masses through the medium of the mass meeting, and soliciting the involvement of the Grenadian masses in every stage of the struggle through mass demonstrations".

However, those tendencies were not sustained and as the revolution progressed there was growing evidence to suggest the "deliberate transformation of the NJM from a party of mass mobilization to a closed, secret conspiratorial vanguard party" (Joseph 2015b, 161). Joseph proposes a number of arguments for why the tendencies towards Jamesian democratic practices were superseded in preference for more centrist and vanguardist approaches. Amongst the factors identified include: the growing urgency of the necessity of seizing state power, which demanded a shift in tactics from mass democratic mobilization to a concentration on military and tactical considerations; the growing influence of factions of the party more steeped in Leninist politics at the expense of the older more centrist and populist NJM types of the early to mid-1970s anti-Gairy struggles (Joseph 2015b, 160–61); the growing perceptions of the backwardness of the economic structure of Grenada which were seen in classical Marxist logic as resulting in a strong petty bourgeoisie and an under-developed, ideologically weak working class, and as such resulting in the necessity of leadership from ideologically and politically advanced groups (Joseph 2015, 162); the increasing reliance on authoritarianism and militarization by Gairy and the experience of the NJM's electoral defeat in the 1974 General election which resulted in a skeptical and practical rejection of the formal electoral system as a means of effecting political change (161–62).

The growing impact of these developments on the evolution of the Grenada experience away from the Jamesian ideal, with the resultant effect of the alienation of the Grenadian masses from the revolutionary process, have been neatly captured in a comment by Brian Meeks (in Joseph 2015b, 162–63):

> Each Leninist measure which made the party more capable of taking power, also increased its tendency towards hierarchical decision-making and enhanced the autonomy of the leadership both from ordinary party members and the people... If Leninism was the necessary ingredient for victory then it had to be implemented. Leninism prepared the party for insurrection, but also at the same time it made it more hierarchical. The populist elements in the Jamesian approach had been thrown out with its tactical weaknesses.

It should be noted however that while the failures of the 'vanguard party' have been broadly categorized as a 'Leninist' failure, important distinctions should be made between the later Stalinist corruptions and the notion of the vanguard party as developed by Lenin himself. It is also important to appreciate the political context which shaped Lenin's thinking on how a revolutionary party should be organized given the specific challenges faced by a revolutionary movement in the context of Feudal Russia in the early 1900s. This is important to avoid the loose caricaturing of any indications of authoritarian centralization of power as Leninism. This is also important for appreciating James's anti-vanguardist ideas itself, since James was far more sophisticated in his understanding of Leninism, the vanguard party and the later Stalinist corruptions than the broad conflating of Leninism with Stalinism, by both Marxists and anti-Marxists, have suggested. Indeed, the Coard faction of the Grenada revolution might have been conveniently or erroneously associating themselves with Leninism rather than Stalinism, given the abiding need for legitimacy both before and after the collapse of the Grenada Revolution.

Significantly, Marcel Liebman, in an important study, has been at pains to show that Lenin's vanguard Party model, in the words of Ernest Mandel (1975) has been the product of orchestrated "myths, dear to the bourgeoisie and petty-bourgeoisie...to discredit Bolshevism and, therewith, the proletarian revolution, by means of Stalin's crimes". According to Liebman (1975, 31),

> A number of passages in What Is To Be Done? show that the author was above all concerned to make fully effective the spontaneous activity undertaken by the masses. Whenever he deals with action, far from condemning spontaneity, he urges the revolutionary organization to assume the leadership of such movements, even affirming that 'the greater the spontaneous upsurge of the masses and the more widespread the movement, the more rapid, incomparably so, [is] the demand for greater consciousness in the theoretical, political and organizational work of Social-Democracy'. Surveying the historical achievements of the Russian labour movement, Lenin noted with satisfaction that 'the upsurge of the masses proceeded and spread with uninterrupted continuity.' He regretted only 'the lag of leaders...behind the spontaneous upsurge of the masses;' 'the spontaneous struggle of the proletariat will not become its genuine "class struggle" until this struggle is led by a strong organization of revolutionaries'. Here we see already an approach to a dialectical attempt to transcend the contradiction between the spontaneity and the organization of the proletariat.

Separating vulgar Stalinism from Lenin's more nuanced and contextual development of the vanguard party, is important for understanding C.L.R. James's stance on the Grenada revolution itself. Far from dismissing the revolution and its denouement on the basis of an ideological stance towards 'vanguardism', James's main pre-occupation at the moment when the internal crisis of the Grenada revolution was at its peak, was to, as was the case with most of the leading Marxist activists and thinkers all over the globe, seek to intervene to bring about an amicable solution. In a cable dated 17 October 1983, addressed to the Political Bureau of the New Jewel Movement, St. George's Grenada, and copied to the George Weekes and Darcus Howe, writing from 165 Railton Road London, C.L.R. James stated the following:

> An issue of importance not only to Grenada but the whole of the Caribbean must be solved through the mass of the population, unions and the party... Primary is the safety of Bishop, for himself and for the respect of the people of Grenada and the general public" (James 1983).

It is clear therefore that in the midst of the Grenada crisis, C.L.R. James understood that his prescription of mass mobilization from below, was the surest safeguard to forestall the fatal and disastrous machinations of a small clique unchecked by popular censure and guidance.

Later, in his own analysis of the demise of the revolution, James would point to the failure of the leadership, namely Bishop to "do anything" concrete to fulfill in a timely fashion the onerous demands of the local population, a situation, which in James's view, forced the people to turn to the army. According to James (1985, 61),

> a mass movement above all needs leadership, and if the political leader does not give it people turn to another organization, often the army. The army consists of organization commanders, lieutenants, majors, etc. So when people want somebody to take steps it is not surprising that they turn to the army. It has happened repeatedly in the course of revolution.

In short, therefore, James's recognition of the relationship between the mass and the role of an advanced leadership, responding effectively to the demands from below, was no different from Lenin's own understanding of the role of a vanguard in relation to the spontaneous actions of the mass of the population.

Despite his appreciation for the how and why of the Leninist vanguard, as seen earlier, James had felt that the shifts in technology and the general growth in consciousness of the working class, had meant the vanguard party could be transcended and replaced by other forms of direct action.

The Jamesian Vision and Socialist Possibility in the 21st Century

These then have been the weaknesses and failures of the experience of socialism in the Caribbean in the twentieth century, when assessed from the Jamesian perspective.

However, if the decade of the 1990s ended as the decade in which Leninist vanguardist forms can be said to have faced their deepest crisis, the decades since the 2000s can be seen as the period in which global anti-capitalist movements began to approximate most closely in their features and underpinning logic, James's anticipated expectations of post-Leninist socialist revolutions. Thus, from as early as the year 2000, the world witnessed a number of spontaneous anti-capitalist mass social movements, striking in their autonomy from any centralized decision-making vanguard and delinked from formal party leadership – liberal, social-democratic or communist. These anti-capitalist revolts included: the anti-globalization movements of the late 1990s to early 2000s, the Occupy Wall Street Movement, the Black Lives Matter Movement (BLM), the Arab Spring, the Rhodes Must Fall and Fees Must Fall student movements in South Africa, the *gilet jaunes* revolts in France, the popular protests in Algeria and the Sudanese popular uprising against President Al-Bashir, and the End SARS anti-police violence movement in Nigeria.

A more thorough analysis of the political efficacy and strength, weaknesses and failures of these will be seen later. However, despite their inability to sustain themselves, or to advance the aims of workers or traditional trade-union type or anti-racist interests, it is important to acknowledge that these movements, have had a profound impact on global and domestic politics and, in the wake of the collapse of European Communism, appear, in validation of James, to point to a potential revolutionary future that goes beyond the twentieth century modes of political organization. The perspective of one observer, Hunziker (2018), although referring specifically to the Yellow Vest movement, captures effectively what is novel and distinct about these movements, and their potential for challenging the dominant capitalist order in the twenty-first century:

> All of [this] describes the future of revolutionary activity throughout the world. It is seamlessly simple and frighteningly powerful. In Algeria, protestors donned yellow vests in response to a failing system... In Tunisia, a new group called "Red Vests" issued a call for protests of a Tunisian political system that promotes "systematic impoverishment." In Belgium, police violently cracked down on angry groups of Yellow Vests with similar demands. In Basra, Iraq Yellow Vests criticize widespread contamination of drinking water and poor city services and corruption... "Yellow Vest" has become a catchall for all of the grievances of working people. Indeed, this is how revolts commence in earnest... The precursor for the present insurrection was identification of an elite class, or the 1%. Throughout history, revolutions aspire to confrontation once lines of division have been clearly drawn, e.g., the Boston Tea Party, or the fall of the Bastille, or today's "One Percent," which clearly divides the world into "haves" and "have-nots." Certainly, the One Percent is one of the clearest, easiest targets of all time.

Despite the clear conformity of these developments to the ideas of James, there has not been a flood of publications by Caribbean writers applying his work as an explanatory tool for understanding the current trends. One notable exception to this is Horace Campbell, who has applied the ideas of James to explain the popular movement which emerged around the election of the forty-fourth President of the United States, Barack Obama (Campbell 2010). In a section of his book entitled, "Beyond Vanguardism in the Twenty-first century", Campbell focuses on a number of features of the

Obama campaign which signaled departures from vanguardism and which pointed to novel tendencies in mass uprisings against contemporary capitalism. Campbell touched on several issues addressed by James. In Campbell's view, the "self-organization and self-mobilization of the different social forces" in the US 2008 election campaign "raised new directions for understanding of revolutionary organization" (Campbell 2010, 16). He described the Obama campaign as being one in which "every volunteer was seen as a potential community organizer", clearly echoing James's claims of the erosion of the distinction between the "party and being" and the "party as knowing". Finally, Campbell noted that "tech savvy volunteers were able to break the distinction between the professional and amateur political campaigner" (2010, 135). In Campbell's view,

> the dynamics of innovation throughout the campaign ensured that national goals were rooted in the capabilities of grassroots efforts and not imposed from the headquarters in Chicago. This was indeed bottom politics, and it was clear in grassroots fundraising (2010, 135).[7]

Despite the force and visibility of these global movements, and though Caribbean scholars have made important theoretical contributions to their understanding, the Caribbean itself has been comparatively less marked by popular mass movements of the *gilet jaunes* and BLM variety. Caribbean mass movements have largely conformed to the traditional party or trade-union led experiences and spring up around moments of industrial disputes or electoral contests. Where such spontaneous mass movements have emerged, they can be largely described as 'low impact' and have not heralded the potential collapse of either existing regimes or the system of government itself.

The relative quiescence of these movements in the Caribbean, however, does not mean their total absence. Nor does it mean that James's outlook is irrelevant as an explanation for the future directions in Caribbean anti-capitalist protests. Indeed, while Caribbean mass movements have continued to be dominated by political parties and trade unions, there have been several episodes and issues which stand out as marking a shift away from traditional radical politics, and there have been many instances of mass struggle which have occurred independently of trade union and political party leadership. While these movements have not had the large political impacts on Caribbean society as the earlier discussed global mass movements have had on their respective theatres, their very emergence have provided glimpses into the alternative forms of action that can transcend the traditional forms and validate the Jamesian view. The level of political development of the Caribbean working class, therefore, is in many ways itself a reflection, of the level of development of these mass movements and how they have been woven into the fabric of Caribbean political life.

Since the year 2000, a number of these movements have emerged in the Caribbean. These movements have largely sprung up around environmental issues, or against exorbitant giveaways to foreign investors particularly in the tourism sector. In some cases, these issues have been intertwined. They have also sprung up over historical instances of marginalization around racial and class lines. Despite the tendency of post-modernists to treat these "new social movements" as representing a disavowal of traditional Marxist concerns, these movements cannot be separated from long-standing Caribbean political struggles for self-determination, democratic equality, and domestic control of economic and other resources. More recently too, these independent social movements have sprung up around demands for sexual minority rights and for the rights of minority religious groups to equality of treatment, such as for instance, in the struggle by Rastafari groups for the legalization of marijuana for sacramental purposes.

Certainly since 2015, there have been a number of notable protests which can be cited as examples of spontaneous expressions of anti-systemic activity in keeping with the Jamesian vision. One such episode was the anti-Desert Star Holdings

(DSH) protests in St. Lucia. During this protest, St. Lucians demonstrated en masse against a giveaway investment facilitated by the overtly neo-liberal and anti-nationalist Allen Chastanet-led administration in St. Lucia between 2016 and 2019. Another such movement was a beach access (Save our Beaches) movement in Jamaica, led by ordinary citizens protesting the fact that private beaches in Jamaica constitute the norm rather than the exception, effectively debarring the poor and the powerless from accessing an abundant gift of nature (see Cooper 2021). There have also been protests in Tobago, Trinidad over a tourism investment project by one of the Caribbean's leading hotel brands, Sandals, that threatened environmental damage. The Caribbean has also witnessed an internet and community-based protest movement against a waste-to-energy project that was being proposed by an unpopular Democratic Labour Party government in Barbados in the period leading up to the 2018 general election. Finally, there have been protests which can be said to have been simultaneously inspired by the Caribbean reparations movement and the Black Lives Matter movement, such as the 'Tek Down Nelson' campaign in Barbados, which was aimed at the removal of a slave-era statue of English naval captain Lord Horatio Nelson from a prominent location in the city of Bridgetown.[8] While none of these movements galvanized their respective populations on the scale or intensity of the global mass movements, they provide a sufficient basis for identifying the manner in which they have departed from the traditional approaches to the conduct of radical anti-systemic politics, more familiar to the Caribbean region.

In assessing these movements, two distinct tendencies can be seen. On one hand, are the movements which can be seen as direct spillovers of global mass movements, like the Black Lives Matter Movement for example. On the other, are those movements which are rooted in the autonomous Caribbean problems, but which have spawned spontaneous uprisings that deviate from the traditional vanguard-led, trade union or political party struggles.

There is little doubt that the US's BLM movement has manifested itself in a direct way on political developments in the Caribbean. However, except in the case of the afore mentioned "Tek Down" Nelson protest and a copy-cat BLM protest in the vicinity of the American Embassy in Grenada (see Now Grenada 2020) these BLM protests have not taken the form of large masses of people on the streets. Instead, the reflection of the BLM movement in the Caribbean has largely taken the form of internet protests against prominent businesspersons whose public stances were at variance with the political objectives of the movement. Despite the absence of overt and large eruptions of mass protests, what was significant however, is that these episodes helped to ignite deep-seated racial and class tensions, especially when the individuals targeted were members of the dominant exploiting classes in the region. In a series entitled "*The Black Lives Matter Effect in the Caribbean as Seen Online*", one writer has provided informative commentary on specific episodes which ignited online criticism and business boycotts of prominent business-persons in Jamaica and Trinidad and Tobago, whose online stances suggested opposition to the Black Lives Matter movement (Digital Business 2020a; Digital Business 2020b).

Among the most prominent of these episodes was the decision by Adam Stewart, the son of Sandals Hotel chain magnate Butch Stewart, to post a picture of Sandals' owners posing with US President Donald Trump captioned with a retweet of Trump's offensive threat to black US protestors, "when the looting starts; the shooting starts". The public response to Stewart's post exposed many underlying racial and class tensions not readily addressed in the formal political system. Many persons called for a boycott of the hotel. A post, critical of the hotel chain, highlighted the fact that Sandals was "spending some of its ad dollars on Fox News, a channel that is unapologetically pro-Trump", some of which was airing on specific shows headed by the likes of Tucker Carlson and Laura Ingraham, who had "reputations for not being very fond of black people or Black Lives Matter" (Digital Business 2020a). These developments led to a tremendous internet backlash against the Sandals chain. While the main impact of the backlash took the form of internet denunciations of the Stewart family, the attendant commentary helped to bring to the fore the problems of racial and class inequity in Jamaica and the Caribbean, often left untouched in the regular conduct of electoral politics.

A similar situation was reported in Trinidad and Tobago, where a popular tea house featured a sugar-icing design with the words "All Lives Matter". This led to business boycotts and internet verbal censures, not only of the business involved, but of other business owners who had taken public stances in support of the offending tea house (see Digital Business 2020b). In one poignant display of political consciousness, a small chocolatier who had been a reliable supplier to one of the offending businesses, decided that she could no longer avoid taking a personal stance on the issue. She terminated her business relationship with the buyer, on the basis that the time had come to "to remove the coon/sellout parts of my mentality a little towards liberation". While surmising that she would feel the economic pain of losing one of her larger clients, she resolved the issue by asking: "Can I afford to sell self-respect, integrity, and racial solidarity for a few pieces of silver? You know the answer. Some things have no price" (Digital Business 2020b).

The striking features of these developments from the Jamesian perspective are the ways in which they point to the transcendence of the political party as the ideational and practical vanguard, leading the way forward to Caribbean revolutionary activity and the politics of progressive change. It is notable that amidst a concerted global debate about BLM and the questions of race, inequality and the need to overturn historical marginalization, the dominant political parties in the Caribbean have been largely silent on these questions and have not been at the centre of these popular struggles. Apart from a token but formal resolution moved in the Barbados House of Assembly to express support for BLM (see Barbados Government Information Service 2020)

Caribbean governments' commitment to these issues have not been translated into a concerted and deliberate party program nor have they been reflected in the approach to domestic policy formulation or political practice. What the moment has represented is a definite shift in which popular adoption and identification with a global ideology and movement has taken place above the direction and influence of the formal political parties as the main organizational forces in Caribbean countries. In other words, the Caribbean involvement with this movement has not been mediated by the 'middle-man' political parties and trade unions serving as vanguards. This perhaps marks one of the most important shifts in Caribbean politics from the 1950s and 1970s to the early twenty-first century. Further, as James had predicted, not only is the spontaneous free creative political mobilization of the mass movement occurring autonomously of the direction of the mainstream parties, but given the nature of the issues being contested, those parties are now finding themselves incapable of advancing progressive politics in a manner demanded by the mass of the population. Given the "tied" nature of the region's mainstream political class to the Caribbean racial and economic elite, and given the structure and philosophy of the region's dominant economic developmental model as revolving around dependency upon the local and global former colonial elite, the Caribbean mainstream leadership was glaringly exposed and surpassed by the BLM movement.

In addition to these "spillover" movements from BLM and other global mass uprisings, there have been other distinctive movements of local origin which capture many features of the "free creative activity" type popular movements envisaged by James.

The popular demonstrations against the Desert Star Holdings investment in St. Lucia following the election of an extremely neo-liberal and single-mindedly pro-capitalist Allen Chastanet as Prime Minister, can be seen as an instance of a Jamesian-type mobilization not linked to the global BLM movement.

The DSH controversy surrounds the decision by the Chastanet administration to agree to the terms of investment, which among other things, gave the company sixty-five acres of land for the setting up of a horse racing track and related developments and an additional ninety-two acres to the south of the international airport, occupying a significant beach front for the purpose of a tourism project inclusive of hotels, a marina, and casinos (Government of St. Lucia 2016, 4–5), with a further possibility of an additional ninety acres for the planned establishment of offshore tertiary institutions (4).

Significantly, the initial discussions for the investment had taken place under the St. Lucia Labour Party (SLP) prior to its defeat in the 2016 general election, but the SLP delayed the investment due to several concerns. Among these included, the large amount of acreage conceded to the developers, the fact that the proposed project was expected to displace several key existing economic and social infrastructure projects including a meat processing plant, a solid waste landfill, the national stadium and a wildlife mangrove. Perhaps the most controversial aspect of the DSH investment was the fact that the land was being offered to the developers at an extremely low cost, with either the option of purchase at between US$60-90,000 or lease at a cost of US$1 per acre for ninety-nine years (Government of St. Lucia 2016, 6). In addition, the government would agree to bear the cost of all private land acquisitions that would be necessary to transfer property to the developers (5), as well as all the cost of any remedial infrastructural works associated with the project, inclusive of decommissioning a nearby landfill. In addition, DSH would be exempt from income tax on interest earned; value added tax; property tax (commercial and residential); aliens landholding licenses; stamp duties and vendors taxes; customs duties of imports; corporate tax; and any other exemptions prescribed in the Tourism Incentives Act (Government of St. Lucia 2016).

Given the exorbitant giveaways and the neo-colonial nature of the DSH project, the country witnessed sustained protests particularly in the south of the island in the Vieux Fort area where the investment was domiciled (see *St. Lucia Times* 2016). These protests shared many similarities with the global post-vanguardist protest movements seen elsewhere. Among the significant features of the protests were their spontaneous nature and the fact that they had been organised particularly by young people independent of the direction of the political parties. The protests were also accompanied by the democratic eruption of talk shows, newspaper articles and heated town-hall meetings, with informed citizens offering educated criticisms to the project.

However, the anti-DSH movement exhibited many weaknesses inherent in 'spontaneity' as a political tactic. Amongst these weaknesses is the fact that mass 'mobilization' does not easily translate into realizable political objectives. In the case of the St. Lucian DSH protests, the government of St. Lucia, was able to get its way with the project, though the flagship horserace track and other advertised features of the project have stood as rusting monuments, given the absence of a horseracing culture in St. Lucia. Secondly, the anti-DSH movement was not fully free from the direction of political party leadership. The official opposition, buoyed by the protests, organized and led some of the major public marches on the issue, and saw the anti-DSH movement as a useful platform from which to regain its foothold following its defeat in the 2016 election. Indeed, the SLP's electoral victory in July 2021 cannot be divorced from the momentum which it gained from the DSH and related protests. In this sense therefore, the DSH movement, from a Jamesian perspective, did not shift the dynamic of anti-systemic political organization decisively away from traditional party-based organization, particularly since no lasting, permanent, or legacy-remnant social movements were left behind following the period of heightened activity.

Unlike the anti-DSH struggle in St. Lucia, the beach access movement in Jamaica facilitated a process of mass mobilization which transcended partisan political concerns. The movement can be described as a loose association of citizens, newspaper contributors, academics, and community activists, advocating for access to Jamaica's beaches as a recreational right of all citizens. Its main concern is the fact that private beaches in Jamaica have been accepted as the natural order of things, in contrast to what obtains in the rest of the independent English-speaking Caribbean. Further, with each new tourism development, the rapidly diminishing areas of "public beaches" become even more threatened.

Given the entrenched nature of the culture of private beaches in Jamaica, and given the entanglement of this culture with the main tourism development thrust of the country, the beach access movement, developed naturally as a bottom-up mass pressure movement, enforcing its will on reluctant party and government leadership across the political spectrum. Further, the very nature of the issue, shifted the discourse away from the traditional economic exploitation questions, and touched upon questions of human rights, equity and racial justice, which the main political parties have been reluctant to address. This does not mean that the thrust of the struggle did not have implications for the traditional questions of elite minority and expatriate capital control of the resources of the country. Indeed, the proliferation of private beaches as the norm rather than the exception in Jamaica, cannot be divorced from the related questions of racialized patterns of ownership and power, particularly around developments associated with tourism expansion.

The reflection of Carolyn Cooper, a University of the West Indies (UWI) based academic, and one of the leading public voices for the beach access movement, captures the sense in which the movement was pursuing its objectives ahead of a trailing and ambivalent, formal political class. Writing in a moment when the movement had successfully blocked one of the remaining public beaches from falling into private hands, Cooper (2018) observed that,

> Discovery Bay community groups have won a major victory. Peach Beach is not going to be privatized. It will soon be upgraded by

the Government and maintained as a public beach. It took a lot of hard work. A 'Save our Beaches' campaign was launched. There were protest meetings in the square, media interventions, and negotiations with politicians. Just a constant struggle!... Citizens shouldn't have to resort to these extreme measures to ensure public access to beaches. Our Government should be guarding our right to enjoy the natural resources of this country. It's not only tourists who should come to Jamaica and feel all right. We should all be at home in our own country.

Despite celebrating the short-term victory of successfully staving off another capture by the private sector of yet another public beach, and while expressing optimism that government, under pressure from the Save Our Beaches movement, would "actually keep its promise and... ensure that there's at least one well-maintained public beach in each parish", Cooper's reflections reveal the subordinate nature of the movement and its dependence on state authority for the realization of its objectives:

Community groups have shown that public pressure can compel politicians to do the right thing. But there's many a slip between the cup and the lip. Or, in this case, between the talk of politicians and their actions! (Cooper 2018).

Just as in the case of the anti-DSH movement in St. Lucia, the Save Our Beaches movement in Jamaica, raised issues about the efficacy of mass-based autonomous movements, in achieving their revolutionary objectives independent of their traditional reliance on the party and the state. While their success could be measured around their ability to mobilize around deeply entrenched issues, they however remained constrained in their ability to translate pressure into policy. More importantly, these movements have not replaced the political party as organs of revolutionary action, in the manner envisaged by James. While these movements have provided an indication of a maturing of the proletariat, their growth in consciousness, organizational capacity, their relationship to technology, and their interconnection with global political activity, when compared to the working class of the mid-twentieth century, their full emergence as new governmental structures may still depend on the unfolding of further qualitative contradictions and transformations in global capitalism.

A similar observation can be made with respect to other episodes of spontaneous mass activity which have occurred within the first three decades of the twenty-first century. Thus, for example, the struggle of the Barbadian public against the establishment of a questionable waste-to-energy project, witnessed the mobilization of engineers, environmentalists, and community activists against a government proposal to offer a foreign company Cahill exclusive right to the waste of Barbados for conversion into energy. The movement was centred mostly around town hall meetings, newspaper interventions, internet blogs and critical commentary on popular radio and television talk-shows. Significantly, an internet blog, Barbados Underground, appeared to be ahead of the formal parties in revealing confidential documents, inclusive of a previously unknown secret Memorandum of Understanding (MOU) between the government and Cahill and other details of the project. In effect Barbados Underground had eclipsed the formal opposition party as the leading voice in the struggle against the Cahill project.

A resolution tabled by the official Leader of the Opposition of Barbados, Mia Mottley, in the House of Assembly on August 25, 2015, in which she demanded that the hitherto secret MOU between the Government of Barbados and Cahill, be tabled formally before parliament, revealed several features of the belatedly revealed MOU and the related process by which Cahill established itself in Barbados, that proved troubling to the Barbadian public. In her resolution, Mottley, revealed that Cahill Energy Limited had agreed "to construct a $480 million Plasma Gasification Waste to Energy Plant"; and that the actual cost would be $700 million notwithstanding the fact that Cahill and its subsidiaries had "no previous experience in constructing, outfitting and operating a WTE plant"; that the Government of

Barbados had signed an Implementation Agreement and a Power Purchase Agreement "reflecting a range of legal commitments binding the Government and taxpayers of Barbados... until 2048" (in *Bajan Reporter*, September 1, 2015).

Despite the apparent lead taken by the official opposition in bringing the issue before Parliament, what was significant about the anti-Cahill movement from the Jamesian perspective was the fact that the impetus of the movement had been driven by popular forces independently of the involvement of the official opposition party. Indeed, the intervention of the official opposition can be seen as a belated development, piggybacking on the protests that had begun by the self-mobilized population. The impetus for the movement was the largely internet based, popular whistle-blower blog called Barbados Underground (see Barbados Underground July 29, 2015). Just as in the case of the Wikileaks exposures at the global level (Silfry 2015), the impetus for the resistance to and eventual overthrow of the proposed investment came from the ability of the activists to locate and place in the public domain, documents and private exchanges which otherwise would have remained hidden from public view, or which would otherwise have been kept within the small circle of governmental officials (vanguard) supposedly acting on behalf of a disempowered public.

A report of a town hall meeting held by the proposed developers as a public relations exercise to stave off the increasing public acrimony to the project, provides a sense of the consciousness of the public, their intellectual sophistication in responding to foreign investors and their level of self-organization and self-confidence in resisting the development. Speaking of their open confrontation with the lead spokesperson for Cahill, Clare Cowan, who in her opening statement "communicated the main purpose of the Open House was to debunk untruths being posted on the blog (Barbados Underground) and Facebook", the report speaks of a packed auditorium of a "very informed crowd", leaving "unhappy because key questions were not answered or were deflected". The report observed that the two main issues concerning the crowd were firstly, their unawareness of "a plasma gasification plant built on any island of similar size to Barbados anywhere in the world" and secondly, the issue of "how would environmental standards be enforced" (Barbados Underground 2015). Quite significantly, the anti-Cahill protests were occurring at a time when a very unpopular ruling administration was facing an election, following two-terms of instability, and a series of popular national protests led by trade unions and the private sector over the government's poor handling of the economy.[9]

Despite the success of the anti-Cahill protests, the reality was that the outcome of the struggle was too closely interlinked with the electoral moment in Barbados to separate the abandonment of the project from the formal politics of the election itself. Indeed, the non-implementation of the proposed Cahill project, as might have been observed from the interventions of the Leader of the Opposition, Mia Mottley, might have been more the result of electoral change, rather than the popular protest itself. Further, like the other movements examined, the Cahill protests ended with the election itself, and have not perceptively been translated into a qualitative transformation of the politics of Barbados, nor has it resulted in a sustained movement against the dominant capitalist order.

Despite these limitations, the Cahill protests conformed to several Jamesian expectations of future global revolt. First, the Cahill struggle revolved around an increasingly more sophisticated and educated working public. This was evident in their ability to critique and unpack the complex scientific claims of a waste-to-energy project, and their use of technology to mobilize action and public opinion and to conduct a sustained public relations campaign. While these features may be shrugged off as taken-for-granted, banal and commonplace in the twenty-first century, it may be useful to remember that at the time of James's reflections, in the mid-twentieth century on free creative activity and the eventual maturation of the proletariat, the material conditions which would have allowed the Caribbean working-class to evolve into the kind of tech-savvy, educated, globally connected social actors that was evident during the anti-Cahill protests, did not yet exist. To James's credit however, he foresaw the eventual lessening in significance of vanguardism, in his recognition that the very exposure of the working class to capitalism would result in their own capacity for self-organization and self-emancipation. That was the essential meaning behind his own understanding of the "invading socialist society" (James, Forest and Stone 1972) most effectively described in Facing Reality (James, Lee and Chaulieu [1958] 1974).

Similar tendencies can be said to have emerged in protests over tourism investments in Tobago, Trinidad. The protest by environmentalists led by an enterprising blogger and writer, Elspeth Duncan, who opposed the environmental damage to the coastline of Tobago and who was instrumental in leading to the abandonment of a tourism investment project by Jamaican-based Sandals, is further illustrative of the new tendencies. An account in *Trinidad Newsday* of Elspeth's struggle against the Sandals Hotel chain's planned investment reveals the nature of the spontaneous resistance, and how it was diametrically opposed to the standard strategies of reliance on foreign investment at the expense of local interests. According to the writer, (Surtees 2019), "Elspeth, like some in the tourism sector, said that she prefers small businesses in Tobago to be supported to growth by government investment, rather than international chains being helped to expand their profits and market share. He quotes Elspeth as saying "tourists don't come here to experience a mass-produced hotel chain... They come to meet down-to-earth people, taste a basic and simple life and enjoy our unique services and offerings" (Surtees 2019).

Conclusion

The broad conclusion which can be reached in reflecting on the relevance of C.L.R. James's notion of socialism to the period spanning the late twentieth century to the early twenty-first century Caribbean, is that it has opened the door connecting socialism to democracy.   It was inherently anti-authoritarian. James's anti-authoritarianism did not spring from a moral perspective, but it emerged as a logical outcome of his understanding of the evolution of the working class. The creeping development of democracy, political consciousness and independent activism, in James's vision, would be a natural outcome of widening education and the expansion of technology and the wider development of global connectivity of a worldwide socialist movement.   It is these developments which assist in freeing the working-class movement from the overlordship and direction of the formal parties and trade unions which always play a mediating role in the sustaining of capitalism.   In James's view therefore, the objective development of the proletariat would lead increasingly towards new modes of political organization and new modes of anti-capitalist struggle, which transcended the vanguardist forms which had shaped the revolutions of the twentieth century.

What can be surmised however, is that the Jamesian-type movements which have been observed thus far in the Caribbean, are still in their infancy. While they have sustained radical and anti-capitalist struggles in the wake of the reversal of twentieth century socialist projects, they have not eclipsed the traditional parties, nor have they transcended the state as the central and legitimate organs of governmental authority to the extent that James anticipated when he studied the soviets during the Russian revolution and the Workers Councils in Hungary and Poland in the latter half of the twentieth century.

However, the relative infancy of these movements in the Caribbean, does not lessen their significance as new forms of political expression, signaling new directions in Caribbean radical politics. First, they represent something new. Secondly, they remain important challengers to state-supported capitalism in the Caribbean, in the context of the reversal of the options for radical politics around which the project of global transformation had been launched in the twentieth century. Thirdly and perhaps, most importantly, the new modes of radical expression have assisted in overcoming the non-democratic and authoritarian features of Marxist revolution, particularly those which had become institutionalized and modelled against Lenin's revolutionary tactics and Stalin's state practices. In short, despite the current absence of evidence to suggest that the new forms of revolutionary organization and governance have eclipsed and replaced the party and the state as formal institutions of proletarian power, James's insights into the collapse of vanguardism and their replacement by the politics of 'free creative' activity, continue to be relevant and evident in the manner in which concrete struggles are being waged against capitalism in the era of global neo-liberalism.

Conclusively, however, perhaps the most important contribution of the thought of C.L.R. James to understanding Caribbean radical politics in the early twenty-first century, is the marriage which it facilitates between the Caribbean's democratic traditions and the socialist projects of transformation which were pursued in the twentieth century. It is the failure to come to terms with the democratic possibilities of socialism which is perhaps one of the most critical failures of the Caribbean experience of socialism as was seen in the case of the Grenada revolution, for example. Indeed, one of the main lessons of the Grenada revolutionary experience is that the movement for socialism should not be divorced from the movement for democracy. From the Jamesian perspective these two processes are not mutually exclusive but are inextricably intertwined. Socialism cannot be 'decreed from above' but must involve the active participation of the people at every stage of the process. As Marable (1987, 248), echoing Rose Luxemburg, notes, "without democracy, democratic centralism becomes the rationale for authoritarianism".

Conversely, it is James's intertwining of socialism and democracy which provides yet a further and deeper basis for understanding the possibilities of Caribbean revolutionary transformation in the early twentieth century. This aspect of his thought has not been given the full attention that it deserves, particularly in the context of the concrete failures of authoritarian models of socialism. A full appreciation of James's marriage between socialism and democracy is of critical importance, therefore, for understanding how a radial project of Caribbean transformation can be pursued, considering the objective material realities of the twenty-first century.

The task following is to examine how James understood Caribbean democracy, to demonstrate how his conceptions of democracy were intertwined with his socialism, and to discuss the meaning of his marriage of socialism and democracy for understanding current directions in Caribbean democratic development.

4.

The Marriage of Socialism and Democracy: Towards a Jamesian Democracy for the 21st Century Caribbean

Representative government – what we have been taught to call democracy – was in short, an industrial technology for assuring inequality.

Alvin Toffler – The Third Wave

The major devices by which liberal theory continues to guarantee liberty while securing democracy – representation, privacy, individualism, and rights, but above all representation – turn out neither to secure democracy nor to guarantee liberty. Representation destroys participation and citizenship even as it serves accountability and private rights. Representative democracy is as paradoxical an oxymoron as our political language has produced; its confused and failing practice make this ever more obvious.

Benjamin Barber – Strong Democracy

Democracy – The Jamesian Focus

Given the marriage between socialism and democracy in the Jamesian construct, a discussion of C.L.R. James's socialist thought makes an analysis of his views on democracy seem almost unnecessary. This is because to James, the achievement of a "balance between the individual and the community" can only be fully realized under socialist society, where social and economic inequalities, the exploitation of man by man, and by extension political inequality have ceased to exist. The question of the establishment of a balance between the individual and the community, and "what is the relation of the individual his rights, his liberties, his freedom, his possibilities of progress to the community in which he lives as part?" was to James (1960, 5) "one of the fundamental problems of politics". The answer to this question is, to James, the solution to the problems inherent in both 'actually-existing' socialism, and 'actually-existing' democracy.

To James, democracy is a process whereby individuals exert an increasing degree of control over their lives free from any direction or delegation of that control to forces over and above themselves. 'Delegation' which is obtained under parliamentary, representative democracy, and other systems of representation, where the authority and power of the individual is transferred to his or her representatives, is the problem. James's critique of democracy is therefore applicable to both socialist and capitalist democracy. In a 1985 conversation with Jan Hillegas, James clarified his understanding of the relationship between socialism and democracy when he noted that,

> some people use the word socialism, but socialism as Marxism used it was government of the people, by the people, for the people. Today, socialism is government of the people for the people, by the bureaucracy... [T]he trouble is so far that people have tended to believe that democracy was parliamentary democracy. That is not so (James 1986a, 25).

Elsewhere James (1984c, 110) clarified his specific understanding of democracy when he argued that the only barrier to dictatorship is "when for the people democracy is not a carefully doled out concession that rulers make to people, but an inherent part of their conceptions of themselves". He saw democracy as an inherent "possession" which ordinary people "exercise and defend because they cannot conceive of existence without it".

James's perspective of democracy, by necessity, moved beyond that of the classical seventeenth, eighteenth and nineteenth century theorists such as Thomas Hobbes, John Locke, Alexis de Tocqueville, Montesquieu, and John Stuart Mill. While these theorists were generally aware of inherent shortcomings in representative democracy, they nevertheless saw it as being the most practical and realizable form of government, in terms of its ability to maintain a minimal level of political participation, to act as a safeguard against tyrannical and arbitrary government, and to ensure the preservation of the rights of citizens. The clearest formulation of this perspective was seen in Thomas Hobbes (1914) who perceived the need for the creation of a central governing authority without which life would be "solitary, poor, nasty, brutish and short" (Hobbes 1914, 65). The "extreme" nature of Hobbes's formulation resided in his assumption that the central governing authority should itself be above the law (Hobbes 1914, 104).

While John Locke's position proved to be more enlightened than Hobbes's in its insistence on the consent of the governed and in its awareness that "there remains still in the people a supreme power to remove or alter the legislative" (Locke 1924, 192), Locke was still unable to transcend the need for representation. Sabine and Thorson (1973, 492) have noted that "Locke regarded the setting up of a government as a much less important event than the original compact that makes a civil society", since, once a majority has agreed to form a government, "the whole power of the community is naturally in them". Crucially, Sabine and Thorson (1973, 492–93) make a clear distinction between the democratic thought of Locke and that of later theorists among whom C.L.R. James can be included. They note that,

> the power of the people over government, however, is still not quite as complete in Locke as it came to be in later and more democratic theories. Though he called the power of the legislature a fiduciary and a delegation from the majority that acts for the community, he retained the older view that the grant of the community divests the people of power so long as the government is faithful to its duties (492–93).

Similarly, other democratic theorists like Alexis de Tocqueville and Montesquieu continued to accept the view that the role of the people should be concerned with creating a government rather than with governing per se. The view of democracy which they expound, can only perceive greater liberty for the individual as being determined by the extent to which one can limit the effect of government on the individual, as seen through such mechanisms as the separation of powers and the adherence to term limits, rather than by increasing the individual's scope for action. Such a view of democracy understands freedom in the negative sense of 'freedom from' only, and not in the positive sense of 'freedom to' (Gould 1988). Tellingly, Gould (1988, 31) observes that the classical theories of eighteenth and nineteenth century liberalism "have proven to be inadequate to the demands for greater freedom and equality in the twentieth century". They therefore assert that "despite the abiding virtues that these theories retain" there should be "a new and enlarged conception of democracy and for the articulation of its philosophical foundations" more suited to the material bases since the latter half of the twentieth century.

In a related argument, Benjamin Barber in a work entitled *Strong Democracy* (1984) has suggested that one of the greatest failings of 'liberal democracy' particularly in its institutionalized forms, is that it is inherently contradictory, since the concept seeks to simultaneously balance three mutually-opposing tendencies, which he called "anarchist, realist, and minimalist". According to Barber (1984, 5–6),

> while the three dispositions may share a belief in the primacy of conflict, they suggest radically different approaches to its amelioration. Put very briefly, anarchism is conflict-denying, realism is conflict-repressing and minimalism is conflict-tolerating. The first approach tries to wish conflict away, the second to extirpate it, and the third to live with it. Liberal democracy, the compound and real American form, is conflict-denying in its free-market assumptions about the private sector and its supposed elasticity and egalitarianism; it is conflict repressing and also conflict-adjusting in its prudential use of political power to

adjudicate the struggle of individuals and groups; and it is conflict-tolerating in its characteristic liberal-skeptical temper.

Most significantly Barber points out that the practice of liberal democracy has been too heavily influenced by individualistic and private concerns, the furtherance of which early theorists such as Locke saw as the primary reasons for the establishment of government. Barber laments the fact that such an emphasis on individualistic and private motivations militates against the possibility of perceiving a form of democracy which is designed to foster communal and collective concepts such as justice, equality, community, citizenship or participation (Barber 1984, xiv). He asserts that, "autonomy is not the condition of democracy, democracy is the condition of autonomy", and he insists that "without participating in the common life that defines them and in the decision-making that shapes their social habitat, women and men cannot become individuals" (Barber 1984, xv).

C.L.R. James's construction of democracy is based on the realization that genuine individual self-interest and a thorough expression of individuality cannot be safeguarded upon the basis of representative democracy. James found support for his critique of representative democracy in the work of Jean-Jacques Rousseau (Henry 1992, 229). James saw in Rousseau's thought, the most uncompromising critique of representative democracy (James 1960, 19–21). In his famous lectures on western political thought delivered to a Trinidadian audience in 1960, James made it clear why he saw Rousseau as more relevant to the post-representative forms of democratic politics that he felt were emerging. In James's view,

> Rousseau thought that representative government was an absolute farce. He says the moment you give your vote and give your power to some other people, they begin to represent themselves or other interests, not the interests of the people. Rousseau thought that representative government deceived the people. And political parties too deceived the people. Rousseau said that as soon as political parties get together and start to quarrel with one another,

all sorts of private or special interests come into play and the
interest of the population is lost (James 1960, 20).

Rousseau's perspective was based largely upon his view of the
relationship between the citizen and government and on what he
perceived to be the basis of sovereignty. Rousseau was insistent
that sovereignty lay with the people who formed the government
and not in the government which the people formed (Michels
1962, 73–74). Like James, Duverger (1964, 140) has argued that one
of the main contributions which Rousseau makes to democratic
theory is that "sovereignty cannot be delegated". He insists that,

> all legal artifices concerning the representation of the mandator
> by the mandatary cannot conceal this truth: that the mentality of
> the delegates is never the same as that of those who delegate them,
> with the result that every additional stage of delegation increases a
> little more the gap between the will of the base and the decision of
> the apex (Duverger 1964, 140).

It is factors such as these which account for James's hostility
towards ideas which restrict democracy to an institutional
arrangement which allowed only for a narrow, representative
interpretation of the concept. To James, like John Stuart Mill,
the constitutional arrangement is not in itself an indication
of democracy and should not be treated as an end in itself.
Instead, the constitutional structures should be nothing more
than a reflection of a peoples' conception of democracy and the
corresponding institutional structures should seek to ensure that
such a conception was realized in practice. In the words of J.S. Mill
(1975, 154),

> in politics as in mechanics, the power which is to keep the engine
> going must be sought for outside the machinery; and if it is not
> forthcoming, or is insufficient to surmount the obstacles which
> may reasonably be expected, the contrivance will fail. A nation
> therefore, cannot choose its form of government. The mere details,
> and practical organisation it may choose; but the essence of the
> whole, the seat of the supreme power, is determined for it by social
> circumstances.

It is for this reason that James (1984c, 115) points out that "democratic government does not create democracy. Democracy creates democratic government. It is held together by the habits and practices and expectations of people". It is this historically and sociologically conditioned aspect of democracy – the recognition that the institutional arrangements for ensuring democracy are subject to transformation as the expectations and political consciousness of people change – that James seeks to highlight in his formulation of democracy.

Though largely attacked as Eurocentric, James's openly avowed admiration for ancient Greek democracy, was the result of the ability of the Athenian model to attain a 'balance between the individual and community'. James applauded the fact that the system allowed the ordinary male citizen not only to elect his representatives, but to participate in the actual process of government itself. James also deeply admired the hostility of ancient Athenian democracy to arbitrary and tyrannical government. James was particularly drawn to Athenian democracy because he was aware that the decision to adopt a participatory mode of government was a conscious and deliberate one, since the representative alternative had been known to the Athenians (James 1986a, 1–2). James felt that it was significant that philosophers such as Plato, Aristotle and Socrates resisted participatory democracy even though their views were perceived as subversive by the authorities (G.G.M. James [1954] 1988). To James such a development was evidence of the fact that such a mode of government had to be consciously defended by the people against the view held by those like Plato, that government should be undertaken by experts and not by the common people (James 1986a, 2).

In his pamphlet *Every Cook Can Govern*, James (1986a, 1–2) establishes the case for the transcendence of representative democracy and its replacement by participatory forms. James argued that "before the democracy came into power, *the* Greeks had been governed by various forms of government, including government by representatives", and they "knew representative government and rejected it". He claims that the Athenians "refused to believe that the ordinary citizen was not able to perform practically all the business of government". As a result of this historical experience, James was emboldened with the belief that Caribbean states in the late twentieth century, could adopt participatory forms along the lines established by the Greeks:

> we today who are faced with the inability of representative government and parliamentary democracy to handle effectively the urgent problems of the day, we can study and understand Greek democracy in a way that was impossible for a man who lived in 1900, when representative government and parliamentary democracy seemed securely established for all time (James 1986a, 14).

It is a post-representative, participatory democracy such as that established by the Greeks, that James believes Rousseau's concept of the general will sought to achieve. James is aware that Rousseau's general will cannot be realized under a representative form of government. He felt that Rousseau's concept of the General Will represents a leap from the democracy propounded by the classical liberal theorists and, by its rejection of representative democracy, seeks to lay the foundations of participatory government. James (1960, 21) claims that,

> Rousseau... is seeking a form of political organisation in which the individual will feel himself in relation to a government in much the same way that the Greek citizen felt in relation to the city-state. And that is why he is not afraid of one man - a legislator - if that fellow will express the general will. But he is pretty sure that parliament and political parties as he has seen them will not express it. Once you put them there, they acquire ... [through] the objective circumstances ... a life of their own which is separate from the life and the interests that they are supposed to serve.

These aspects of Rousseau's thought – the concept of the 'legislator' and the question of the 'diminished importance of government' – appear to be inherently contradictory since Rousseau's 'legislator' is in effect a concession to the necessity for some form of central governmental authority which would have the will and force to initiate and implement collective goals. Rousseau's vision of a government totally subordinate to society has generally been viewed as largely unworkable since it ignores the practical question of the autonomy and power needed by governments – the traditional question of the legitimacy of the centralized state – to effectively determine and execute society's goals.

It is significant that the Jamesian view of democracy as well as its institutionalized expression, the mass party which seeks to make government subservient to society, has been criticized on similar grounds of its apparent 'impracticability'. What is often forgotten however, is that the theoretical basis for the subordination of government to society has been thoroughly explored within Marxist theory and is an inherent aspect of the socialist project. It has found its most acute theoretical expression in Marx's advocacy of the 'withering away of the state' and concrete practical manifestation in the Paris commune, the soviets, and workers' councils of the nineteenth and twentieth centuries in Paris, Russia and Hungary, as discussed in the previous chapter. In fact, to James, modern politics is characterized by a constant struggle between government and society, the latter relentlessly trying to wrest from government the power which government has derived, and could only have derived, from society.

There are sufficient historical grounds therefore, for avoiding the temptation of viewing James's preoccupation with Athenian democracy as a subjective, idealistic, nostalgic belief in a form of democracy whose reappearance is currently unrealizable. James himself was fully aware of the view which held that this direct democracy was suitable only for the city state, and was "unsuited to large modern communities" (James 1986a, 2). One of the more justifiable arguments in this regard, is the claim that Athenian democracy was possible only because it was built upon a foundation of slavery and the exclusion of women and foreigners or *metics*, and as such resulted in the creation of a parasitic, leisure class which was able to devote time and effort to the business of

politics (Sabine and Thorson 1973, 20). While it can be agreed
that James himself did not question adequately the foundations
of slavery, national chauvinism, and sexual discrimination upon
which Athenian democracy was established, the claim that
such a democracy was possible only under the social conditions
of Athenian antiquity is largely untenable. Indeed, later in this
chapter, it will be argued that the objective material conditions
for a participatory democracy similar to, and beyond that of
the ancient Greek city-states, exist today and are daily being
advanced (Toffler 1981; Barber 1984; Osborne and Gaebler 1993;
James 1986a).   Every new breakthrough in communications,
transportation and information technology makes void the claims
that the system of direct democracy was suitable only to the Greek
city-state. As James himself notes in a 1985 conversation,

> most people when they think of democracy, they think in terms
> of parliament and speeches ... I'm looking at something else. The
> means of communication, means of information today are such
> that it is impossible to believe that as time goes on it does not mean
> greater and greater communication between people, which means
> ultimately, a democratic system of some sort... I'm speaking in
> particular about the objective materials, physical means of living,
> means of communication, means of spreading information. That
> is going on every day. That's what I look at and say the tendency
> towards a democratic relation between people is bound to follow
> (James 1986a, 26).

Relatedly, it has also been suggested by writers such as Walton
Look Lai (1992, 183) that James was "often close to suggesting
that the social intimacy and small size of the West Indian islands
were approximations of that closeness and humanism that
characterized the ancient city-states".

Socialism and Democracy: The Jamesian Synthesis

The work of James, and in particular his notion of democracy,
challenges very strongly, the commonly held view that democracy
is synonymous with capitalism. Not only does James's democratic
thought reject the 'thin' democracy that is associated with

capitalism, but by logical extension, it also recognizes that a participatory-democratic political relationship cannot be established within the existing capitalist relation and can only be established under socialist economic and social relations. This point has been made by Samir Amin (1990, 12–13) who has argued that while "Western democracy is ... restricted to the political domain... economic management continues to be based on non-democratic principles of private ownership and competition". He argues persuasively that "the capitalist mode of production does not of itself require democracy, but its characteristic oppression is in fact hidden in economic alienation." On the other hand, he suggests that it is "the socialist project of a classless society, free of economic alienation" which "implies a democratic structure", since "social relations based on co-operation among workers, and not on their subjection, are inconceivable without a full flowering of democracy".

From a Marxist perspective, the establishment of participatory democracy such as that envisaged by C.L.R. James cannot be achieved unless the economic inequality upon which representative democracy is based, is abolished. This perspective recognizes that, "there is no democracy in general, neither are there general and abstract criteria of it, existing independently of the rule of certain classes" but that the "characteristic features of democracy are linked with the rule of definite classes" (Kiss 1982, 152). It is this realization that pushes the Jamesian conception of democracy beyond the mere reproduction of the Athenian model. James was aware that the establishment of a democracy similar to that of the Greeks could only be founded on a more advanced, material, socio-economic base than that of the Greeks (James 1960, 21).

James was aware too, that the new expressions of participatory politics should also include "demands for economic democracy [since] the events of the French revolution, by putting the question of mass poverty on the public agenda, made a simple return to Greek political democracy impossible" (Henry 1992, 230). In other words, the new socio-economic realities of the twentieth and twenty-first centuries, would by necessity create the conditions for advancing beyond the racial, national, and sexual chauvinism of the ancient Greek world. It is on this level, theoretically, that the Jamesian synthesis of socialism and democracy became established and why the two concepts remained mutually inextricable throughout his thought. In the Jamesian perspective, "the struggle for socialism is the struggle for proletarian democracy. Proletarian democracy is not the result of socialism. Socialism is the result of proletarian democracy" (James, Forest and Stone 1972, 4). To James therefore, any advance in democracy is an advance towards the establishment of socialism.

From a class analysis perspective, it is not difficult to understand why capitalist democracy is restricted only to 'representative' democracy. The existence of capitalism means a situation in which certain classes have a more deeply vested interest in the economy than others. To safeguard that interest, the capitalist state and its attendant institutions such as parliaments, political parties and trade unions, ensure that the decisions taken are in the interest of the capitalist and supportive classes. It is only with total economic equality that a system of participatory democracy can work; where everyone can exert an influence on the decision-making and implementation process similar to that exerted by the capitalist class within the framework of capitalist society.

James saw in the commune, workers' soviets, and workers' councils, mechanisms which ensured both political and economic equality and facilitated the direct participation of all citizens in the business of government. As a result, he saw these as institutions of socialist society. In stark contrast to what obtains under capitalist democracy, these institutions, by their very structures, recognize that the political and economic cannot be artificially separated as is done by the mechanism of parliament. This for example, is what James had identified as one of the most significant achievements of the short-lived Paris commune of 1871 (James, Lee and Chaulieu [1958] 1974), as indeed had Marx himself:

the commune was to be a working, not a parliamentary body, executive and legislative at the same time... Instead of deciding once in three or six years which members of the ruling class was to represent the people in parliament, universal suffrage was to serve the people, constituted in communes, as individual suffrage serves every other employer in his business (Lenin 1943, 39).

Paget Henry (1992, 230) has argued that the new structures offered up by the soviets and workers councils were, in essence "the solution to the post-representative government that James inherited from Marx". He argues that it "was a form of social organisation in which political and economic power came to rest on such organisations as the councils into which the workers of the Paris commune had quite spontaneously organised themselves", and he asserts that "such councils would then become the primary bases of mass consent and sources of legitimacy for both political and economic decision-making". This, he argued, would result in a situation in which "politics and economics would then become less removed from popular control and from each other".

The fact that these institutions embodied within their structures a solution to the political disempowerment of the ordinary worker which emanates from their economic marginalization also accounts for their suitability as organs of participatory democracy, and by extension, socialist democracy. In addition to this, however, they were primarily organs of action, as distinct from debate (Arendt 1963; James, Lee and Chaulieu [1958] 1974; Lenin 1943). This lies in stark contrast to what is achieved within political parties, trade unions, parliaments and other institutions of 'capitalist democracy' which serve ultimately to militate against any form of direct action on the part of the people. This emphasis on direct action is the hallmark of socialist democracy. It forms the basis of the much misunderstood notion of the withering away of the state (Lenin 1943, 84) and it is in this sense that James spoke of the 'dictatorship of the proletariat' (James 1960, 35). In James's words these organs of socialist democracy, in contrast to those of capitalist democracy are "based not on the control of people but on the mastery of things" (James, Lee and Chaulieu [1958]

1974, 6). Organization is needed merely for the implementation of society's goals in the interest of all and not for the subjection of the majority in the interest of the few.

Ralph Miliband (1982, 38) captures the true essence and limitations of parliamentary, representative democracy, and by extension, helps to clarify the more advanced democratic nature of participatory forms of socialist democracy that James was seeking to advance, when he observes that "in conditions of capitalist democracy, with universal suffrage, political competition, and the capacity of the working class to exercise different forms of pressure, the crucial problem for the people in charge of affairs is to be able to get on with the business in hand, without undue interference from below". He argues that the "point is not to achieve popular exclusion altogether" since this would be "dangerous and ultimately self-defeating". Instead, he argues that "the point is rather to give adequate and meaningful scope to popular participation" while at the same time aiming to "'depopularlize' policy-making and to limit strictly the impact of the market-place upon the conduct of affairs". In his view "parliamentarianism makes this possible" since it "simultaneously enshrines the principle of popular inclusion and that of popular exclusion".

The perspective which recognizes that the structures of the commune, soviets and workers' councils constitute the basis for participatory democracy, also suggests that they provide the mechanisms for overcoming the bureaucratic inertia which characterizes the administrations of the developed and developing world (Osborne and Gaebler 1993; Toffler 1981; Drucker 1969; James, Lee and Chaulieu [1958] 1974). C.L.R. James recognizes this bureaucratic encumbrance as a product of industrial-capitalist society. He sees the capitalist bureaucracy as a device or 'technique' which was once beneficial and functional, but is now unable to meet the administrative needs of a new participatory democratic model. In short, the shift to a new organizational model to sustain participatory democracy, would necessarily result in transformations, not only in the 'political-democratic' institutions, but in the 'bureaucratic-administrative' systems as well. James (1986a, 45) was therefore fully confident that since the existing "bureaucracy is the result of the capitalist tradition" and "is not required by the new industry", that in the process of transition to the new order "they will overthrow it... [b]ecause the bureaucracy will be incompetent or will be leading the country in all ways".

James's argument is echoed by Osborne and Gaebler (1993, 15) in their highly acclaimed book *Reinventing Government,* in which they sought to show how new technologies associated with the internet revolution and globalization have impacted on administrative processes. They note that,

> the bureaucratic model developed in conditions very different from those we experience today. It developed in a slower-paced society, when change proceeded at a leisurely gait. It developed in an age of hierarchy, when only those at the top of the pyramid had enough information to make informed decisions. It developed in a society of people who worked with their hands not their minds. Today, all that has been swept away. We live in an era of breath-taking change. We live in a global marketplace which puts enormous competitive pressure on our economic institutions. We live in a knowledge-based economy, in which educated workers bridle at commands and demand autonomy.

James had seen the workers' councils and soviets of the early twentieth century as the harbinger of the death of the old bureaucratic structures with their outmoded concepts of democracy. These structures sought to ensure that 'every cook, to a man', took part in the administration of the economy and the state (James 1977b, 202–203). These organizational structures also provided a solution to the government/party contradiction inherent within all political parties (James 1977b, 202–203). This is because there was no scope for political divisions within the councils along party lines since the councils were in effect simultaneously legislative and executive bodies. It is for this reason too that they failed to adhere to Robert Michel's 'iron law of oligarchy' which, in any case, was a discussion of a tendency within liberal political parties (Michels 1962). This is not to suggest that the soviets were not susceptible to differences of opinion, nor perhaps indeed can the fact be ignored that the banning of all parties by the Bolsheviks might have contributed to the apparent uniformity of purpose of the soviets. However, what is critical in understanding James' admiration of the soviets is the fact that they represent a new form of decision-making apparatus that overcame the separation of parliamentary debate and executive decision-making, the artificial split between economics and politics, and the distance between elite decision-makers and subservient decision-implementors inherent to liberal bourgeois-democratic political practice.

It is upon these premises that C.L.R. James forges a synthesis between socialism and democracy. Prior to James, a similar synthesis had been made by V.I. Lenin, in *State and Revolution* (1943), first published in 1917. In that work Lenin (1943, 84) had sought to show a link between the growing levels of political consciousness and administrative competence within the population on one hand, and their capacity for self-government and direct democracy on the other. Lenin had anticipated a moment when "all members of society or even only the overwhelming majority, have learned how to govern the state themselves" as a moment in which "the need for any government begins to disappear". It was in this sense that Lenin understood the 'withering away of the state', since: "the more complete the democracy, the nearer the moment when it begins to be unnecessary... The more democratic the 'state'... the more readily does every state begin to wither away (43). Indeed, Lenin had made a similar argument in the pamphlet "Can the Bolsheviks Retain State Power?", written in response to the claims by various anti-revolutionary groups that the proletarian forces would be incapable of occupying and managing the 'bourgeois' state apparatus. Lenin's rebuttal to this charge was to reinforce the assertion that the aim of the revolution was not to occupy the bourgeois state apparatus but to replace it: "the proletariat *cannot* 'lay hold of' the 'state apparatus' and 'set it in motion'. But it can *smash* everything that is oppressive, routine, incorrigibly bourgeois in the old state apparatus and substitute its *own*, new apparatus. The Soviets of Workers', Soldiers' and Peasants' Deputies are exactly this apparatus" (Lenin 1917).

Having explored the theoretical foundations upon which C.L.R. James forges his synthesis between democracy and socialism, it then becomes necessary to identify the concrete weaknesses in Caribbean democracy which James confronted.

'Actually-existing' Democracy in the Caribbean: The Limits of Representative Democracy

One of the strongest indictments of representative democracy is that, even when accepted on its own terms, it fails to live up to its promise of guaranteeing the establishment of a government which "reflects the 'voice of the people' and frustrates the emergence of government in accord with the will of the people" (Jamadar 1989, 3). The election systems, political parties, 'checks and balances' and other institutional and constitutional arrangements which are designed to guarantee representative democracy have, in the practice of Caribbean politics, fallen far short of their desired goal. These shortcomings result in large measure in growing disillusionment and political apathy on the part of the Caribbean electorate as reflected in the level of voter turn-out in Caribbean elections as highlighted in the work on Caribbean general elections by Patrick Emmanuel (1992, 13; 17), and re-affirmed in Barrow-Giles and Joseph (2006, 89).[1]

The nature of Caribbean democracy and its wider political culture have been shaped by the process of decolonization and the context in which the independence constitutions were taking shape. These constitutions are therefore a reflection of "what its designers wished to discourage, emphasize and even add" to the process of decolonization and democracy (Munroe 1972, 147). In the actual practice of Caribbean democracy, because of the nature of the Caribbean political environment, the levels of education of the Caribbean electorate, and the absence of a 'critical mass', the promise of Caribbean representative democracy is not actualized. Carlene Edie (1991, 9) identifies as perhaps "the most neglected fact about existing democracies in developing nations" the reality that "although the form of political institutions may resemble those in western democracies, the substance is significantly different and is often anti-democratic". She rightfully argues that the "the substance tends to be undermined by a host of internal and external economic and political factors".

These anti-democratic tendencies manifest themselves in the most basic of the structures which form the bedrock of Caribbean representative democracy – the political party. It is not by chance that James's critique of Caribbean democracy sprang from a critique of the Caribbean political party (James 1984c). His critique of the Caribbean party expands upon his criticism and analysis of the party during and around the Russian Bolshevik revolution. The tensions between the "party as government" and the "party as mass mobilization", which were mentioned in chapter two, manifest themselves particularly strongly in the Caribbean. Several commentators (James 1984c; Best 1971; Fanon [1967] 1983; Gittens 1983) have described Caribbean political parties as mechanisms to stifle mass mobilization and as institutions which concentrate more heavily on the 'government' aspect of the contradiction. They have also argued that Caribbean political parties can be more correctly described as state-machines rather than popular organisms (Best 1971, 7). The structures of these parties are strictly hierarchical and centralized with key decisions such as leadership and candidate selection, and governmental policy being decided by a disproportionately small clique within the party (Singh 1972, 114). There are very few mechanisms within the party structure to facilitate a decentralized, bottom-upwards decision-making process which would make these institutions more truly representative of the will of the people.

Carlene Edie (1991, 55) describes the People's National Party (PNP) of Jamaica under Michael Manley as a "pyramid", in which the base "consists of thousands of members of the party who do not participate in decision-making and who therefore can easily be manipulated". In between, in the "intermediate level", is the "constituency committee" which is "in charge of recruiting members and expanding the mass base". She describes the upper echelons of the pyramid as those who control the "power apparatus in the party" inclusive of the "councillors and MPs" who are "given an enormous amount of control over the mass" and who act as "the key intermediaries in the management of political interactions between the electorate at the base and the party hierarchy and vice versa" (55). This control of the 'power apparatuses' by the party leadership at the exclusion of the mass base of the party is characteristic of every political party in the English-speaking Caribbean. It is this dilemma which C.L.R. James sought to resolve through his creation of a mass party (James 1984c), and which will be examined more fully in a later section.

In addition to the larger questions surrounding the inherently anti-democratic nature of Caribbean political parties are also more "technical" issues inherent in the electoral practices which also serve to deepen the anti-democratic culture of the region. The electoral mechanism used in all the English-speaking Caribbean territories, except Guyana – the first-past-the-post system – has for a number of reasons, resulted in the creation of a number of governments which have been unrepresentative of the will of the electorate.

One of the main reasons for this, particularly in 'plural societies' such as Trinidad and Tobago and Guyana, is the tendency to vote according to racial and ethnic demarcations. The first-past-the-post system, with its emphasis on the selection of a government that is determined by the support given to candidates within separate constituencies has often resulted in governments which fail to reflect the true level of representation of less dominant ethnic groups (Jamadar 1989). The Caribbean's noted Nobel Laureate economist, and student of democracy, W.A. Lewis has noted that one of the critical democratic challenges in plural societies is to "create political institutions which give all the various groups the opportunity to participate in decision-making since only thus can they feel that they are full members of a nation, respected by their more numerous brethren and owing equal respect to the national bond which holds them together" (in Ryan 1989, xviii). Lewis argues that in plural societies the emphasis on winner-take-all mechanisms is inherently counter-productive, and he recommends that in such societies "it is necessary to get away from the idea that somebody is to prevail over somebody else" and of "politics as a zero-sum game" (Ryan 1989, xviii).

In addition to the failure to fully reflect the true level of numerical representation of minorities in the society, the first-past-the-post or 'winner take all' system often results in situations where the party gaining the largest proportion of the national vote, fails to secure the largest number of seats (Emmanuel 1992, 18).[2] These are not aberrations but are built-in features of the system, and the problem has persisted into the twenty-first century. In addition, since under the first-past-the-post system, a lost vote is equivalent to a "wasted" vote, supporters of minority parties or independent candidates, tend to withhold their votes rather than to vote for a losing party or candidate (Jamadar 1989, 26). Such voters are, in a sense, virtually disenfranchised by the electoral process which has been designed for the formation of a government which is supposed to be 'representative' of the will of the electorate. It is for all these reasons that Jamadar (1989, 18) writing on the experience of the first-past-the-post system in Trinidad and Tobago has argued that its use has "not resulted in any general election from 1950 to date, in which the parliament accurately represented the main trends of opinion within the electorate. He concludes that "parliament has never reflected the image of the feelings of the country" and that the "true tenor of the voice of the people has never been heard".

Despite its superior capacity to reflect the true spread of political opinion, the proportional representative system, as practiced in Guyana, also fails to offer a solution to the problem of representative government. Indeed, the proportional representative system results in further marginalization of rank-and-file party members since it involves the selection of candidates from various party lists and effectively neutralizes the capacity of citizens to directly elect their parliamentary representatives. As such, it widens the scope for arbitrary power and decision-making on the part of the party's leadership. Under the proportional representative system candidates owe their loyalty to the party leadership rather than to their constituents since the fate of party candidates is dependent upon the patronage of the party leadership rather than support from below. These tendencies have been more than amply witnessed in the post-colonial electoral and political history of Guyana, which continues to be plagued by contentious election results and tendencies towards authoritarianism, all resulting from the absence of direct intervention of the people in the election and removal of individual representatives from parliament. The political tensions in Guyana surrounding the events related to the 2020 general elections illustrate clearly the dysfunctionality of the system, as well as the exclusion of the electors from intervening decisively in the process.

In addition to these "technical" failures of the electoral mechanisms used to ensure 'representative' democracy, the Caribbean experience has shown that the anti-democratic tendencies continue to manifest themselves in other aspects of the system, such as the parliament and in government, beyond the elections themselves. The power of the ruling party in parliament and in its role as cabinet, often approximates as a daily practice, the 'tyranny of the majority' against which Alexis de Tocqueville ([1945] 1989, 1:259) had counselled. Opposition members and senators are powerless to 'oppose' and check government policy. Moreover, the first-past-the-post system has thrown up several instances in which a single party has been able to win the total number of seats in parliament, leaving no formal opposition, despite the large levels of support that the other party or parties may enjoy in the country as a whole. This has happened in the cases of St. Vincent and the Grenadines in 1989, Jamaica in 1983,[3] and it has become even more frequent in the twenty-first century as seen in the cases of Grenada in 2013 and 2018, and in Barbados in 2018 and 2022.[4]

These episodes of single-party representation in parliament have had implications for the constitutional provision of the office of Leader of the Opposition, which was originally intended to serve as a countervailing check on government. The failure of the first-past-the post system to allow for this as a mandatory practice, further limits the effectiveness of Caribbean representative democracy. As noted by Trevor Munroe (1972, 163), "the provision for only one leader of the opposition, however divided the legislative voice of those who do not support the government of the day" suggests "an intensity of opposition to the recognition of a third party", and one might add, other forms of minority political opinion and expression. Further, there are a number of factors within the workings of parliament, such as the concept of collective responsibility, the right of the prime minister to appoint and dismiss ministers of government and to dissolve parliament, which have justified the description of Caribbean representative democracy as "cabinet dictatorships" (Jamadar 1989, 33).

However, these anti-democratic institutional arrangements could not have been sustained were it not for the historical authoritarianism embedded in the Caribbean's political culture. C.L.R. James has argued strongly against the popularly held view of the Caribbean as possessing a democratic tradition. He rejected the idea that the Caribbean had cultivated democratic practice through its experience of British colonialism (James 1984c, 111). On the contrary, James instead, observed that in the Caribbean, "the tendency is to naked power and naked brutality, the result of

West Indian historical development". He argues that "the greatest danger in the whole of the West Indies is that no class in the islands has ever been able to make the conception of democracy an integral part of its existence. The experience of upper and lower classes in the West Indies was the tradition of power and obedience or terrified silence or rebellion" (James 1984c, 111–13).

The absence of a democratic political culture and consciousness has been manifested in the marked absence of vigilance in the attainment of democratic rights and a nonchalance in the defense of such rights on the part of the governed classes. It is also reflected in the tendency towards autocratic and authoritarian rule on the part of the governing classes. In the early twenty-first century, the Caribbean is only beginning to embrace as a central part of its political discourse, issues such as the protection of minority religious rights and issues of gender equality and minority group sexual rights. This culture of authoritarianism is reflected in a tendency to erode the democratic gains of Caribbean people, most notably following periods of challenge to governmental autocracy. The most notable example of such a tendency is the anti-democratic legislation, euphemistically referred to as 'public order acts', implemented in all the Caribbean territories following the upheavals of the 1970s. This tendency to curtail the rights to freedom of expression and public protest has persisted well into the twenty-first century, despite the democratic credentials which are uncritically claimed for the Caribbean region (see Dominguez 1993). Carl D. Parris (1983, 318) identifies the main features of the public order legislation which was introduced in Trinidad and Tobago, following the 1970 Black Power protests, as being intended, among other things to: " (1) Regulate public meetings and marches; (2) Penalise persons inciting others to racial hatred and violence'; (3) Prohibit the organization of training of quasi-military organizations and unlawful oath taking; (4) Allow entry to the police for the purpose of search, [and] (5) Enable the minister to make detention orders".

Such anti-democratic measures are ubiquitous throughout the Caribbean. They can be identified in Dominica, with the Seditious and Undesirable Publications Bill euphemistically called the Shut-your-Mouth Bill passed by the LeBlanc-led Dominica Labour Party (Robinson 2006, 38–39), and also the 'Dreads Act' under the Patrick John-led Dominica Labour Party administration which sought to criminalize members of the Rastafarian community who wore long beards and dreadlocks (Campbell 1985,159); in Saint Lucia, where the public order act seeks to limit the extent to which public meetings and demonstrations can be held by making it necessary to obtain the permission of the commissioner of police before such activities can be undertaken; and in Barbados, where the Erskine Sandiford administration in the face of public criticism over the government's economic policies in the 1992–1994 period, amended the 'public order' bill to curb freedom of speech. The amended bill sought to regulate the contributions of callers to the popular radio call-in programmes by making indicatable any statements deemed as being of hostile intent and a threat to public safety.

These reflections on the "actually-existing" nature of Caribbean representative democracy, explain why C.L.R. James emphatically rejected the idea of the Caribbean states as models of democracy, a boast commonly trumpeted by the undemocratic Caribbean leaders themselves. James drew a sharp distinction between the external trappings of democracy and its cultural substance. He insisted that "voting every so many years is not the beginning and end of democracy". He had always felt that the Caribbean possessed only the "semblance of democracy...because it was always guarded by a cruiser". In the absence of cruisers, James argued that "you have to depend on the population" (James 1984c, 119). He observes that "we have been establishing the premises of a modern democratic society: parliamentary government, democratic rights, party politics, etc. The mere existence of these is totally inadequate... We now have to move on to a more advanced stage" (James 1984c, 121). Indeed, it is such an 'advanced stage' of democracy for the Caribbean that C.L.R. James's largely misunderstood recommendation for a mass party sought to herald.

The Jamesian Mass Party: A Caribbean Soviet?

Perhaps one of the least understood aspects of C.L.R. James's political thought is why he devised the mass party and proposed it as a concrete structure or model for a post-colonial Caribbean. Some writers have viewed James's proposal as a retreat from his socialist perspective and as evidence of inconsistency in his thought (Benn 1987, 122). It has also been described as being "somewhat more conventional and more liberal-democratic than social revolutionary" (Lai 1992, 183). Denis Benn (1987, 122) in particular has sought to identify inconsistencies in the fact that while James had "consistently maintained that the traditional vanguard-type party or other similar organisation was outmoded and reactionary and had emphasised instead the principle of spontaneity", James would have proposed a "democratic mass party" as a "vital instrument of social change in underdeveloped territories such as the West Indies". He further suggests that this raises a number of questions about the theory of spontaneity which James had sought "to justify in terms of complex and elaborate philosophical arguments based on the dialectic and the principle of self-activity". According to Benn (1987, 122),

> one must conclude that if there are exceptions to the principle of self-activity with regard to mass action, then the validity of the theory of spontaneity, justified in terms of its universality, must be seriously questioned or conversely, it must be concluded that James's prescription for party organisation in under-developed countries is inconsistent with, and indeed contradicts, his more general theoretical principles concerning social and political change.

Perhaps one of the weaknesses in appreciating the relevance of C.L.R. James's political ideas to the Caribbean, has been the tendency for writers to explain his Caribbean writings, in the narrow terms of his personal experiences arising from his 'actual engagement' in the politics of Trinidad and Tobago, such as his dalliances with the PNM, his electoral participation on behalf of the WFP and his association with the OWTU. James himself, has already offered an account of his break with Eric Williams's PNM in *Party Politics in the West Indies* (1984c), which provides sufficient historical context, for analysis and application of his ideas to proceed. While these moments of personal and direct engagement with the politics of Trinidad are important way-stations in James's life, the difficulty arises when writers treat these as barriers to the application of his more deeply theoretical ideas to the politics of the Caribbean. It is as if James's theories become 'negated' by his years spent in direct politics in Trinidad.

Far from seeing James's mass party as a retreat from his 'free creative activity' and as a reversal of his anti-vanguardism stance, it is being argued here that the proposal was indicative neither of an inconsistency nor contradiction in his thought. Instead, it can be seen as a logical outcome of his synthesis of democracy and socialism. A party, of the type proposed by James, cannot be established without destroying the material foundations and capitalist social relations upon which Caribbean liberal democratic social formations are based. As such, those who treat the Jamesian mass party as a mechanistic 'technical' critique of Caribbean liberal democrcy, independent of his critique of authoritarianism within socialist political formations, fail to understand the dialectical unity connecting James's critique of Stalinist state-capitalism and Caribbean liberal democracy. James saw them both as species of petty-bourgeois leadership standing in the way of the direct political participation of the working people.

In short, the Jamesian mass party was a mechanism designed to foster socialist participatory democracy, like that established by the short-lived soviets and workers' councils of the early twentieth century rather than as a corrective to representative democracy. It will be argued in the final section of this chapter, that the objective material conditions for the establishment of such a party, such as technological and communications tools and subjective issues like the levels of education and consciousness of the ordinary worker, exist more concretely in the twenty-first century, than they did at the time of James's proposal of the mass party.

It is not entirely incorrect to suggest that James had recognized the utility of the role of a party in under-developed countries such as those of the Caribbean. This is reinforced by James's own involvement with the PNM in Trinidad and his later role as an electoral candidate under the banner of the WFP in the 1966 election, following his ostracism by Williams after his break with the PNM. Indeed James had rationalized his involvement with the WFP on the basis that it "recognises the backward character of the economy, it recognises the advanced character of the population-it knows that one of these has to go. Either the population has to be reduced to where it was in 1937, or the economy has to be made into an advanced and a modern economy" (In Teelucksingh 2010, 72). In *Modern Politics* James (1960, 92) had stated, somewhat region-specifically, that the "the party, adapted to local conditions and basing itself upon a careful examination of both the Second and Third Internationals, is still valid for countries which are under-developed, that is to say, where industry and therefore the proletariat is not dominant". In his view, a strong argument justifying the continued relevance of the party in under-developed, formerly colonized countries were the "continuing victories they are winning in country after country" (92).

James's own dalliance with electoral and partisan politics in Trinidad under the banner of the WFP, his involvement in the PNM and even his association with the British Labour Party and trade unionism does not diminish the theoretical clarity of his reflections on the limits of representative democracy. It is clear that when James speaks of 'victories' he is speaking only in the limited sense of the anti-colonial struggle. Further, James's concept of the party is in keeping with his dialectical logic which recognizes that the specific features of the political structures adopted by the working class at any given moment are dependent upon the objective development of the material base of the society. In a moment when the formal process of decolonization has been largely completed, and when the independence project has moved beyond the stage of the anti-colonial struggle, James's recommendation of the mass party can facilitate the establishment of an advanced form of democracy.

The Jamesian mass party was a mechanism designed to facilitate the self-activity of the ordinary membership, not their domination and direction from above, and as a result it is perfectly compatible with his concept of spontaneity and "free-creative activity". James (1984c xix–xx) in *Party Politics in the West Indies*, outlined his proposal in the following way:

> as with any serious political problem, there is much more to this simple programme – the people must organise themselves... It is also a commonplace of history that the people never know exactly how to get what they want: they are not readers of books or students of politics. They do not know who are their real friends or who are mortal enemies – enemies, that is to say, of a new way of life not only for the few but for the many. People find out these answers only by activity, they make experiences and from these they learn ... The people of underdeveloped countries cannot themselves form the government. But by 'independent political activity' they find out what they can do, their privileges and their responsibilities.

It is important to note that James's proposal for the mass party was part of a larger intellectual conversation amongst anti-colonial theorists who were concerned about the failure of the post-colonial state to become truly anti-colonial. Central to this conversation were concerns about the lack of democracy within the anti-colonial parties themselves. The democratic problem was related to the reluctance by the anti-colonial leaders to allow the base of society to influence the nature of the anti-colonial struggle and post-colonial transformation. Often, these questions were expressed in class terms as signifying a difference in the aims between the 'petite-bourgeois' nationalist leadership on one hand, and workers and peasants on the other. Prior to James, these questions had been famously identified and addressed by Frantz Fanon, 'the apostle of real decolonisation' (Munroe 1972,

185). In a tone very similar to that of James, Fanon ([1967] 1983, 85) in calling for the transcendence of the party, argued that,

> the notion of the party is a notion imported from the mother country. This instrument of modern political warfare is thrown down just as it is, without the slightest modification, upon real life with all its infinite variations and lack of balance, where slavery, serfdom, barter, a skilled working class and high finance exist side by side.

Most importantly, however, Fanon had noted as part of what he referred to as "the pitfalls of national consciousness", a tendency for the revolutionary party which has waged a successful anti-colonial struggle, to degenerate into a system of oppression of the masses of the newly independent population. The similarity of the concerns of Fanon in *Wretched of the Earth* ([1967] 1983) and James (1984c) in *Party Politics in the West Indies* suggests another motivation behind James's proposal of the mass party. The party was suggested as a tool to further complete the decolonization process which was being stifled by the middle class leadership whose political ideas and practice sought to minimalize the role of the masses in the decolonization process. It is instructive that Fanon's critique of the anti-colonial nationalist party echoes in striking detail the issues which James was able to identify specifically in Williams's PNM:

> the leader is all the more necessary in that there is no party. During the period of the struggle for independence there was one right enough, a party led by the present leader. But since then, this party has sadly disintegrated; nothing is left but the shell of a party, the name, the emblem and the motto. The living party, which ought to make possible the free exchange of ideas which have been elaborated according to the real needs of the mass of the people, has been transformed into a trade union of individual interests. Since the proclamation of independence the party no longer helps the people to set out its demands, to become more aware of its needs and better able to establish its power. Today, the party's mission is to deliver to the people the instructions which issue from the summit. There no longer exists the fruitful give and take from the bottom to the top and from the top to the bottom which creates and guarantees democracy in the party. Quite on

the contrary, the party has made itself a screen between the masses and the leaders (Fanon [1967], 1983, 136–37).

C.L.R. James's mass party was designed to facilitate socialist democracy. It was a model which served to ensure a continuous flow of decisions from the bottom upwards and not from the top downwards. Moreover, it was designed to widen the decision-making structure to include every member of the rank-and-file of the party and to break the decision-making monopoly of the leadership – or more accurately, the leader – of the party. James's mass party was therefore, designed to facilitate the practical emergence of participatory democracy in its concrete expression. It was designed to transcend the structure of 'representative' politics where the party leadership makes all the key decisions and the role of the people is merely to support the programme that has been determined from above. Echoing Rosa Luxemburg on the need to trust the spontaneous creative impulses of the people, James (1984c, 116) notes that, "politics is an activity" and it is "not merely to support something or somebody". In his view, "it is to discuss and plan and to carry out some programme or perspective of your own and then to judge how far you have succeeded or failed, and why. It does not limit a government. The more of this a people do, the more it can defy its enemies. Otherwise as sure as day you find you have to shoot them down".

The mass party, as devised by James, if implemented correctly in practice, could normatively serve to overcome the division of labour between the party as "consciousness" and the party as "being". Similarly, it can resolve the contradiction between the party as government and the party as mass mobilization which James had identified as existing within the party (James 1977b). This tendency, which James (1984c), Fanon ([1967] 1983) and Gittens (1983) have identified in the party as a mechanism to stifle mass initiative and to take decision making power from the people, is a result of the dominance of the "government" aspect of the contradiction within the party, at the expense of its "mass mobilization" aspects. Thus, in his criticism of the anti-democratic tendencies within the PNM, James (1984c, 153) had lamented that while "Williams formed a party... his main concern is not the party but the government". He complained that under Williams's leadership, as was typical of most Caribbean political parties, the expectation was that "the masses are to be whipped up to give the leaders the authority and power. After that the government will do everything. Modern democracy has gone a long way from that" (James 1984c, 153).

This observation reopens several questions about the merits and demerits of centralization of power versus decentralization, which had been seen in early twentieth century debates between VI Lenin and Rosa Luxembourg. One of the major arguments in favor of greater centralization is that it furnishes government with the required strength to implement policy unhindered by mass pressure. What should be noted however, is that in modern capitalist society, under representative democracy, governmental power is required not merely for the implementation of society's projects, but for the suppression of society's under-classes. Moreover, as part of the maturation of the Caribbean democracies, and given the greater levels of education and the wider possibilities allowed by new technology, the objective conditions now exist for greater levels of mobilization and scrutiny from below, to check authoritarian governments, while it should be added, the advances in technology have also created the conditions for greater levels of governmental control and repression of their populations.

It is important to note that the contradictions associated with the tensions between centralism from above and mass democratic participation from below are compounded in post-colonial states existing under a neocolonial relationship with the metropolitan powers. Under such conditions, the dominant economic class interests which governments are expected to serve, are external interests. Both James (1984c, 129) and Fanon ([1967] 1983, 119–20) had lamented the fact that the middle-class leadership which inherited political power from the metropolis, was not a true 'ruling' class since they lacked economic power.

The subservience of the local governing groups to a metropolitan ruling class largely explains why their political organizations tend to be concerned more about stifling the participation of the masses rather than encouraging and fostering such participation. It is on this basis that the Jamesian mass party, with its emphasis on bottom-up decision-making, can be said to be a mechanism for socialist democracy and is incompatible with capitalist or neo-colonial existence. Given the proclivity of the post-colonial leadership to accommodate itself to external power, James's mass party was meant to serve as a bottom-up check on the decisions of the center, as a buffer against neo-colonialism.

One of the 'controversies' surrounding James's recommendation was its explicit advocacy of a one-party state for the Caribbean. Given the cultural socialization of the Caribbean people and the historical political and constitutional development of the society towards liberal democratic political practice, the insinuation of the possibilities of a one-party-state inherent in James's recommendation appeared to conflict with these external manifestations (rather than the substance) of liberal culture. However, James's insinuations of the possibilities of the one-party state were rooted in notions of the natural and 'organic' transcendence of the limits of competitive democracies rather than in any 'mechanical' abolition of competitive party politics. So certain was James that his model of the party would represent a new, organic and dialectical leap in the attainment of democracy that he was adamant that with such a party, the need for the illusion of political competition at a multi-party level would disappear. According to James in *Perspectives and Proposals* (1966b, 28–29),

> [in] an underdeveloped country, if a political party organises itself properly and has a real program devoted to the mass of the people and the improvement of their situation, it will become a one-party state. But the opposition can take place, but there is no real room in most underdeveloped countries for any opposition to a party which is a genuinely mass party... And that is the situation, that is the cut-throat business that is taking place in underdeveloped countries between two parties because no party puts forward a

genuine mass democratic program. So they have the opposition and all this business. There is no need for the opposition party and the government party.

It is clear therefore that James's proposal was not motivated by any authoritarian or 'anti-democratic' outlook. Instead, it was driven by his awareness of the limitations of two-party electoral competition, which, contrary to the defenders of formal, institutional practice, did not indicate any substantive measurement of qualitative democracy.

Perhaps James can be accused of being too far ahead of standard Caribbean practice in his conceptualization of the mass party and his related perception of democracy. James's dialectical consciousness meant that, in studying a phenomenon, his focus had always been on its internal movement and transformation, where it is going rather than what it is. His methodological approach was always geared towards discerning, from what existed in bare outline, what would be the dominant tendencies in future politics. His perception of democracy and the role and nature of the party was consistent with this outlook. His awareness of the bankruptcy of representative democracy forced him to identify the outlines of its alternative within the very system he was seeking to overcome. His proposal of the mass party was intended to transcend liberal democratic practice, and as a result, it went against the narrow, empirical practice of democracy, particularly in its Caribbean expression. According to Paget Henry (1992, 238),

> because of its critical nature, Jamesian theory tended to stay too far ahead of Caribbean actualities. Although the theory was carefully historicized when applied to the Trinidadian case, it is clear that James did not get close enough. Given local perceptions of the unfolding pre-independence events and the absence of experience with self-government, James's concerns must have seemed rather distant.

The following closing sections examine the extent to which the objective conditions for the establishment of a Jamesian democracy have matured, and the extent to which these have been reflected in twenty-first century political practices within the political parties, even if only in embryonic form.

Is the Jamesian Democracy Feasible?

There are several objective factors and transformations which make a form of participatory democracy attainable in the Caribbean, and which strengthen the validity of James's assertions. These transformations include advances in communications, information, and transportation technology, increases in the level of education, wider availability of information, greater levels of interpersonal and intercultural interaction, increases in individual and group consciousness and awareness of minority rights and individual liberties. These developments do not only point to the possibility and feasibility of participatory democracy, but their objective existence also suggests that representative democracy can no longer operate, untransformed under the weight of these factors (Bruce 2019). From a Marxian perspective, it can be argued that the continued persistence and retention of the organizational forms and institutionalized expression of representative democracy has now become a "fetter" on the free development of organizations and principles of participatory democracy.

Alvin Toffler (1981, 446) in *The Third Wave* has claimed that the extent of democracy practiced in any given society depends more than anything else, on the "decision load" being carried by decision makers. In Toffler's view, "a heavy decision load will ultimately have to be shared through wider democratic participation". In his perspective, democracy is not so much a question of ideology, but of practical necessity depending on the size of the 'decision load'. In his view, "so long as the decision load of the social system expands... democracy becomes not a matter of choice but of evolutionary necessity". Toffler, in the early 1980s was witnessing a process (now variously called globalization, the internet revolution and other descriptors) in which the world was experiencing a period of fundamental transformation in its infrastructure and superstructure. These transformations were increasingly expanding the 'decision load' which governments had to bear, and as a result, he was pointing to new emerging social pressures being placed on governments in the late twentieth century aimed at widening the decision-making structure.

Significantly, Toffler (1981, 438), like James, is aware of the long tradition of forms of direct democracy frustrated in their emergence at specific historical periods. He suggests that while the demand for direct participatory democracy is not new, what is different in the twenty-first century, is the objective technological, material and social means for its realization. Referring to the "inventors" of representative democracy as "second wave" revolutionaries, Toffler (1981, 438), argues that they were "well aware of the possibilities of direct as against representative democracy". He argues that,

> there were traces of direct, do-it-yourself democracy in the French revolutionary constitution of 1793. American revolutionists knew all about New England town halls and small-scale organic consensus formation. In Europe later on, Marx and his followers frequently invoked the Paris commune as a model of citizen participation in the making and execution of the laws. But the shortcomings and limitations of direct democracy were also well known – and, at that time more persuasive (Toffler 1981, 439).

While Toffler's concept of the "decision load" offers a useful materialist explanation for the practical necessity for more inclusive forms of democratic decision-making, Toffler's weakness, however, lies in the fact that he ignores the role played by class interests in determining the democratic structures adopted by the second wave revolutionaries. In other words, despite its materialism, Toffler's argument ignores the "economic power" dimensions which frustrate the emergence of alternative institutional forms. His perspective is too heavily centred around a struggle of technologies rather than a struggle of classes. The role which class interests played in determining the victory of representation over participation in the case of the United States, has been thoroughly addressed by Charles Beard ([1913] 1965) in *An Economic Interpretation of the Constitution of the United States*. Similarly, in the present, new forms of political practice are unlikely to emerge through technological change alone, devoid of a struggle of competing economic interests.

It is important to observe, however, that the conversations on democracy which are framed around questions of the sharing of a decision load, have also opened the door to conservative, bourgeois and neo-liberal notions of the 'rolling back' of the state. Thus, roughly since the 1980s, in the post-communism moment associated with the rise of neo-liberal globalization, governments have sought to 'transfer' many of the functions which had once been considered the exclusive preserve of the state, to private firms and non-governmental organizations (Osborne and Gaebler 1993). Under the new ethos of privatization, renewed emphasis has been placed on 'small government' as the solution to the crisis of democracy (Toffler 1991, 252). This shift to privatization has had the opposite effect of popular democratization and has resulted, since the 1980s, in a disempowerment of the Caribbean working people and the further enrichment and aggrandizement of the holders of capital. Further, the shift to privatization has not meant that future possibilities of the working class to gain control of industries and other avenues of wealth creation and economic empowerment, remain closed. The implications of privatization for the Caribbean and the manner in which such a thrust can be viewed within the Jamesian framework will be examined more fully in the final chapter.

Despite the short-term potential challenges to the Caribbean working class in the current moment of state deregulation and withdrawal, James's dialectical approach allows for an understanding of the potential avenues for democratic empowerment of the Caribbean working people, that emanate as a positive side-effect of these policies. It was James's optimism in the long-term political empowerment of the non-owners of capital in the Caribbean that drove his demand for the widening of the decision-making base of Caribbean politics and which guided his call for the involvement of the masses in such a process. James had grasped fully the fact that twelve, seventeen, twenty-four, thirty or forty-two elected representatives scattered across the various parliaments in the Caribbean did not capture the full spectrum of available wisdom and knowledge and could not solve the problems confronting the West Indies. Moreover, a solution could not be implemented without the active involvement of the people through education, sharing of ideas, and commonality of purpose. In speaking of the economic crisis of the neo-colonial West Indies in the 1960s, James (1984c, 129) had lamented the glaring inability of the ruling Caribbean middle class to confront the challenges without the involvement of the mass of the population:

> this middle class with political power minus economic power are still politically paralysed before their former masters, who are still masters. The only way of changing the structure of the economy and setting it on new paths is by mobilising the mass against all who stand in the way.

James (1984c, 130) however was fully aware that the governing middle class – the local agents of metropolitan power – would be opposed to demands for more inclusive and participatory forms of democracy. He argued that in the eyes of the middle class "any topic which may enlarge the conception of democracy is particularly dangerous because it may affect the attitude of the mass of the population". In response to demands for democracy, James suggested that the "middle classes point to parliamentary democracy, trade unions, party politics and all the elements of democracy. But these are not things in themselves. They must serve a social purpose and here the middle class are near the end of their tether".

There is little doubt that the political, social and economic crisis which James had identified in the 1960s, deepened considerably in the first three decades of the twenty-first century. Since the 1980s the Caribbean middle class has had to contend with: the collapse of colonial-era trade preferential arrangements which undermined the main economic pillars on which their post-colonial economies were built; the loss of benefits previously enjoyed in the bi-polar Cold War world; the challenges of endless adjustment of several aspects of their economies to the shifting demands of neo-liberal policy re-orientation; the ravages of climate change and natural disasters and other economic challenges consequent upon their existence as small island developing states (Gonzalves 2019); a crisis of the global financial system in 2008; the ravages of the devastating global COVID-19 pandemic of 2020-21; and the general and continuing weakening of the post-colonial independence project through neo-liberal globalization (Joseph 2011). Thus, the concerns raised by James in the 1960s for a further democratization of the Caribbean, have become even more urgent in the twenty-first century.

A participatory democracy for the Caribbean has not only become necessary because the expanded 'decision load' has made liberal representative democracy unworkable, but it has also been made more realizable through transformations in technology (Bruce 2019). Toffler (1981), James (1986a), Barber (1984), Osborne and Gaebler (1993) and others, have all insisted that one of the political consequences of transformations in communications technology is an inevitable expansion of the concept of democracy. They note that modern technology has made it possible to bring information to the public as quickly as their representatives receive it. Advances in communications technology also make it possible for ordinary citizens to have an input into governmental decisions. Benjamin Barber (1984, 274), for example, has noted that while "the capabilities of the new technology can be used either in civic and constructive or manipulative or destructive ways", it is clear that these technologies "can be used to strengthen civic education, guarantee equal access to information, and tie individuals and institutions into networks that will make real participatory discussion and debate possible across great distances". He suggests that "for the first time we have an opportunity to create artificial town meetings among populations that could not otherwise communicate" (274).

Several decades after Barber's observations, it is now taken-for-granted that internet communications platforms such as Zoom, Skype, Facebook and WhatsApp, and even the most basic forms of radio talk shows have now created mechanisms for mass meetings and decision-making procedures which can now result in the transcendence of the closed and exclusive parliaments which have historically been the preserve of the specially chosen.

Despite the advances in technology which are used in everyday communication in the Caribbean, the possibilities for widening democracy have not fully been tapped. While there has been some movement such as the live airing of parliamentary debates on dedicated channels, and the proliferation of talk shows, call-in programmes, town hall meetings and "live chats" involving government officials, the tendency has generally been to stifle the possibilities presented by the existing technology. There has not yet been clear evidence of organic shifts in the formal political institutions, practices, legislation or even policy to suggest that new mechanisms for democratic inclusion and practice have emerged on the backs of the existing technological platforms. Though the technologies exist in concrete form, the revolutionary transformations commensurate with their possibilities, have not yet emerged. A case can most certainly be made, for example, for the popular call-in programmes to be used more fundamentally as mechanisms for genuine public participation in decision making rather than as entertainment talk shops, or as fodder for popularity ratings. Further, existing internet technology allows for new voting mechanisms that can facilitate direct people participation, plebiscites and direct decision making, which have not been considered in the Caribbean. Similarly, other forms of workplace democracy offered by the internet and other institutional mechanisms are yet to be explored or discussed, in debates about democratic and constitutional reform in the Caribbean.

The increases in the levels of education of Caribbean peoples, increases in their awareness of their rights, transformations in their relationships and attitudes to governments, increased access to information about global and regional events, have all deepened the capacity of Caribbean people for participatory democracy and are rendering representative democracy untenable. The rationale used to justify representative democracy, namely that people are not properly informed and that their representatives are better placed to make informed and educated decisions, has become untenable given the narrowing of the gap between the educated and uneducated and given the equality of access to information. Many of the responsibilities borne by central governments can now be easily performed by local government units in every Caribbean island (Singh 1972). Moreover, many of the decisions that are left to the consideration of governments, because of their highly personal and private nature, are ideally suited for participatory decision-making. For example, it is difficult to perceive how a dozen or more individuals (mostly male) sitting in parliament can legislate effectively over an issue such as abortion which is increasingly perceived by Caribbean women, as an issue which touches upon the sovereignty of their bodies, and therefore is an issue upon which no one but themselves possesses the competence or legitimacy to decide upon.

If one considers the Marxian adage that "mankind... inevitably sets itself such tasks as it is able to solve" (Marx 1970, 21), then the most compelling factor which suggests the readiness of the Caribbean for a Jamesian-type democracy is the concrete activity which can already be discerned, which indicates that decision-making has already been moving away from the hands of governments and towards civil society. In referring to such concrete activity a clear distinction is being made between the traditional partisan anti-government mobilizations on one hand, and the mass mobilizations, independent of political parties, to reform the political and economic system, on the other. Indeed, there is a long tradition of the latter form of struggle in the Caribbean, and it is there that the Jamesian notion of "free creative activity" finds its resonance.

The "Black Power" movement in Trinidad and Tobago in 1970 can serve as the first example of the pressures being put upon a West Indian government by the people with a view to shaping government in the image of the masses. James himself in his article, *The Caribbean confrontation Begins*, interpreted the Black Power Movement as the concrete validation of his critique of the authoritarianism of Williams' PNM (in Oxaal 1982, 272–73). The movement for the establishment of Peoples' Assemblies in Grenada in the 1970s during the anti-Gairy struggle was also an attempt to supersede the structures of representative democracy in the country (Hodge and Searle 1981).

The clearest historical moment in the Caribbean which can be generally described as being 'Jamesian' and through which the feasibility of a Jamesian 'soviet' in the Caribbean can be assessed, was the 1970 'Black Power' February revolution in Trinidad witnessed an army mutiny and in which consciously Jamesian political associates were involved, the more ideologically 'Jamesian' later grouping themselves under the banner of the New Beginning Movement. The account of the Jamesian practitioners in the concrete context of the 1970s 'revolution' is important therefore in connecting James to concrete Caribbean politics and in closing the distance between theory and practice.

A useful account of the 1970s, revolutionary period can be found in Walton Look Lai's pamphlet called *The Present Stage of the Trinidad Revolution,* published under the auspices of the New Beginning Movement (1974). Lai's account is thoroughly Jamesian. He argues that the "difference between the 1937/38 riots and the [1970 February revolution] is that the former paved the way for the first stage of the anti-colonial struggle, whereas the unrest now sweeping the Caribbean regions signals the second stage of that struggle" (1974, 4). In his view, there were two features of the second phase which advanced the struggle to a new phase. The first was that "with the achievement of political independence an accomplished fact... the mass movement is now pressing for its logical conclusion – economic independence" (1974, 4–5). More importantly, he argued that in the new struggle, "the workers, peasants and unemployed have seen fit to organize themselves and move not just against the colonizer and the imperialists who are still there, but also against the indigenous bourgeoisie and petty-bourgeoisie who have gone over to the side and are now standing in the way of the people" (Lai 1974, 5).

In reflecting on the nature of the class forces and ideological tendencies within the mass movement and the distinctions which separated them from the New Beginning movement, Lai (1974, 7) identifies "Lloyd Best's TAPIA organization and James Millette's MOKO organization which eventually became the United National Independence Party", as being in the forefront of the movement. He however argues that their "conception of what was to take the place of foreign domination of the society was to work towards the creation of an indigenous capitalist class... who had been shut out of the system for the last four centuries. That was their idea of a new society; a society dominated by a native capitalist class, as opposed to a foreign capitalist corporation" (Lai 1974, 6). In Lai's view, the February uprising had shifted the revolutionary potential of the society and had rendered the perspectives of Millette and Best's perspective 'backward', since "for the first time, the masses of the people – the unemployed, the workers, the farmer – came into the streets and began to carry that opposition began by the middle class, and began to articulate from their own class viewpoint what they saw wrong with the political and economic system, and what they felt the new society could be like. And by doing that they carried the consciousness of the entire society onto a higher level, a revolutionary level" (Lai 1974, 7).

It was on the basis of the creative energies of the mass movement therefore, and the features of the new society which were being demanded during the revolution itself as seen in their creation of "people's parliaments", that assured Lai of the transformative and revolutionary capacity of the mass movement in line with the perspective which had been a central feature of C.L.R. James's thinking:

> During the eight weeks of the upheaval, all kinds of popular
> political institutions began springing up in the country, named

the 'peoples' parliament'. It started in Woodford Square, next to the official Parliament, and they said that "this was *our* parliament over *here*, and *their* Parliament over *there*". From Woodford Square, the "People's Parliament" spread throughout the country. There, the people discussed and decided upon everything under the sun (Lai 1974, 9).

In Lai's view, while "there were many defects in the operation of this form of direct democracy" what was significant was "what the people were actually creating in the middle of an upheaval" since "these spontaneous creations of the people always point an objective way out...". He therefore saw in the people's parliaments, despite their defects "a popular alternative to the present bankrupt political system, with its fake democracy which shuts out the people and prevents them from taking charge of their own lives" (1974, 9). Significantly Lai (1974, 8) observed that the main criticism of the mass movement of the political system was that "British-style parliamentary democracy... was not designed for ordinary people to participate in any meaningful kind of way". Insofar as the response of the mass movement to the economic situation was concerned, Lai (1974, 9) felt that they carried "anti-imperialist discussion a stage further" since "they were not only anti-imperialists, but also anti-capitalists".

Many of these developments, suggested that a qualitatively new stage had been reached by the events of the February revolution. In keeping with the Jamesian outlook which identifies the ideas from below as critical to the future post-capitalist society, Lai made much of the fact that "during the middle of the 1970 uprising, one of the unemployed youth addressing the Peoples Parliament hit upon the key to the entire thing: he suggested that with all the people's parliaments now springing up all over the country, that it may not be necessary to have a government in the old sense anymore; that what they could do is link up all the people' parliament and they could become the new government" (21). On the basis of all of these developments, Lai concludes that "the movement in 1970 raised politics in Trinidad and Tobago onto revolutionary dimension and posed not just a reform of the existing economic and political but its total abolition" (1974, 9).

In much of this, critical elements of the Jamesian analysis such as the emphasis on government from below, the emergence of new organizational forms, the imminent arrival of alternatives to the Westminster system and top-down party politics, and the realization of worker self-management all came to the fore. While the February revolution would come to an end and Eric Williams was able to consolidate his power throughout the decade of the 1970s, the demand for peoples' assemblies would find renewed expression in the politics of the New Jewel movement in Grenada and found its most concrete expression in the NJM manifesto of 1973, which declared that,

> since politics deals with the making of decisions, and since politics is largely the process which decides who gets what how and when, New Jewel does not consider it to be the function of an 'exclusive club'. NJM stands solidly behind Peoples' Assemblies as the new form of government that will involve all the people all the time. Through this form, people will be assured of both their political and economic rights. To us, People's Assemblies will bring in true democracy (NJM 1973, 9).

It was clear therefore that the revolutionary 1970 to early 1980 period in the Caribbean witnessed many developments which suggested the actualization of the Jamesian perspective, despite the fact that these various revolutions would have faced their respective defeats between 1970 and 1983. Following the collapse of the socialist experience in the English-speaking Caribbean in the late 1980s and early 1990s, the demands for new forms of democratic participation and economic inclusion and ownership have not been silenced.

Since the 1980s, there has emerged a concerted set of demands for democratic reform and for the re-organization of government to facilitate more inclusive forms of democratic engagement. In Barbados, for example, the public interventions of Val McComie, a former ambassador to the Organisation of American States (OAS), in calling for new models of governance, was typical of the kinds of pressures being placed on Caribbean governments for democratic reform. Using the local media to call for the setting up of a citizens forum to examine citizens' rights in relation to government, and to advocate the setting up of a participatory-democratic, political environment, McComie, (1993, 10A) argued that "examination of the relationship which has existed between government and people of Barbados since independence, suggests that successive governments have not regarded themselves as servants of the people". Arguing that, "governments have ignored the right of the people to be actively involved in the decision-making process" by denying "us the information which we need to make informed judgements on matters of policy, and most importantly" by failing to "discharge their fundamental obligation to be accountable to us for their actions". McComie insisted that the time had come "to break this dependency syndrome and to recover from government our right to active participation in the democratic process". To achieve this, he called for need to "restructure our social institutions, such as the government, the legislature, the legal system, the financial institutions, the civil service, the information media, and the system of education, to make them more responsive to the will of an independent people in search of a just society".

The early embryonic concerns raised by McComie for greater levels of accountability and transparency in the early 1990s, have been reflected in the 2000s and beyond, in the formation of "Integrity and Transparency" organizations focused on issues of good governance, 'integrity in public life', anti-corruption and access to information. Thus, in Jamaica for example, the former head of the communist-oriented Workers Party of Jamaica (WPJ), Trevor Munroe, is now better known as the main source of energy behind the NGO, National Integrity Action, devoted to advancing legislation and institutional changes to foster good governance practices in Jamaica (see National Integrity Action 2021). Barbados too has witnessed the emergence of groupings such as Integrity Barbados and a rise in activism by academics and other professionals around questions of corruption and governmental accountability and integrity in public life (see Barrow-Giles 2017). While these interventions have largely taken the form of 'technical' recommendations for legislative and policy changes to make governments more transparent and accountable, and while they have been led largely by sections of the professional middle class like lawyers, accountants, management specialists and academics, and while they do not approximate the mass transformations in the political party systems anticipated by James, they nevertheless point to important shifts in Caribbean political practice from the authoritarianism of James's day to more realizable efforts at the inclusion of civil society in Caribbean governance (see Hinds 2019, 62–66).

These kinds of demands which were emerging in the early 1990s have been reflected in more concrete actions by some of the governments, which came to office in the late 1990s into the early 2000s, in undertaking measures which were reflective of the need for greater levels of inclusion and accountability. One clear example of these tendencies can be found in the 1997 manifesto of the St. Lucia Labour Party which was redefined as a "contract of faith" and which made overt references to the issues of recalling parliamentarians, allowing for greater access to information and the strengthening of integrity legislation (Saint Lucia Labour Party 1997, 3–4). Most importantly, the manifesto promised to "recognize representative social, economic, and cultural organizations as legitimate voices expressing citizens' concerns on vital societal issues" and it proposed that these civic bodies would "receive a new emphasis as vehicles of direct participation in the governance of the country". These new mechanisms included the strengthening of the National Social and Economic Consultative Council which was organized as a civil society advisory body to the government. In addition, the SLP was able to formalize, as part of its own internal reform mechanisms, processes for selection and deselection of candidates via a 'run-off' or primary system which contributed, albeit minimally, to the empowerment of the mass base of the party.

Similar and related levels of democratic inclusion were also witnessed in Barbados under the Owen Arthur-led Barbados Labour Party (BLP) administration, with the strengthening of a social partnership between government, the private sector and labour in the wake of an IMF structural adjustment programme in the post-1994 period when the harsh economic crisis confronting Barbadian society required new forms of consensus building (see Carmichael and Robinson 2020). Conversations around these kinds of concerns and institutional practices are reflected in varying degrees, in all Caribbean countries, albeit with divergent levels of concrete actualization. As a case in point for example, the work of Jamaican activist Lloyd D'Aguilar, convenor of the Justice Now and People's Anti-Corruption Movement in championing grassroots calls for human rights and for exposing acts of public corruption suggest that organic movements are being spawned to expand democratic and social freedoms in the region.

To what extent then are James's notions of democracy and the mass party reflected in the current state of Caribbean political parties and the democratic process in the early twenty-first century? It is clear that the rare revolutionary moments such as February 1970 in Trinidad and the Grenada revolution from 1973[5] to 1983 where Jamesian-type people's parliaments emerged as possible democratic alternatives to liberal representative democracy have not been sustained. It is also true that James's mass party with its deep democracy in which the rank-and-file constitute the nerve centre and vanguard, determining the direction of the leadership in a workers' council or soviet, has not been approximated in practice as a concrete and lasting model of Caribbean democratic practice. Nor too, has the mass party and its democratic efficiencies developed to such an extent that James's vision of the transcendence of two-party competition been reflected in reality. It is instructive however that recent Caribbean elections such as in Grenada in 2013 and 2108 and in Barbados in 2018 and 2022, the political responses of the NNP and the BLP to the existing challenges had been so holistic (relative to the limits of electoral contestation) that these parties were able to garner the totality of the seats in their respective parliaments.

What can be gleaned from the democratic evolution of Caribbean society since the intervention of James, is that there has clearly been movement in the direction of greater levels of ground-up inclusion in decision-making, increased checks and balances on government, wider use of technology, and increases in levels of education and consciousness. These changes create the context for the kinds of democratic transformations anticipated by James. In short, the expected shifts to greater democracy which James had called for in the 1960s which appeared then to be 'ahead of his time' are now being actualized daily in the politics of the Caribbean. These demands are now being seen in formal moves at constitutional reform in the Caribbean to bring the inherited constitutions more fully in line with the expectations of Caribbean people for greater levels of inclusion and for greater reflections of themselves in the constitution (see Meeks and Quinn 2018). The most recent stage of this development to date was the decision by the Barbados government to move to republican status in 2021, and to embark on its own formal process of constitutional reform, a move which appeared to have opened up the debate on republicanism in Jamaica and the other remaining Eastern Caribbean countries which continued to retain the British Monarch as their head of state after independence.

On the other hand, these demands have not yet been met with organic, revolutionary transformations in the main institutions of the inherited liberal democratic forms. The political parties, the legislature, and the executive branch of government have not been materially transformed into qualitatively new institutions, despite the advances in technology and despite the continuing pressures from below. The new forms of civic organizations and the rise of more variegated 'social movements' now organizing around questions of gender, sexuality, race, religion and cultural movements, have not qualitatively overturned the internal dynamics of the party systems in the Caribbean.

Their emergence however, is perhaps one of the most important features of the political environment which distinguishes 1950 to 1980 from 1990 to 2020. James's notion of free creative activity is indeed being reflected in the manner in which these movements have by-passed the political party as the vanguard in present-day struggles, but the corresponding organic and qualitative transformation of the institutions of government into new 'soviet' or 'council' or 'mass party' type formations, has not occurred. Given the nature of current demands for continued democratization and economic empowerment of the mass of the Caribbean population, James's democratic expectations remain very relevant to twenty-first century Caribbean politics, but their concrete actualization will depend on the emergence and maturation of future Caribbean revolutions.

Perhaps, the clearest way in which to close this assessment of the possibilities of a Jamesian politics for the twenty-first century Caribbean, is to reflect on what James himself saw as the nature of the Caribbean person and what he felt were the conditions shaping the Caribbean's relation to the rest of the world and the Caribbean's potential for crafting new democratic and post-capitalist economic possibilities. Much has been made of James's reflections in *The Making of the Caribbean Peoples*, which explain how James saw the Caribbean as a fully modern and globalized people. Much later in his life however, in the 1980s, James would repeat this theme of optimism in the revolutionary capacity of Caribbean people in an extended interview in the Trinidad *Express Sunday* newspaper of December 12, 1982, with Anthony Milne. After listening to James speak on global and African politics Milne asked James, "how does all this relate to Trinidad and Tobago and the Caribbean?" James responded as follows:

> The Caribbean is a very special place. The most important social factor in the Caribbean is that there is no peasantry. There are no peasants in Jamaica or Trinidad. Have you ever been to Africa? When you go to Africa and begin to walk through Nigeria, you

see peasants. You see them in Venezuela. There are none in the Caribbean. Everybody knows everything... Peasants are people surrounded by forest, and so on. They are people isolated from the centres of civilization by the very objectives in which they live. Nobody in the Caribbean is isolated from anything. Nobody. Everybody speaks modern languages. They all read modern newspapers, listen to modern music, travel up and down by air, go to America and England. Social backwardness does not exist in the Caribbean. Not only do they have special capabilities, but the circumstances in which they live prevent it. And that is the situation that [government] has to deal with. A highly concentrated, highly modernised population (Milne 1982, 7).

5.

James, the "Race Question" and 21st Century Caribbean Politics

Ancient Egypt was a Negro civilization. The history of Black Africa will remain suspended in air and cannot be written correctly until African historians dare to connect it with the history of Egypt... The African historian who evades the problem of Egypt is neither modest nor objective, nor unruffled; he is ignorant, cowardly and neurotic. Imagine, if you can, the uncomfortable position of a Western Historian who was to write the history of Europe without referring to Graeco-Latin antiquity and try to pass that off as a scientific approach.

Cheikh Anta Diop – The African Origin of Civilization

I believe that when we look across millennia at what Europe has done to civilization, but particularly what it did in the last five centuries a process of struggle between civilizations can be identified. A struggle starting essentially 2,500 years ago representing a definite decline of black global power. A period of 2,500 years of envy and revenge by the European world and initially by the Eurasian hordes against the glory of Egypt. A period and process essentially of European anti-thesis. It ought to be part of the destiny of the "Negro left" to resolve this contradiction.

George A.V. Belle – The Collapse of the Soviet System: Implications for the Caribbean Left

C.L.R. James and the "Black Marxist" Enigma

There is indeed little doubt that, in addition to his direct intellectual contributions to understanding the political questions surrounding the intersection of socialism and democracy, another of the more significant contributions of C.L.R. James to Caribbean and global political theory has been his treatment of the contradictions emergent from racism and racial inequality as a central feature of the modern capitalist world-economy. This role was forced upon James by the inherently contradictory factors of his skin color, his social and political experiences as a Caribbean national and his adherence to Marxism – a perspective which, in some of its later incarnations, if not in its original manifestation, has been accused of being conspicuously silent on the realities of non-white, non-western European society (Cummins 1980; Hobsbawm 1964; Singham 1970). Similarly, Marxism, in its latter interpretation and praxis has been accused of being primarily focused on economic factors, and at worst, totally ignoring the contradictions resultant from racial inequality.

James's adjustment of the race question into his Marxian framework was a perfectly logical development since according to Charles Mills, "it is in this area, the ideational resistance to racism, that Caribbean people can be said to have made their most original contribution to global thought" (Mills 1991, 25). The disproportionate number and profiles of Caribbean activists and theorists involved in the various pan-Africanist and race consciousness movements attest to this fact. A list of the names of Caribbeanists involved in such activities reads like a Who's Who of the politics of race. Henry Sylvester Williams, T. Ras Makonen, Marcus Garvey, Amy Ashwood Garvey, George Padmore, C.L.R. James, Stokely Carmichael and Walter Rodney can all be cited in support of such a claim. What marks out the thought of James from other similarly concerned theorists, except perhaps Walter Rodney and Amilcar Cabral, is the fact that he was able to fit his perspective on race within the Marxist paradigm while other Marxists and race theorists, such as Marcus Garvey for example, generally saw the two as being mutually exclusive and incompatible.

Before a full and thorough analysis of C.L.R. James's treatment of the race question is undertaken, it is first necessary to address some enduring misconceptions which have pervaded Western political thought, especially its Marxist variant, and which by extension, have impacted adversely the attitude of black political thinkers and generations of black scholars towards Marxism in general. These distortions inherent in the race question and Marxism can be said to exist on two levels. First, they can be seen in the perspectives which deny the role of a 'black' contribution to European thought, and in ideas which can be construed as expressions of European chauvinism towards the non-European world. Secondly, they can be seen in misconceptions surrounding Marxism and Marx himself on the race question. These distortions have resulted in a hostility by black, non-Marxists towards thinkers such as James, who have attempted to adhere to both a Marxist and a race perspective, and it has contributed to wider, anti-Marxist positions. The treatment of the race question in general, and the examination of how James addressed the race question in Marxism, is necessary for any general rethinking of Marxism, and for appreciating the application of James to the twenty-first century Caribbean.

This chapter therefore has three main aims. First, attention will be paid to addressing the intellectual controversies arising out of the race/class dilemma within Marxism which have impacted on the efficacy of radical, anti-colonial and pan-Africanist politics. As part of resolving these contradictions, two issues which were not central to the Jamesian task, but which are relevant to his mission in the twenty-first century will be addressed: the question of the impact of ancient African philosophical systems on European and by extension Marxist thought; and the overcoming of doubts about the incompatibility between Marxist class consciousness and racial consciousness as critical elements of radical politics.

Further, this latter task will also necessitate a re-examination of widely held claims of the silence of Marx and Marxism on the race question. Secondly, following this, the strengths and weaknesses of James's own approach to the race/class dilemma and his marriage of Marxism and Pan-Africanism will be examined. Thirdly and finally, the chapter will close by examining new and emerging critical questions of the politics of race and Pan-Africanism relevant to Caribbean politics in the twenty-first century, and will offer an assessment of the perspectives of James which remain relevant to these twenty-first century questions.

Overcoming Unresolved Contradictions within Marxism and Pan-Africanism

Ancient Africa and Its Contribution to European Philosophy

One of the main barriers to the resolution of contradictions between Marxism and Pan-Africanism is the enduring understanding of Marxism as specifically a 'white man's ideology'. The task of resolving the contradiction between Marxism and Pan-Africanism therefore involves a process of 'standing Marx on his head' in terms of re-examining the relationship between the foundational philosophical principles of Marxism – the dialectic and economic materialism – and the ancient African past. Thus, in much the same way that Marx had 'stood Hegel on his head' by unlocking the potential of the dialectic and applying it to the material world, similarly, the task confronting black Marxists is to unlock the potential of the consciousness of racial conflict and Pan-Africanism and to connect it with Marx's critique of capitalism as a way of advancing anti-systemic politics in the wake of the collapse of European communist state models. It must begin by demonstrating historically and scientifically the anteriority of black political theory to European thought, and in particular the discovery of dialectical and materialistic conceptions of the world prior to Marx or even the European predecessors of Marx such as Hegel, Plato, Aristotle and Heraclitus. Such a task necessitates, among other things, an examination of the contribution of Egypt, a civilization which had a profound influence on ancient Greece, to European political thought (Diop 1974, 1991; George James [1954] 1988).

In making explicit the implications of this task of uncovering the historical relationship between European philosophical contributions and its borrowings from the ancient African world, and its connection to C.L.R. James's own Marxist contributions, Belle (1994, 109) has insisted that,

> mankind will solve many of the social problems of the 21st century if the "black left" can in a fashion repeat Marx one step on. Where, while Marx said he had turned Hegel right side up by replacing "world spirit" with forces of production. So too the "black left" must turn Plato the philosopher of Europe on his head and "political greatness and wisdom" would thenceforth be among the people. James's "free creative activity as necessity" would have come to pass. Egypt's cosmological negation, an Aristotelian responsibility and determination would have been negated.

The Senegalese scholar Cheikh Anta Diop, has made some critical interventions which have assisted in clarifying some largely un-acknowledged facts about the relationship between Europe's intellectual traditions and its African past. Diop has argued conclusively and convincingly that ancient pharaonic Egypt was a Negro civilization (Diop 1974, 1981, 1991). In one of his major works, *The African Origin of Civilisation – Myth or Reality* (1974), he relied on factors such as the descriptions and perceptions of the early Egyptians of themselves, the descriptions of the Egyptians by their European contemporaries such as Herodotus, the 'father of History', as well as archeological evidence which demonstrate the black African basis of Egyptian civilization. Moreover, Diop exposed historical and contemporary attempts by European Egyptology and historiography to deny the black world of a contribution to Egypt's past and by extension to European thought.

Writers like Martin Bernal (1987) and W.E.B. Du Bois (1965) have noted that the denial of acknowledgment of Africa's contribution

to world civilization is an endeavour which coincides closely with
the emergence of trans-Atlantic slavery, because the admission
of the former would undermine irreparably the foundation and
basis of the latter. Bernal (1987, 1:2), for example, has argued that
the denial of an African contribution to European thought gained
currency only in the 18th and 19th centuries, the period marking
the beginning of European domination and conquest of the
world. Such an environment he maintains, made it impossible to
adhere to the historical fact of an African contribution to Europe.
He contends that, "the paradigm of 'races' that were intrinsically
unequal in physical and mental endowment was applied to
all human studies, but especially to history", but he notes that
following the period of European colonial domination in the
nineteenth century "it was now considered undesirable, if not
disastrous, for races to mix". Moreover, according to Bernal, given
the newly found global power of Europe, not only did European
civilization need "to be 'racially pure'" but it "became increasingly
intolerable that Greece – which was seen by the Romantics not
merely as the epitome of Europe but also as its pure childhood
– could be the result of the mixture of native Europeans and
colonizing Africans and Semites" (Bernal 1987, 1:2).

However, the significance of establishing the Negro basis of
civilization does not rest at demonstrating this historical fact
in isolation, but necessarily goes further in highlighting the
contribution of Negro Egypt to European learning. It is only on this
basis that one can challenge the claim that Marxism, is distinctly
a "white-man's" ideology and is inapplicable to the experiences of
persons of African descent. Cheikh Anta Diop (1991, 3) has seen
this question as being of uppermost significance in the rediscovery
of the Negro Egyptian past. He observes that,

> insofar as Egypt is the mother of Western cultures and sciences...
> most of the ideas that we call foreign are often-times nothing but
> mixed up, reversed, modified, elaborated images of the creations
> of our African ancestors, such as Judaism, Christianity, Islam,
> dialectics, the theory of being, the exact sciences, arithmetic,

geometry, mechanical engineering, astronomy, medicine, literature (novel, poetry, drama) architecture, the arts, etc.

Similarly, it has been demonstrated by other writers, most notably by George James ([1954] 1988) in his book *Stolen Legacy*, that Aristotle, Plato and Socrates had all, at various points, come under the influence of black Egyptian pharaonic philosophy and that many of the works which have been ascribed to the ancient Greek philosophers represent cases of vulgar plagiarism or accidental distortions of Egyptian thought.

Indeed, evidence in support of Martin Bernal's claim that knowledge of Europe's philosophical debt to black pharaonic Egypt was far more widely accepted in the pre-eighteenth century period than is currently acknowledged, can be found in the words of Marx himself. Aware of the heavy dependence of the early Greek philosophers on Egyptian learning, Marx observes in *Capital* that,

> in so far as the division of labour is treated in [Plato's *Republic*], as the formative principle of the state, it is merely the Athenian idealisation of the Egyptian system of castes, Egypt having served as the model of an industrial country to many of his contemporaries, also amongst others to Socrates, and it continued to have this importance to the Greeks of the Roman Empire (Marx 1906, 402).

Cheikh Anta Diop (1991), in his magnum opus *Civilization or Barbarism*, has attempted to demonstrate the existence of a philosophy inherent in Egyptian cosmogony (Diop 1991, 310), and more importantly for the purposes of this work, he has identified the origins of dialectical reasoning, which became central to the Marxist world view, in Egyptian cosmogony. In outlining the major essential features of dialectical thought which the Europeans owe directly to the Egyptian cosmogony, Diop, (1991, 340–41) observes that,

> The essential principle of the Egyptian cosmogony, which Plato faithfully copied without admitting it, should always be kept in mind: the Egyptian cosmogonic philosophy is integrally evolutionist and transformist... The internal primordial matter without beginning or end, is engaged in an evolution, a perpetual becoming, thanks to the intrinsic property which is the law of transformation, elevated

to the level of a divinity. Matter, together with the evolutionary movement that always pushes it to change its form, to evolve, are both eternal principles. There did not exist in Egyptian cosmogony a period designated as zero, at which point the being, matter, arose out of nothing, out of non-being...[I]ts fullness excludes a priori even the hypothetical possibility of non-being, of nothingness, as supreme absurdity. Nothingness or non-being in the Egyptian philosophical cosmogony, is equivalent to concrete matter in disorder, in the chaotic state of the Nun, of the primordial abyss. But this Nun contained in it, in the form of a desire toward order and beauty (so many notions allegedly Platonic) a force capable of assuring its evolution, in the same sense used by Marxists (Lenin) when they say that movement is an intrinsic property of matter.

Diop (1991, 311) demonstrates further that the first element in Egyptian cosmogony in the creation of the world was "materialistic in essence; for it is professing a materialistic faith when postulating the existence of an uncreated eternal matter, excluding nothingness and containing its own principle of evolution as an intrinsic property". He notes however that it later takes an idealist aspect, through the appearance of the demiurge Ra, since Ra achieves creation through the word. Diop (1991, 310–11) observes further that, "the objective idea of Hegel is nothing but the word (of Ra) of God without God, a mythicized version of the Judeo-Christian religion, as Engels remarked". This final observation leads to a direct challenge to Marx's claim of having stood Hegel on his head by uniting the dialectical and the material. Such a link can be identified thousands of years before Marx, in Egyptian thought.

Resolving the Race/Class Dilemma and the Claims of Marx's Eurocentrism

The absence of general awareness of the African origin of some central aspects of Marxist philosophy, has been an important, though not the only factor impacting upon black scholars' acceptance of Marxist theory. The reluctance on the part of black theorists to embrace Marxism and their general suspicion towards European political ideas have resulted in the emergence of several alternative perspectives out of the Caribbean. These Caribbean perspectives seek to address problems of exploitation and oppression from a 'race first' perspective, or within a modified class perspective, with varying degrees of compatibility with Marxist theory. The Africa for the Africans movement of Garvey (1969), Black Power (Rodney 1969), Pan-Africanism (Padmore 1972), and plantation economy theory (Best 1968; Beckford 1972) are all examples of Caribbean perspectives which sought to centre race and culture and to create indigenous theories that would address directly the problems confronting formerly colonized, black-majority societies.

There are several arguments which propose that Marxism in its original theoretical expression, and in its practical expression in the communist revolutions of the twentieth century is unsuited to the specific modes of oppression experienced by the black and colonized peoples of the world. These arguments have had a long and enduring impact on the perception of Marxism as 'white man's ideology' (Cummins 1980) and have coloured discussions of Marxism's applicability to black liberation struggles. A.W. Singham (1970), for example, remarking on the question of racism in Marx's thought, has pointed to Marx's description of the 'Asiatic Mode of Production' as being typical of this built-in Eurocentric negation of Africa. According to Singham (1970, 84),

> Marx had shown himself to be hopelessly confused and little informed on the colonial question, introducing a novel but hardly scientific concept to explain the traditional colonized societies of Africa and Asia. In dealing with European societies Marx used analytical categories, but for these societies he coined the non-analytical term 'Asiatic mode of production' to imply the total power enjoyed by the state apparatus, that is, landowners and bureaucrats in preventing change... Historically this is not surprising, for Marx shared the contempt of most bourgeois intellectuals of Western Europe at that time for non-Western, non-White cultures. At one point, for example, Marx wrote quite contemptuously that 'India had no indigenous history, but was rather a tale of successive invaders who founded their empires on the passive basis of that unresisting and unchanging society'. The dialectic apparently worked for Europeans but not for Asians.

Related to this is the deeper question of the well-traversed arguments about Marx's "economic determinism", his emphasis on the causal relationship between infrastructure and superstructure, which it is argued, relegates racial prejudice to the sphere of the superstructure and as a result, greatly determines the level of importance attached to it in terms of its potential for revolutionary transformation. In short, this question revolves around the long-held issue of the problem of the primacy of race over class in Marxism. The Jamaican philosopher and world-famous author of *The Racial Contract* (1997), Charles W. Mills (1991, 28) has argued strongly against some of the major claims to the 'universalism' in key Marxian formulations. In his view the pre-determined notion that "ethnicity is largely constructed, and ultimately decomposable in class terms, needs to be reconsidered as a corollary of Marx and Engels' questionable 'universalism' which... represents as supranational and colourless what is really European and white" (Mills (1991, 28). He suggests that because of this tendency, "the crucial psychic dimension of the struggle for black personhood...with its links to historical reclamation and redemption, rests crucially on the assumption that ethnicity is part of one's identity". He argues that this claim is "difficult to handle within a Marxist conceptual framework in which 'class', 'economic' and the relation to the 'means of production' are truly the 'objective' and 'determining'" (Mills 1991, 28).

The implications of these discussions become even more critical when the obvious truth is brought to the fore, that Eurocentrism is not confined to Marxism.[1] The dilemma of the 'race question' within Marxism is indeed symptomatic of a wider problem. A pervasive and inbred Eurocentrism can be identified in every aspect of Western political theory. It is as a result of the often taken-for-grated, unnoticed but pervasive racism in Western thought that C.W. Mills insists upon a specific role and necessity for an Afro-centric perspective. Mills (1991, 29) has noted that "given the pervasiveness of racism as a structuring ideology deeply imbricated in European thought for the past few hundred years, we should expect that on matters involving race there are likely to be systematic lacunae and distortions in Western intellectual schemas devised to explain society and history". It is the role of black political theorists to offer counter-narratives since "sometimes it is only through the emergence of alternative views and voices that one begins to appreciate how much of what had seemed genuinely universalistic was really particular" (Mills 1998, xi).

Among the examples of the supposed pervasive Eurocentrism in Marx, frequently cited by Afro-centrists, include his thesis on pre-capitalist economic formations, the aforementioned Asiatic mode of production, as well as his views on the transformation from feudalism to capitalism (Marx 1964). It is a commonly held claim that Marx's views on these questions were influenced heavily by "the pattern of development experienced by Western European societies" (Cummins 1980, 175) and presented as a universal rule. To these critics, Marx's 'Asiatic mode of production' was characteristic of a,

> fundamentally static form of society, whose stationary character Marx attributed to its lack of private property in land, to the central government's control over public works, including irrigation, and to the combination of agriculture and manufacture characteristic of the village system... It was the self-sustaining nature of the village economy, in which the individual was unable to become independent of the community, that explained the fact that the 'Asiatic form necessarily survive[d] longest and most stubbornly'. Only when brought into contact with the universalizing and dialectically superior capitalist mode of production introduced from the West would this village system disappear (Cummins 1980, 173).

In short, the 'Asiatic mode' was viewed negatively by Marx.

Cheikh Anta Diop (1991, 29) has argued that the features of what Marx describes as the "Asiatic mode of production", can be identified first in Black pharaonic Egypt and should therefore be properly described as the "African mode of production". Contrary to the offhanded dismissal by Marx of the Asiatic mode as an anomaly, Diop contends that it represents the norm since, in its African manifestation, it survived for more than three thousand years, while European capitalism is scarcely three hundred years old (Diop 1974, 225). In *Pre-colonial Black Africa*, Diop (1987, 147–48) cautions that "the accidents of European history which led to the systematic expropriation of the peasants are not general laws". Instead, he argues that, "without this phenomenon of expropriation, capitalism would not have come to be". He therefore questions the Marxist claim to universal and "immutable sociological laws which explain the necessary passage from the stage of domestic economy to capitalism in all societies" and "why the politico-social balance of Africa was broken only at contact with an external influence". He insists therefore that wherever capitalism is found it is "a European export and not the result of natural local evolution" (Diop 1987, 147–48).

Diop insists that the special conditions which led to the development of capitalism in Europe were absent in the territories in which the misnamed Asiatic mode of production existed. These 'special conditions' include, for example, factors such as private property in land, in contrast to Africa where land was "within everyone's grasp, with no need to forfeit one's freedom, like the serf bound to the soil, in order to make use of it to 'possess' it" (Diop 1987, 150). Another major factor responsible for the absence of dynamic in the African case, as opposed to the Graeco-Latin situation in which case the social conflict resulted in the emergence of feudalism, was the size factor, which made it difficult for an all-embracing social revolution to occur (Diop 1974, 207). In explaining the differences in levels of social stability between the states of Graeco-Latin and African antiquity, Diop (1974, 225) observes that, "the appearance of a state with an Asiatic economic system... did not spring abruptly from the brutal contact of two races, one of which enslaved the other and thus created from the outset, the conditions for the development of the class struggle and private property". A major aspect of the process of rethinking Marxism, especially in the light of concerns of its relevance to the problems of race, therefore requires a re-examination of Africa's pre-colonial past and its subsequent transformation upon contact with European capitalism. Such a re-examination should necessarily involve discarding what is Eurocentric and chauvinistic in Marx himself while retaining in essence his methodology which remains independent of any unacknowledged and subcutaneous Eurocentrism in his perspectives (Rodney 1981; Cabral 1969).

It is significant that Eric Hobsbawm (1964), in his preface to Marx's *Precapitalist Economic Formations* has acknowledged the possibility of Marx's limited understanding of the pre-conquest modes of production of most of the non-European world. Hobsbawm (1964, 20–21) notes that "neither a classical education nor the material then available made a serious knowledge of Egypt and the ancient Middle East possible". Similarly, Ian Cummins (1980,175) has noted that "Marx's view of historical change was essentially a Eurocentric one. More precisely his Eurocentrism was based on the pattern of development experienced by Western European societies".

While these observations lend credence to the claims of Eurocentrism in Marx, and have resulted in a schism between black radicalism and Marxian political struggles, it is also useful to be guided by recent scholarship which has sought to challenge the notion of a Eurocentric Marx. An examination of this counter-narrative to the Marxist anti-black claim is necessary for carving a space for overcoming the rejection of James as a 'black Marxist', and by extension, for further clarifying his relevance to the politics of Pan-Africanism and black liberation and anti-racist struggles in the twenty-first century.

One such effort is the work of Kevin Anderson (2010). Anderson has explored Marx's discussions of the possibility of revolution outside the main capitalist centres of Europe. Anderson's aim was to show that, contrary to the widespread assumption of Marx's 'dismissal' of the possibility of revolution in non-European contexts, Marx did raise a number of issues which supported the possibility of revolution in 'underdeveloped' societies and within non-European contexts of exploitation. Amongst the areas studied by Marx and highlighted by Anderson were, "India to Russia and from Algeria to China – and their relation to capitalism and colonialism" and his "writings on movements for national emancipation". Of specific significance was Marx's "theorization of race and ethnicity in relation to class, with respect to both black labour in America during the Civil War and Irish labour in Britain" and his writings on societies that were for "the most part peripheral to capitalism during his lifetime" (Anderson 2010, 1–4). The main implication of Anderson's work, has been to show that Marx's expectations of the possibilities of revolution in the 'peripheral' underdeveloped world were far more optimistic than has been commonly accepted particularly by black radicals suspicious of Marx's Eurocentrism (Anderson, 2010, 1–4).

The preceding analysis provides a sufficiently solid philosophical and theoretical base for contextualizing and understanding C.L.R. James's Marxism as a black Caribbean thinker, unaffected by the hostility to Marxism as a result of his racial emphasis. How James addresses the perceived conflicts between Marxism and Pan-Africanism, may also serve to inform current treatment of the issue, particularly in the context of the retreat of both Marxist and global pan-Africanist movements in the early twenty-first century. Specifically, how James addressed the "race/class dilemma" can assist in informing the stances of black and formerly colonized radicals in confronting squarely the problems of race, class and other forms of oppression in a manner relevant to the local and global expression of radical movements in the early twenty-first century.

The Race Question in the Jamesian Perspective

It is not difficult to grasp why sections of the black left express an ambivalence towards C.L.R. James's race consciousness, and its relative positioning vis-à-vis his class consciousness. The early twentieth century "English public school" colonial Trinidad context within which James was educated neither equipped him with the scientific and historical knowledge of the anteriority of black political philosophy to European thought, nor did it furnish him with the tools to analyse the political and social implications of such a reality. James's fascination with antiquity was largely confined to its Graeco-Latin aspects. In *Every cook can Govern* for example, James (1986a, 8) in diametrical contrast to perspectives of Diop (1974; 1981; 1987), Bernal (1987, vol. 1), Du Bois (1965), George James ([1954] 1988) and others, was never able to hide his belief in the superiority of ancient Greek culture, while exhibiting ignorance of its pre-Greek foundations. Adhering to the standard Eurocentric interpretations, James had always viewed the early Greeks as laying "the intellectual foundations of Western Europe" and had uncritically attributed to them the origins "of politics, democracy, oligarchy, constitution, law..., oratory, rhetoric, ethics;... tragedy and comedy;... history;... sculpture and architecture" (James 1986a, 8).

Similarly, James's early hostility to thinkers such as Garvey whose philosophy he famously described as "pitiable rubbish" (James 1969, 79), his description of himself as a "black European" (Bracey 1981, 25) and his frequent claims that the experience of European-organised slavery and the severing of Caribbean blacks from their African ancestry had transformed the Caribbean into a "fully Europeanised People" (James 1966a, 3;15), all paint James as a "soft" Pan-Africanist, more aware of the impact of Europe, rather than Africa on his political consciousness. Joseph (2022) has argued that these assertions all indicate a limited appreciation of the African past as having autonomy and agency, in shaping Caribbean consciousness and, by extension, in offering alternatives to European notions of development and progress. These notions hold profound implications for the possibilities of revolution in the twenty-first century particularly in a context where European-based ideas of Marxist revolution have encountered crises in the late twentieth century.

These assertions from James however, do not represent a final or closed understanding of his contribution to racial discourse and Pan-Africanism and their place in revolution.   These statements by James, must be weighed against his constant and early writings on Africa, his work in and around pan-African revolutionary organizations and politics, his writings on revolts and revolutions in the pan-African world and his engagement in theoretical discourse on race and revolution. Thus, in contrast to Bogues (1997, 46) who suggests that James had a "long way to go to come to terms with Africa's distinctive contributions to human civilization", Høgsbjerg (2014) has been arguing that a history of James in the UK would show a far longer commitment to Africa and African issues, than has been fully acknowledged. On the basis of these perspectives, it is simplistic and misleading to attribute to James any underdeveloped or "soft" racial or pan-African consciousness without appreciating how his discourses on race and pan-Africanism were meant to achieve an analytical synthesis with Marxism, and how race, anti-colonialism, Pan-Africanism and revolutionary democracy were always treated as a singular whole in the advancement of anti-capitalist revolution, in the Jamesian perspective.

It is not without significance that one of James's most important books, *The Black Jacobins*, his history of the Haitian Revolution, was motivated by the need to respond to the fact that "they are always talking about West Indians as backward, as slaves, and continually oppressed and exploited by British domination", so it was necessary to "write a book that showed the West Indians as something else" (MARHO 1983, 267). It is significant too that it was in *Black Jacobins* that James made one of the most overt expressions of his race and class, (Marxist and pan-Africanist) theoretical synthesis. According to James, "the race question is subsidiary to the class question, and to think of imperialism in terms of race is disastrous. But to neglect the racial factor as merely incidental is an error only less grave than to make it fundamental" (James 1989, 283).

While this statement can be viewed as being consistent with the typical Marxist position with its claim that the "race question is subsidiary to the class question", what is more important is James's preoccupation in overcoming the twinned oppressions of race and class in the colonial context and in the context of racism in mature capitalist countries. Indeed, James viewed any movement for racial equality as being part of a movement towards the abolition of classes. This marriage between black revolt and socialist transformation emerges very clearly in James's article on *Black Power* (1992a), in which he defends the centrality given to the race question by Black Power advocates such as Stokely Carmichael and criticized the Marxist parties for not fully embracing the Black Power movement. There, James reiterated to the Marxist parties the position which he had adopted on the role of the black struggle in the United States of America. Essentially James's argument was not only that "the independent struggle of the Negro people for the democratic rights and equality with the rest of the American nation... had to be defended and advocated by the Marxist movement" but that the "Marxist movement had to understand that *such independent struggles were a contributory factor to the socialist revolution*" (James 1992a, 372). [Emphasis in original].

James's clearest statement on the role of the black struggle and its significance for the attainment of socialism, can be found in his 1948 article entitled *The Revolutionary Answer to the Negro Problem in the U.S.A.* In this article James is adamant that the black struggle in the U.S.A. should be seen as the vanguard of the revolutionary struggle in the U.S.A., and should not be subordinated to the dictates of the Marxist parties since, "the Negro struggle is able to exercise a powerful influence upon the revolutionary proletariat, that it has got a great contribution to make to the development of the proletariat in the United States, and that it is in itself a constituent part of the struggle for socialism" (James 1992f, 183).

In a similar way, James, in a 1939 meeting with Trotsky in Mexico, demonstrated his commitment to the view that the black struggle should not be subordinated to the need to establish socialism. In this conversation, James reinforced his commitment to his notion of 'free creative activity' by expressing the view that blacks, through their own autonomous organizations and activity, should decide on what the objectives of their struggle should be. James, though he was opposed to the calls for territorial separation and political self-determination on the part of more militant North American blacks, a position opportunistically adopted by the official communist parties, was willing to support such a move once it had the backing and support of the majority of the blacks (Richards 1992; Martin 1984). Richards (1992, 146) argues that James, "while questioning the appropriateness of the slogan of black self-determination or territorial... separatism rejected any Marxist approach which failed to distinguish between black and white workers regarding both as simply the victims of class oppression". James's readiness to accept the autonomous activity of black nationalists, his awareness that such activity could serve to further the socialist cause, as well as his rejection of attempts by Marxists to dominate and stifle the black movement, demonstrate his willingness to revise the Marxian categories to allow the "most oppressed section of American society and the most discriminated against" to become "the very vanguard of the proletarian revolution" (James 1992f, 188; Richards 1992, 149).

James's recognition of the need to adjust his Marxism to accommodate the realities of racial oppression and the necessity of black liberation, was not confined to the realities of the U.S.A. Indeed, his most novel and profound ideas on the 'race question' were expressed in relation to developments occurring in the Caribbean. James's analysis of the development of plantation slavery in the Caribbean for example, led him to the conclusion that a modern, totally westernized proletariat had been created in these territories (James 1966a). It is such a reality which, to James, explains the level of rebelliousness which has characterized the populations of the Caribbean territories from the earliest days of slavery to the present period. In remarking on James's analysis of West Indian slavery and its relation to the Marxist framework, A.W. Singham (1970, 86–87) posits that James,

> made his own unique and important modification in dealing with a special variant of imperialism, the Caribbean states. While Marx, Lenin and even Trotsky and Luxemburg saw the traditional states of Africa and Asia as reflecting the 'Oriental' peculiarity, James showed how the Caribbean was the first modern society to arise outside Western Europe, where both institutions and populations had been transplanted. It was to be a replica of Europe outside Europe. The settlers bought with them a 'modern' socio-economic organisation to exploit agriculture... There was a commitment to the principles of hierarchy and rationality, which characterized the modern capitalist states.

Singham further demonstrates the implications of James's Marxist analysis when applied to the concrete historical experiences of Caribbean peoples, in James's treatment of the Haitian revolution. He argues that,

> James was demonstrating concretely that not all national revolutions followed the same patterns, nor did all colonial societies have the same type of economic structure. In San Domingo a new type of hybrid had emerged from the imposition of a capitalist form of economic organisation, the plantation, on the pre-feudal structure of slavery. This bore no relation to Marx's Asiatic mode of production, but had produced a new kind of contradiction. Thus, San Domingo under Toussaint was able to 'leap over the stages of national development'. Like Lenin, but with more concrete evidence James stressed the flexibility in the stages of history of different societies (Singham 1970, 85).

It should be noted too that James was also building upon Trotsky's theory of 'uneven and combined development' which had been expressed in his *History of the Russian Revolution* where he had emphasized that "the development of historically backward nations leads necessarily to a peculiar combination of different stages in the historic process. Their development as a whole acquires a planless, complex and combined character" (Trotsky [1932] 1965).

This novel application of Marxist methodology to the realities of Caribbean political development, effectively challenge the popularly held notion that James's Marxism had little bearing for the Caribbean. It also challenges the questions raised about the application of Marxism to non-European socio-political contexts and assists in overcoming the view that racial consciousness was a form of 'false consciousness', located in the ideational superstructure. In *The Making of the Caribbean Peoples,* James (1966a) emphasizes that it was the experience of European slavery in the Caribbean which created the seeds for the transformation of Caribbean society, and specifically, defined the nature of Caribbean freedom. It was James's application of a Hegelian "qualitative leap". He argues that,

> liberty means something to us that is very unusual. There were many generations of slaves in Africa, of that we are quite sure. And in Africa, they took it and no doubt fought against it at certain times. But when we made the 'middle passage' and came to the Caribbean we went straight into a modern industry - the sugar plantation - and there we saw that to be a slave was the result of our being black. A white man was not a slave. The West Indian slave was not accustomed to that kind of slavery in Africa; and therefore in the history of the West Indies there is one dominant fact and that is the desire for liberty; the ridding oneself of the particular burden which is the special inheritance of the black skin (James1966a, 4).

In a strikingly similar mode of thought to James, Cheikh Anta Diop (1974, 225) offers a perspective which captures the manner in which the divergent historical experience of ancient slavery and private land ownership in Europe and Africa, helps to explain the later emergence of forms of oppression and consequent actions for liberation, in the two societal formations. According to Diop (1974, 225),

> The Greek city-state was founded from birth on slavery and the intangibility of private land ownership. In contrast, the appearance of a state with an Asiatic economic system, as described by Marx and Engels, shows that it did not spring abruptly from the brutal contact of two races one of which enslaved the other and thus

created, from the outset, the conditions for the development of the class struggle and private property... In sum, it suffices for societies with an Asiatic mode of production to be reduced into slavery... for them to insert themselves into the historic cycle of humanity. The worldwide emancipation of all the former European colonies, which, without exception were dependent on that mode of production, illustrate the idea.

The creative manner in which James applied the Marxist dialectic to understanding the problems of racism in the capitalist centre and in peripheral black-majority post-colonial societies, challenges the Eurocentric label and debunks the claims of the inapplicability of Marxism to 'underdeveloped' post-colonial societies. Indeed, given James's concern with dialectical synthesis, no absolute and final label can be applied when assessing the place of racial consciousness in his broad philosophy. Indeed, James's treatment of the race question becomes progressively more sophisticated with the maturity of his thought. Towards the end of his life, in stark contrast to his earlier descriptions of Garvey's philosophy as 'pitiable rubbish', he had accepted Garvey's call for black pride and racial consciousness as one of the leaps necessary for the emancipation of the black race (James 1984c, 167). He had also, much earlier, using his J.R. Johnson pseudonym, written a respectful obituary to Garvey acknowledging the success and unprecedented scale of Garvey's organizational abilities (James 1940). In a similar vein, too, James did begin to make more open declarations of the African connection to Caribbean culture. To James, genuine independence – an independence which breaks completely with the European past – can only be achieved by returning to the African past. This "return to Africa" was, to James, one of the most significant achievements of the Haitian revolution. James (1984c, 167) writes that,

> after the successful revolution for Haitian independence in 1802, the Haitian intelligentsia tried for nearly a hundred years to build a model French civilisation and culture in the West Indies. Their failure is of great importance to us today... Recognizing this failure to make themselves French, they turned back home. What they

found and built up was the African heritage which the Haitian peasants more than all others in the West Indies had preserved.

Further, there was much in James's intellectual evolution which suggests an increasing recognition of Africa's contribution to global intellectual development and its possibilities for Caribbean development alternatives, suggesting a redefining of his earlier overwhelming European focus. In a radio series with Robert Lalljie, the transcripts of which were published in (1990, 69), James made clear his own awareness, if not open acknowledgment of ancient Egyptian civilization's African origins and its anteriority to Europe:

> I believe I have hopes for Africa which astonish people. I say when you go to Egypt, that the persons who helped to build them came from Asia; the Mediterranean; but they came from central Africa too! And when you look at what they have built, the African is there! His face! One of my main... favourite topics, I don't talk about it too much, but the historians believe that civilisation originated in Tanzania. Now I don't mean to say that it did, but I prefer that it originated there than it originated in England (Lalljie 1990, 69; see also James 1966a, 1).

It is expressions such as these, coupled with James's concrete activities in the quest for the liberation of Africa through his various pan-Africanist struggles, and his creative application of Marxism to incorporate his race perspectives which represent the hallmark of James's treatment of the question of race and which negate any attempt to attach a label of Europhilism to James with any finality. The implications of James's specific outlook for the concrete practices of pan-African, anti-racist and anti-capitalist organization and revolt in the twenty-first century, will later be explored. However, as a necessary corollary to this, it is important to address specifically how James addressed the race/class tensions in Marxist thought and how his position is distinguished from other competing tendencies such as the race first perspective of Marcus Garvey and the post-Marxist black nationalist argument of George Padmore, since these remain important perspectives impacting on contemporary Caribbean radical politics.

James, the Race/Class Dilemma and Implications for Praxis

Having acknowledged, unpacked and discussed the complexities of the place of Africa in James's thought, it should be equally acknowledged that he offers a unique treatment of the problems arising out of the tensions which exist between race-centered or class-centered approaches to political struggles. To many Marxists, any approach which sees social oppression as arising out of one's skin colour and forming the basis for social revolution, serves to elevate to a central position what is essentially a problem arising out of one's relation to the economic means of production. At the other extreme is the position adopted by several black activists in whose view, "the crucial psychic dimension of the struggle for black personhood... with its links to historical reclamation and redemption, rests crucially on the assumption that ethnicity is part of one's identity" (Mills 1991, 28) and should not be construed as merely a by-product of class oppression.

The "race first" perspective however, is in itself a unidimensional perspective and has the tendency to result in the overemphasis on one form of social oppression, ignoring totally, other deeply rooted forms of exploitation and oppression. Such a consequence can be clearly discerned in Marcus Garvey's *Philosophy and Opinions* whose arguments, as Azinna Nwafor (in Padmore 1972, xxxi), in an introduction to George Padmore's *Pan-Africanism or Communism* observes,

> were directed, not against the fact of imperialist domination and colonialism in itself, but rather against European, *white* domination. Indeed, were Africa held under the imperial subjugation of black ruling classes as opposed to whites, Garvey would have been unruffled by such a situation... "why", he asked in *Philosophy and Opinions*, "should not Africa give to the world its black Rockefeller, Rothschild and Henry Ford?"

The gulf which exists between these two diametrically opposed perspectives at the theoretical level, has manifested itself even more conspicuously in the practical sphere, and had a profound impact on the unfolding of radical politics in the twentieth century, inclusive of the Caribbean and continues to have implications for twenty-first century politics. The relationships which existed between the Marxist parties and the race consciousness movements in several of the predominantly white-dominated, multi-racial societies, such as the USA and South Africa, reveal clearly the practical organizational difficulties created by the opposing viewpoints of the two perspectives. A stark example of the negative political impact of the race/class contradiction was seen clearly in the case of pre-liberation South Africa, where the 'Marxist socialists' adopted the slogan "workers of the world *fight and unite for a white South Africa!*" during strike action by white miners between 1907 and 1922 (Roux 1964, 148).

Given the dynamics of the race/class divide, Marxists and pan-Africanists have often manifested greater hostilities towards each other than towards the exploiting classes against which their energies should be directed. As Tony Martin ([1976] 1986) shows in his book *Race First* which studied the organizational struggles of Garvey's Universal Negro Improvement Association (UNIA), the greatest obstacles to Garvey came from the North American Marxist parties. This rivalry emerged from the fact that they were mobilizing and organizing within the same oppressed community of persons. As Martin ([1976] 1986, 222) observes, "the necessity of winning over the black workers and peasants would assume even greater importance for the communists when they belatedly awoke to the realisation that the black masses, as the most exploited section of American society would have to occupy a critical position in their thinking if they were ever to seriously entertain any hopes of overthrowing American capitalism".

It is such divergences in outlook between 'race first' and Marxist perspectives which have resulted in the emergence of similar anti-Marxist, yet radical tendencies in the Caribbean. Rastafarianism, Black Power, the plantation economy school, as well as the wider pan-Africanist perspective of George Padmore, all grew out of a rejection of the class-centered outlook of Marxism and a need to replace it with more autochthonous perspectives. The plantation economy theory of George Beckford (1972) and Lloyd Best (1968), though not a race first perspective per se, and which can perhaps be described as a Caribbean cultural nationalist perspective with a heavy political-economy flavour, fits perfectly into this mould. The theory is explicitly presented as attempt at indigenous theorizing to account for Caribbean social and political reality in contrast to what is perceived to be an alien and inapplicable Marxism.   Arguing against the applicability of Marxist class analysis to Caribbean realities, Best (in Oxaal 1982, 298), claims that,

> there is no 'bourgeoisie' here because we have had no 'bourgs'. Nor have we had feudalism or any dynamic class of natural capitalists so there need not be any 'socialists' or 'communists'. What is the meaning of 'middle class'? In almost every family we can find represented the full spectrum from professional through artisan to labourer. Tapia[2] rejects all these imported categories and we seek to understand what is going on in terms of *Caribbean* definitions. When we do that, we see all kinds of very rich possibilities for national integration and economic transformation. And we make all kinds of fresh interpretations.

The analytical value of James's political thought for Caribbean political theory resides in its potential for resolving the problems created by the race/class schism among radical political thinkers. James's thought expresses an overriding commitment to Marxist class analysis while at the same time, confronts the social contradictions of societies structured along racial configurations. It is this commitment to class analysis which serves as the greatest strength of the Marxist outlook and conversely, it is the absence or denial of the necessity for the incorporation of class by the other schools which constitutes their greatest weakness. The thought of James reveals constantly how his methodology allows for his fusion of racial consciousness and class analysis. In *The Revolutionary Answer,* James (1992f, 183) shows how addressing racial inequalities in the USA must necessarily include confronting the problem of the economic marginalization of blacks:

on the question of the state, what Negro, particularly below the Mason-Dixon line, believes that the bourgeois state is a state above all classes, serving the needs of all the people? They may not formulate their beliefs in Marxist terms, but their experience drives them to reject this shibboleth of bourgeois democracy.

This synthesis of the race and class question can also be discerned clearly where James (in Stanton 1980, 28), arguing against the participation of blacks in the US military during the second world war, had claimed that since the "average Negro lives like an outcast in the North" they would have no difficulty rejecting the claims of "a democrat like Roosevelt... [who] tells everybody (including the Negro, of course) that the war now being fought in Europe is a war for 'democracy'".

James's synthesis of race and class invites comparative analysis with the ideas of two other prominent black Marxists, namely, Walter Rodney and Amilcar Cabral, who had exhibited a similar overriding commitment to Marxism, while remaining conscious of, and organizing politically against, colonial and racial oppression.

Cabral (1969) in *The Weapon of Theory*, while accepting the category of class as an essential component in the understanding of contemporary politics, rejects the view that history begins only with 'class' struggle. Cabral makes a very important contribution to understanding pre-colonial Africa with a modified Marxist lens. He contends that in Africa and other parts of the non-European world, 'classes' in the sense adopted by Marx, are virtually unidentifiable prior to the imposition of European colonialism. He argues that,

> in the general evolution of humanity and each of the peoples of which it is composed, classes appear neither as a generalised and simultaneous phenomenon throughout the totality of these groups, nor as a finished, perfect, uniform and spontaneous whole. The definition of classes within one or several human groups is a fundamental consequence of the progressive development of the productive forces and of the characteristics of the distribution of the wealth produced by the group or usurped by others. That is

to say that the socio-economic phenomenon 'class' is created and develops as a function of at least two essential and inter-dependent variables - the level of the productive forces and the pattern of ownership of the means of production (Cabral 1969, 75-76).

Cabral (1969, 77) insists that to ignore the question of the level of the productive forces is to ignore "the essential and determinant element in the content and form of class struggle". In his view, the emergence of 'classes' is a development that occurs belatedly consequent upon the development of the productive forces, and is not a 'natural' or inevitable development, and indeed occurred only after the European contact with Africa. In Cabral's view therefore, to make the 'struggle of classes' the motor force of history, would be to,

place outside history the whole period of life of human groups from the discovery of hunting, and later nomadic and sedentary agriculture, to the organisation of herds and the private appropriation of land. It would also be to consider – and this we refuse to accept – that various human groups in Africa, Asia and Latin America were living without history at the time when they were subjected to the yoke of imperialism (1969, 77).

Instead of accepting the Eurocentric view that European contact was necessary for African development, Cabral (1969, 87), in contrast, sees the experience of European colonialism as being a "negation of the historical process" of Africa and the non-European world, for it resulted in the usurpation of the critical national productive forces, and as such, took Africa 'out of history'. Despite his rejection of the anteriority of class as a determinant factor in African development, Cabral recognizes that once classes have been formed within any political entity, they remain critical to its future development and evolution.

Like Cabral, Guyanese scholar Walter Rodney, also developed a world view which maintained a commitment to Marxism, despite his awareness and consciousness of the reality of racism as a determinant factor impacting on all aspects of life of non-white, colonized peoples and regions. What is distinctive about Rodney's marriage of class and racial analysis is his deployment of the Marxist dialectical method as a tool for understanding the possibilities of revolution in specific local conditions. Rodney (1981, 4) believes that Marxism, if viewed as a method,

> would exist at different levels, at different times, in different places and retain its potential as a tool [since] a methodology would, virtually by definition be independent of time and place. You will use the methodology at any given time, and any place. You may get quite different results, of course, but the methodology itself would be independent of time and place.

This perspective of Rodney's has been reinforced in his more recent (posthumous) publication on the implications of the Russian revolution for Africa and the Third World (Rodney 2018). Insisting on the relevance of an 'African perspective' despite the commitment to Marxist methodology, Rodney sees the question as residing more critically "in the concept of the two world-views – idealism and materialism – representing fundamentally opposed aspects of consciousness" and which one is applied in studying Africa (Rodney 2018, 4). Fully cognizant of the fact that "there is an area of conflict that arises by trying to reconcile an African world view with the two world views", Rodney (2018, 4–5) addresses the issue in the following way:

> It can be argued that aspects of ideology coming from Europe are irrelevant to the African perspective or the black world view. Conversely, it can and has been said that a world view is either idealist or materialist that the label 'Africa' conveys no meaning and probably mystifies... Whatever uniqueness one may attach to any given African view, it does not dispense with the necessity to recognize (1) the superiority of materialism, and (2) that materialist views are partial and do not take African perspectives into account.

It is therefore as a methodological tool to be applied to the analysis of society, and not as a dogmatic set of ready-made answers to questions about society, that black Marxists like James, Cabral and Rodney use the Marxist method. Rodney, is particularly adept at using the dialectic in this manner and he provides useful examples of how the local historical experiences of racial oppression, can be incorporated within Marxism in understanding the possibilities of socialist revolution in black majority societies. It is the absence of such a methodological tool, and the denial of the necessity for class analysis, which largely separates the approach of the Marxists from other 'black nationalist' perspectives like some notions of Black Power, some branches of pan-Africanist thought and practice, Garveyism, the Plantation Society perspective of writers like Lloyd Best and other sections of the non-Marxist left and other 'race first' perspectives (Oxaal 1982, 298). Similarly, it is this absence of a sound analytical and methodical base which is the greatest weakness of these non-Marxist perspectives.

According to Oxaal (1982, 298-9), it is this factor which best explains the split between Tapia on one hand and C.L.R. James and other West Indian Marxists on the other. Oxaal (1982, 299) argues that "Tapia could be criticized as a reformist movement which, far from destroying capitalism in Trinidad, was actually proposing to do what Eric Williams had failed to do - *strengthen it through the creation of a national bourgeoisie*". Oxaal (1982, 300) notes further that, "the refusal of Lloyd Best to recognize the importance of making a class analysis of Trinidadian and West Indian society is one of... the major weakness of Best's ideology", and that this weakness was based on the "assumption of *Caribbean exceptionalism*". [emphasis in original]

The classic expression of the shortcomings of the race-centric perspectives, can be seen in George Padmore's Pan-Africanism and how it struggled with the reality of class in colonized social formations leading to a settled bourgeois nationalism as an offshoot of anti-European Pan-Africanism (Rodney 1981, 11; Padmore 1972). Worrell (2020, 4), citing Brent Haynes Edwards, informs us that while Padmore had "become a devoted and enthusiastic communist and rose to be an important figure in the Comintern", his involvement with communism was "aimed at a race-specific formation that rejects the Comintern Universalism, adamantly insisting that racial oppression involves factors that cannot be summed up or submerged in a critique of class exploitation". Worrell shows further that once Padmore had left the Comintern owing to Stalin's more accommodationist stance in the lead up to the with the World War II prior to the declaration of hostilities between Germany and Russia, Padmore "turned to Pan-Africanism as the vehicle to liberate Africa and the Caribbean" (4). He argues that during Padmore's early years as a member of the Communist Party of the USA (CPUSA) in the late 1920s, while he had "argued for the primacy of class, he felt that race was also extremely important and should not be entirely incorporated into a rigid class analysis" and that the "Negro Question had racial connotations which demanded special consideration by the party" (Worrell 2020, 33). Worrell notes further that some members of the CPUSA felt that Padmore had "certain black nationalist predispositions that made it difficult for him to adhere to orthodox communist doctrine" (33).

Consequently, it has been argued by Nwafor (1972) that Padmore's Pan-Africanism which was put forward as an alternative to both capitalism and socialism resulted in the establishment of neo-colonialist, capitalist regimes throughout the black world. In *Pan-Africanism or Communism?* Padmore (1972, 317), as Azinna Nwafor (1972) points out, virtually provides a blueprint for the establishment of such regimes, where he warns the colonial powers that,

> the time is fast passing where colored folks will continue to accept their colonial status, which in the modern world signifies racial and national inferiority. If the Western powers are really afraid of communism and want to defeat it, the remedy lies in their own hands... there must be a revolutionary change in the outlook of the colonizing powers, who must be prepared to set a date for the complete transfer of power.

This process of the establishment of time-tables for the peaceful transfer of power has been a central strategy in the formation of neo-colonial regimes in the wake of the withdrawal of formal colonialism. The consequences of this strategy have been well documented in the Caribbean and the other former colonies (Gittens 1983; Lindsay 1975). Belle (1988, 87), for example, observes that in the Caribbean, "the strategy of constitutional tutelage which led to the adoption of a frozen version of the Westminster model was a part of a wider imperial strategy, which was being implemented throughout the empire and it was a policy not perceived by all to be the most positive for a process of decolonization". He cites C.L.R. James for example, who viewed this model of constitutional tutelage as a process of political miseducation and neo-colonial obfuscation. In James's view,

> by delaying the achievements of self-government... by the mean and grudging granting of so many the vote, so many to become ministers and all the palaver and so-called education by which the British government claimed that it trained the West Indies population for self-government a terrible damage was inflicted upon us. In reality our people were mis-educated, our political consciousness was twisted and broken. Far from being guided to Independence by the 1960s... the imperialist government poisoned and corrupted that sense of self-confidence and political dynamic needed for any people about to embark on the unchartered seas of independence and nationhood (James 1966a, 17).

Decades after the earliest successes of race-based nationalism had consolidated themselves in the Caribbean, the consequences of the race-only emphasis could be seen in some of the struggles which belatedly addressed themselves to questions of economic democratization, which apparently had been forgotten in the pursuit of flag independence. A clear example of the inevitable 'pitfalls' of the race-first perspective can be identified, for instance, in the outcome of Hilary Beckles's struggle against the racial exclusion of the black majority of Barbados from economic ownership as a result of the racial-hegemonic power of white corporate power in Barbados (Beckles 1989). Beckles, in seeking to address the wider issue of the economic marginalization of Barbadian blacks sought to focus on the virtual absence of black faces within the boardrooms of local business establishments and in the Barbados Mutual Life Assurance Company in particular.

Beckles himself seems to have been caught by surprise by the logical outcome of such an emphasis, when the white elite simply responded by accommodating a number of token black directors in the boardrooms. Beckles (1989, 16) observes regretfully that, "by the manner in which events subsequently developed... we were essentially opening doors for the repressed, black corporate middle class... It is true that persons so defined, who hitherto had been critical of our concepts of economic change, have requested that we now recede into the background and leave it to them". Further Beckles (1989, 188) would add that, as a direct result of his focus on *race*, it became apparent that the "board surely wanted a few other *black* faces – but ones they could control".

The example above illustrates clearly the consequences of a perspective which underplays or denies the relevance of Marxist class analysis. Theorists adhering to the race first perspective, can be said to "go too far and that in itself results in their not going far enough" (Belle 1977, 26). Millette (1974, 28–32) observes of such theorists that, "while they construct an ideology, it is obvious that they have no ideology, and the most likely result is ultimate collaboration with capitalism". He argues that by

> emphasising the indigenous and racial peculiarities of political and economic change the political revolution is side-tracked into a reactionary, cultural dead-end. The revolution becomes culture bound. That is not to say that culture is unimportant, or that race is unimportant or that indigenous content is unimportant. But the fact is that these things do not make the revolution (Millette 1974, 28–32).

It is the existence of a 'holistic' revolutionary theory of social change in Marxism that explains James's commitment to a Marxian method and theory despite his consciousness of racial oppression in the Caribbean and the former colonized world in general. It is for this reason too that Walter Rodney (1981, 15) concludes his pamphlet *Marx in the liberation of Africa* with the timely reminder from Amilcar Cabral that "there may be revolutions which have had a revolutionary theory which have failed. But there have certainly been no revolutions which has (*sic*) succeeded without a revolutionary theory".

James and the Race Question: Relevance for 21st Century Caribbean Politics

Given its history of enslavement, and the obvious and well documented segmentation of Caribbean society along racial lines, racism, racial exclusion and discrimination against the black majority population, remain central features of Caribbean political life. However, amongst the most striking features of Caribbean political life are the glaring official silences and the failures to engage in deliberate official policy and programmatic responses to the very real presence of racism which is a central aspect of Caribbean existential reality. In contrast, it is to academic sources that one must turn for a discussion of racism as a sociological fact in the Caribbean.

Charles Mills (1991, 24) has claimed that "racial oppression can uncontroversially be categorized as the salient oppression of the region", while Walter Rodney has described the Caribbean as "the laboratory of racialism" (Rodney 1969, 60). Indeed, the history of West Indian slavery in which being a slave was a consequence of being black (James 1966a, 5; Williams 1966; Rodney 1969), the post-emancipation denial of the franchise and other rights to blacks, and latterly, the relative economic disenfranchisement of blacks, (Lewis 1990, 35) all validate the need for an analysis of race in understanding Caribbean political life. Moreover, the racism in the Caribbean is underscored and reinforced by the global marginalization of blacks. As Ali Mazrui (1991, 17) has observed, "blacks are the economic victims of the new economic situation and economic apartheid, partly because many of the economies of Africa are in very bad shape and partly because... there are tremendous pressures on Black countries" in the Caribbean and Africa "to move in directions which seem as yet to yield no positive results".

Despite overwhelming evidence of the existence of racism as a central feature of Caribbean political culture, the natural response of the upper and certain sections of the middle class, is to deny such a reality (Watson 1990b). This denial is consistent with their historical origins as pro-colonial classes which had accepted and coalesced in the racialism of the former colonial powers (James 1984c; Fanon [1967] 1983; Lindsay 1975; Gittens 1983; Beckles 1992; Lewis 1990). Beckles (1992, 12) has argued that a major feature of the West Indian independence experience involved "an alliance of white capital and black politics [which] constituted the ideological basis of a problematic social contract in the post-independence period". He has shown that the two dominant pre-independence political leaders of Barbados - Grantley Adams and Errol Barrow - both had to temper their radical economic proposals in exchange for the support of Britain and the local white monied interests in facilitating both their political aspirations and the independence of Barbados as a whole. Beckles (1992, 12) argues that as a result of this, a "fundamental national division of labour... a post-colonial form of Hobbesian social contract" took shape in Barbados, "having as its principal parties, whites dominating the economy and blacks dominating the state". He argues that central to this social contract were

> two assumptions, both buried deep in the culture of racism. First, that since the whites, with few exceptions, had opposed the rise of popular democracy and independence, they had in effect disqualified themselves for service in the new governmental order... Second, whites mobilised their ideological argument that blacks had no propensity towards big business, and implemented policies to keep them out of the market economy (Beckles 1992, 12).

The work of C.L.R. James is useful in studying the question of racism in the Caribbean, particularly in relation to capturing the role played by privileged Caribbean blacks in the marginalisation of the underprivileged black majority. James, like Fanon, was aware that, with independence, an indigenous black class that was European in its manners, taste, world-view, life-style, and contempt for the black underprivileged classes, had come into being. This was clearly borne out in his criticism of the sixth Pan-Africanist Congress of 1974 and in his recommendations for the establishment of the seventh (James 1977c). James was of the view that while the famous fifth Pan-Africanist Congress of 1945 had made the quest for political independence its main rallying cry, and had achieved its aim in the establishment of independent states in Africa and the Caribbean pioneered by Nkrumah's Ghana in 1957, the sixth congress should have called for a rejection of mere political independence and should have insisted upon complete economic control of national resources. To this end therefore, James (1977c, 43) advocated that the seventh Pan-Africanist Congress be cognizant of the fact that, "there is an African elite in every African country, which has adopted the ways and ideas of western civilization and is living at the expense of the African peasant". Just as he had done for the sixth, he insisted that the seventh congress "must draw a line of steel against those, Africans included, who hide behind the slogan and paraphernalia of national independence while allowing finance capital to dominate and direct their economic and social life" (James 1977c, 40).

James's remarks, though aimed directly at the continental African elite, might well have been aimed at the Caribbean middle-class ruling elite. The tendencies which he observed in the 1960s and 1970s, have deepened rather than diminished in the decades after formal independence leading to the twenty-first century. His aversion to the state-centrism of the sixth congress – a consequence of newly achieved independence – was fuelled by his awareness of the role which the independent state played in perpetuating the racist policies of the former colonial powers and in serving as a barrier to a more far-reaching regionalism or Pan-Africanism. This is particularly true since it was the winning of national independence which had resulted in the abortion of the West Indian federation experiment. It is perhaps for these reasons that James (1977c, 42) stressed that for the seventh Pan-

Africanist Congress, the state should no longer be seen as an idea of any significance:

> when you look at society today, you know that the national state, which began with the United States and the French revolution, is a total failure. The national state is no longer anything that can be looked upon as a political formation with any great significance. The bourgeoisie themselves are breaking up the national state.

Walter Rodney, like C.L.R. James, had understood the necessity of applying the concept of racism to the relationship between the black privileged classes and the poor black underclass in the Caribbean. Following his debarment from re-entry into Jamaica by the Hugh Shearer-led Jamaica Labour Party government, following his attendance of a Black writers Conference in Montreal in 1968, Rodney establishes clearly the basis for such an application of the concept of racism. He notes that his expulsion was, "not very surprising because though the composition of that Government... be predominantly black ... they are all white-hearted". He accused the leadership of serving the "interest of a foreign, white capitalist system" and of pursuing domestic policies which "uphold a social structure which ensures that the black man resides at the bottom of the social ladder. He is economically oppressed and culturally he has no opportunity to express himself" (Rodney 1969, 60).

The link between the racial exclusion of the black majority despite the reality of political independence, the complicity of the Caribbean ruling elite in this exclusion, the role of the globalized neo-colonial state in structurally sustaining racism, and the denial by the ruling elite of the possibilities of Pan-Africanism and the absence of domestic pro-black socio-economic policies, becomes evident in the anti-colonial thought of C.L.R. James. This multifaceted framework of James's arguments against racism, creates the basis for applying his approach to the politics of race in the Caribbean in the twenty-first century, despite the emergence of new issues which were not central, during James's lifetime.

Principal amongst these new issues, is the question of reparations for genocide and slavery (see Beckles 2013), for which there was no organized Caribbean movement at the time of James's writing. However, despite the fact that CARICOM has formally adopted the call for reparations as a legitimate demand to be placed before the European Community as a formal part of the international relations and development agenda, and has appointed a reparations committee under the Chairmanship of Hilary Beckles, reinforced by national reparations committees in each member state, a number of Jamesian concerns can be seen in the politics of reparations.

Just as James had warned of a black ruling elite controlling the pace of decolonization, then similarly, the official adoption of reparations by a post-colonial ruling elite has resulted in major differences between the ruling class and the underclass sections of civil society who had for decades spearheaded the call for reparations when the ruling class was silent or skeptical. Specifically, members of the Rastafari community who had long championed repatriation and reparation as compensation for slavery, have felt that the formalization of reparations has taken the process out of the hands of the underclass and placed it in the hands of state elites who have channelled the demands into formal policy assistance demands indistinguishable from the traditional aid dependency of the immediate post-independence period. This can be seen clearly, for example, in CARICOM's formal ten-point plan of reparation demands, which, in addition to requesting a formal apology and the facilitation of voluntary repatriation, have been framed around a demand for development assistance around cultural institutions, public health, illiteracy eradication, technology transfer and debt cancellation (CARICOM 2014). Many of these demands fit neatly in the policy-aid categories which had always defined Caribbean-European relations in the post-colonial period. As such, CARICOM reparation demands can be viewed as little more than a refashioning of the post-colonial appeals for 'special and differential treatment' which had previously defined Caribbean-European foreign relations in the aftermath of independence. Moreover, CARICOM's approach has ensured that any benefits from reparations would accrue to the state, and not the citizen, reinforcing the Jamesian suspicion of the power of state elites to hijack popular movements. In short, the wider populations have felt themselves cut off from the reparations movement and have little expectation of a direct benefit to themselves from the current effort, in a manner similar to what was experienced during the independence period.

This state-centric and 'ruling elite' policy agenda approach to reparations have given rise to sharp criticisms from the radical left. Accusing reparations and activists of 'playing footsie with capitalism', one writer Ajamu Nangwaya (2017, 2), has criticized the Caribbean reparations movement for not "putting capitalism on trial". Arguing that "reparations should be used to build people power in the region, ultimately to overthrow capitalism" (1), he argues that,

> today we are witnessing the unconscionable, but politically understandable behavior of the neocolonial states in the Caribbean Community (CARICOM), in divorcing their call for reparations from measures aimed at overthrowing capitalism into the cesspool of history. These member states of CARICOM are all committed to the implementation of social, economic and political policies that have enshrined capitalism in the region. They are interested in reparations as a way to deal with their balance of payment, budgetary and development challenges as seen in their call for debt cancellation, technology transfer and a formal apology and not statements of regret in the regional body's Ten Point Action Plan..." (Nangwaya 2017, 3–4).

To address these weaknesses, a Jamesian approach becomes necessary. Nangwaya (2017, 6), therefore proposes that the revolutionary forces in the Caribbean's reparations movement should "work with other progressive forces throughout society to establish a federated system of popular, democratic and horizontal assemblies of the oppressed". He suggests that these "assemblies would function as the direct democratic structures of political self-management that seek to approximate the communist self-organizing concept of the 'administration of things and not the governance of people'".

A fundamental Jamesian criterion for measuring the extent to which a state has succeeded in supplanting the racist ideology of the former colonizing power, was the extent to which the ruling middle-class had become genuine servants of the black masses. It was the failure of Eric Williams's PNM to undertake the kinds of anti-colonial and democratic transformations which James thought necessary and possible, which became a major source of his disagreement with Williams. In his examination of Eric Williams's Trinidad, James was confronted with the unwillingness by the leadership to subject themselves to the political guidance of the black majority (James 1984c). Instead, they pursued the business of government as the servants of the economically dominant classes, in many cases expatriate owners of capital.

James felt that one way in which the racialism of the former colonial power could be overcome was through the mass mobilization of the black population and through the middle class intelligentsia becoming, in Walter Rodney's (1969, 63) words, "the articulate voice of the black masses" and by "attaching themselves to the activity of the black masses". James (1984c, 129), however, observed of the Caribbean middle-class ruling elite that, "not one of them, even the professed communist Jagan, dares to take any such step. They tinker with the economy, they wear themselves out seeking grants, loans, and foreign investments which they encourage by granting fabulous advantages dignified by the name of pioneer status."

In contrast to his criticism of the Caribbean governing class, James was far more positive in his assessment of Julius Nyerere's Tanzania. The conscious and deliberate steps taken by Julius Nyerere to ensure that the independent Tanzanian state existed for the benefit of the Tanzanian peasants and workers account for the high esteem in which James held ujamaa, Nyerere's version of African socialism (James 1969, 140–41; James 1977b). Nyerere in the Arusha Declaration had, among other things, sought to ensure that workers and peasants constituted most members of the government. This, to James, was a repetition of Lenin's approach to the problems which he had encountered with the overthrown Tsarist state of Russia. Although the Tsarist state had been seized by the Bolsheviks, the personnel who manned the state apparatus under the old regime, had basically remained unaltered (James 1977b). Moreover, according to James, a new state can only be created by a new class and, in the case of Russia, no new class had emerged to control the state. It was a dilemma faced by all young revolutions and newly independent states, and James felt that Nyerere's response had been most far-reaching in addressing this challenge. According to James (1969, 140–41),

> it would be a great mistake not to make clear how closely this profoundly creative response to African reality corresponds with and indeed carries further the highest stages so far reached by Western political thought... It is sufficient to know that Dr. Nyerere has seen through the reactionary, bureaucratic colonialist state which he inherited, and has gone further than anyone in the determination to break it up and make a new type of state.

In the twenty-first century Caribbean, racialism is most clearly apparent in the workings of the Caribbean economy. The problem has become even more pronounced with the retreat of global social-democratic projects and the subsequent rise of neo-liberal ideology as the dominant economic model. Neo-liberalism has made it difficult for the independent state to undertake protective interventionist responses on behalf of the poor and vulnerable, on grounds of racial equity, or even in pursuit of advantages for local capitalist development (see Joseph 2011). More importantly however, this shift to neo-liberalism has meant that the very class and racial groups which had enjoyed economic and social power before independence, have been facilitated in the consolidation of their privileges by external agencies which override the decision-making power of nominally independent states. In short, neo-liberalism has facilitated and deepened the problems of economic inequality and racial exclusion, despite the attainment of formal independence in the 1960s and 1970s.

From the early 1990s, there was a growing realization that the problem of racial inequality remained an unresolved problem of the Caribbean independence project. Linden Lewis (1990, 35) observed in the case of Barbados that "when the cases are examined it is black Barbadians and black Barbadians only who are not as integrated into the structures of accumulation and privilege as other racial or ethnic groups in this country". He argued that "such a situation does not occur by chance", but "it is rooted in a long process of institutional racism".

This reality represented the crux of the discussion of Caribbean racism in the 1990s. In the early 1990s, when Hilary Beckles (1992) launched the movement for economic democratization in Barbados, he did so by arguing that Caribbean racism had historically manifested itself in social, political and economic terms. According to his logic, the struggle against Caribbean racism has concentrated firstly, from the period of early colonialism to 1838 at the social level, and secondly, between the years 1838 to the 1930s at the political level. Correspondingly, in the post-1930 period, with the achievement of the universal franchise and the establishment of independence, the struggle for equality in the Caribbean needed to consciously address the economic enfranchisement of the black population. Beckles (1991, 15) argued that "democracy cannot make any sense... unless it is described as economic democracy", and that the time had come "to address the question of who controls and owns the economic resources of our societies".

By the third decade of the twenty-first century, the questions of racism and racial exclusion had gained new momentum largely on account of the global movement associated with Black Lives Matter. This has introduced a new qualitative reality in terms of the possibilities of Caribbean progress in addressing the historical legacies of racism and racial exclusion. Similarly, the meaning and practice of Pan-Africanism holds far greater potential for Caribbean development in the twenty-first century than it did in the twentieth. While in the twentieth century the value of Pan-Africanism to the Caribbean resided largely in its utility as a global African 'solidarity' movement that created space for the self-determination of African and Caribbean states, in the twenty-first century after several decades of independence, Pan-Africanism presents the potential for Caribbean economic development through state-to-state cooperation between the two regions. In addition, the further formalization of the African Union as a modern regional system, and the designation of the diaspora as a specific region within the AU, has meant greater possibilities for Caribbean-African cooperation and mutual development than in earlier moments.

The first sitting of the AU-CARICOM Heads of Government Summit on September 7, 2021 (CARICOM 2021), and the ongoing efforts by the government of Barbados under the leadership of Mia Mottley since 2018 to forge relationships with African states such as Ghana and Kenya (Alleyne 2021; see also *Saturday Sun* June 11, 2022) suggest that important steps are being taken to capitalize on the possibilities which exist. The potential danger however, in these new state-to-state emphases in the twenty-first century, is the transformation of Pan-Africanism into a statist, elitist, top-down opportunistic adventure, devoid of any bottom-up emphasis and separate from the organic pan-Africanist aspirations of Caribbean and African peoples.

Despite these potential challenges, the new directions in Africa-Caribbean relations and the new post-independence potential for Africa and Caribbean participation in the global economy, suggest that James's emphasis on Pan-Africanism, was not an ideological abstraction, but holds real potential for Caribbean development in the twenty-first century.

Socialism, Democracy, Decolonization and Racial Equity: The Jamesian Legacy and the 21st Century Caribbean

What then, is the lasting impact of James's theoretical and practical interventions into the questions of racism, anti-colonial liberation and Pan-Africanism for Caribbean politics in the twenty-first century?

The main lesson which can be gleaned from James's treatment of the race question is that none of the fundamental conflicts existing within Caribbean society can be treated in isolation or divorced from the larger movement towards the establishment of socialism. It is for this reason that James, far from viewing the emergence of race consciousness and the demand for racial equality as an impediment, saw it as being central to the attainment of socialism. The converse also holds true. From the Jamesian perspective, socialism cannot be said to have been truly attained while there continues to exist social divisions on the basis of race. An updated application of James's perspective to the politics of the twenty-first century Caribbean, therefore, requires a synthesis of his understanding of the race question to issues of democracy, socialism and Caribbean development.

This merging of all elements of the struggle against neo-colonial capitalist existence was witnessed in the early 1990s in Barbados when the aforementioned demand for economic enfranchisement, economic empowerment and economic democracy became a central focus of political discourse in the country. As has been shown in chapter three, genuine economic equality necessarily means, and is the only basis upon which a genuine participatory democracy can be established. This fact is clearly appreciated by Neville Duncan (in Beckles 1989) who, in explaining the re-emergence of the race discourse in the Caribbean, contextualized it within the wider framework of the peculiarities of Caribbean decolonization and the movement for democracy and economic equality in the 1990s. His analysis neatly captures the thrust of C.L.R. James's thought discussed in this work. According to Duncan (in Beckles 1989, xiv–xvi),

> our leaders still blindly invoke a notion of democracy which asks people to trust them to provide the answers for all the burning questions of this age... Some continue to maintain a division between the political and economic and restrict by a variety of laws and "hallowed" practices democracy to the political sphere.

He argued further that,

wealth in Barbados was divided up in a condition of great inequality in slavery and maintained throughout the period of colonialism. Independence for Caribbean states represented a transfer of authority in governance but the power of economic wealth and control was maintained by the old oligarchies. Justice has yet to be attained here ... It is the identification of black against white but this is only an accident of history and not an inherent evil...; Nevertheless there can be no evil at all in a people asserting its racial identification based upon an understanding of its disadvantages and beginning to demand, what we should all desire, democracy - the right to participate meaningfully in all the processes vitally affecting the quality of one's life (in Beckles 1989, xiv–xvi).

It is accurate to say the emergence of Black Lives Matter, and the rise of a global political movement and consciousness against racism and racial discrimination in the twenty-first century, has created a context far richer in possibilities for liberation and for achieving the economic enfranchisement demanded in the Caribbean in the 1990s. James's work, as seen in the *Black Jacobins* and in his work in Pan-African organizations between the wars, aimed at African decolonization, was always premised on the notion that global revolutions and global crises would create space for specific liberation movements in the colonized world. There is little doubt that had James witnessed the Black Lives Matter movement, he would have employed his analysis of the Haitian revolution and the history of Pan-African revolt to show how new spaces for Caribbean liberation could be opened by the global anti-racism movement.

Just as in the mid-twentieth century, the wider movement for Caribbean democracy and socialism in the twenty-first, must of necessity, be pursued with the incorporation of the movement against racism, neo-colonialism and imperialism. In the twenty-first century, there are various factors that point to fundamental contradictions within Caribbean society: the experiences of economic marginalization of the black population, the continued domination of Caribbean economies by external interests (as a result of the global hegemony of neo-liberal capitalism), the absence of a genuine and deeply-rooted popular democracy, and the powerlessness and inability of the majority of the population to influence policy decisions. These continue to present a basis for the pursuit of a radical Jamesian response. These contradictions are not separate and mutually exclusive. They require a broad, all-embracing theoretical perspective in order to develop practical mechanisms through which solutions can be derived. Given the theoretical themes and practical activities which occupied the life of C.L.R. James, his relevance to the development of a radical perspective to meet the challenges of the twenty-first century Caribbean, remains beyond question.

The final chapter provides a broad summation of the main political developments impacting upon the Caribbean in the twenty-first century, and closes with a re-iteration of James's relevance to understanding and resolving these issues.

6.

James and the 21st Century Caribbean: Application and Relevance

That there is a crisis probably does not require demonstration. Crisis has become the tedious cliché with which we flaunt our hard-pressed modernity. From the very inception of the idea of modernity, we have portrayed ourselves in the vivid terms of crisis: the crisis of the modern state, the crisis of liberal institutions, the crisis of leadership, the crisis of party government, and the crisis of democracy. These phrases seem so banal only because the realities to which they point are so familiar.

Benjamin Barber – Strong Democracy

The disenchantment with government cuts across national boundaries and ideological lines. It is prevalent in communist as in democratic societies, as common in white as in non-white countries. This disenchantment may well be the most profound discontinuity in the world around us.

Peter Drucker – The Age of Discontinuity

From the 1990s to 2000s: Global Change and Caribbean Politics

There is little doubt that the decades since the onset of the twenty-first century have presented the most severe and testing challenges for Caribbean development since the long independence decade (1960 to 1980). The pervasive sense of crisis – seen in the growing ineffectualness of government; the increasing obsolescence of the sovereign nation-state as a vehicle for anti-systemic politics; the perceived illegitimacy of government by the governed; and the mounting sense of powerlessness by populations whose appetites for civic participation have been whetted by increased levels of education, greater access to information, and changing perceptions of the individual in relation to government – can be accounted for in one all-encompassing explanation: the inability of existing governmental institutions to perform the tasks to which they had hitherto been well-suited. The period since the late 1990s has been largely characterized by significant transformation and contradiction, at the global level, and these transformations have been having a profound impact on Caribbean political life.

The relevance of C.L.R. James's political thought to the realities of twenty-first century Caribbean politics can be analysed against this reality of the growing contradictions between the structures of governmental institutions and the functions which they are designed to perform. James's focus on the perpetual transformation of 'content', which demands in turn a corresponding alteration of the political form, makes his thought particularly suited to the analysis of contemporary politics.

The first and most significant of these global transformations, has been the disintegration of the Soviet Union and the collapse of communism in its Eastern European satellites. The factors which precipitated the collapse provide the clearest instance of a conscious and deliberate attempt by a government to transform twentieth century political institutions to correspond to the democratic aspirations of the governed. It is instructive that in Mikhail Gorbachev's (1988) view, the need to transform the Soviet Union's political system was governed by the realization that truly socialist development was impossible without the active participation of the mass of the population (Gorbachev 1988, 83). He felt that a political system which facilitated the participation of a disproportionately narrow clique, could not effectively meet the needs of the increasingly alienated and disillusioned Soviet population. It should be noted however, that despite claiming responsibility for transforming Russia's institutions, Gorbachev's motives have been questioned by several political analysts. He was accused of double standards since, while he advocated the democratization of soviet society, his commitment to vanguardist notions of political action, as seen in his "revolution from above" approach to *glasnost* and *perestroika*, remained basically unshaken. Aurel Braun and Richard B. Day (1990, 37) for example, suggest that Gorbachev's approach to reform, particularly in his early years in office "reflected the disdain for the soviet people long associated with the vanguard party created by Lenin and Stalin". They argue that when Gorbachev launched his reform program, he had hoped that the "newly elected local soviet would substitute for the decrepit machinery of party control". However, Gorbachev's frustration with government from below quickly became apparent when he,

> complained that the local officials were too busy with political 'meetings' to assume control over concrete affairs. The new people, he contended were not skilled in politics or in practical work. When they were not debating philosophy or procedures, they were deciding issues 'as if they were the supreme soviet of the USSR' (Braun and Day 1990, 40).

Despite these observations, the fact of the overriding historical necessity of the transformations which Gorbachev had advocated, cannot be escaped. The problem was with the anti-socialist manner and consequences of the reforms, and not in the necessity for reforms.

Whatever his motives, Gorbachev's pursuit of glasnost and perestroika confirmed C.L.R. James's long-standing arguments against vanguardism and the Stalinist state and validated his call for 'free-creative activity' as the 'other' of Stalinism. In making a case for his reforms, Gorbachev admitted openly that he had "come to the conclusion that unless we activate the human factor, that is, unless we take into consideration the diverse interests of people, work collectives, public bodies, and various social groups, unless we can rely on them, and draw them into active constructive endeavour, it will be impossible for us to accomplish any of the tasks set, or to change the situation in the country" (Gorbachev 1988, 15). He also claimed appreciation for Lenin's 'remarkable' formula that "socialism is the living creativity of the masses". Gorbachev asserted that "socialism is not an *apriori* theoretical scheme, in keeping with which society is divided up into two groups: those who give instructions and those who follow them" and claimed to be "very much against such a simplified and mechanical understanding of socialism" (15).

What is significant about the collapse of Eastern European communism for the twenty-first century Caribbean however, is not the uniqueness of the events, but their necessity. In the period of the collapse, much of the analysis in the Caribbean focused around questions of the "crisis of the Left" (Mars 1998), or around the implications for development arising from the end of the Cold War, the exhaustion of non-alignment, and the rise of a unipolar world. However, a Jamesian analysis demands an alternative focus. From a Jamesian perspective, the events should not be viewed in the unidimensional sense of a popular rejection of 'communism' but should be better understood as fulfilling the aspirations of popular democracy. When perceived in this way, it becomes clear that Western capitalist society and Caribbean society have not been immunized from similar demands for openness, or for deeper levels of democracy and restructuring. On the contrary, the factors which influenced the movement for democracy in Eastern Europe, have impacted equally powerfully in the advanced capitalist centres of the West.

Far from viewing the collapse of socialism as representative of a "democratic" problem for communist states only, Western writers, such as Alvin Toffler (1981, [1970] 1990) and Osborne and Gaebler (1993), often working within "management" perspectives, had observed that in the 1990s, advanced capitalist societies, were also undergoing democratic stresses, and that governmental apparatuses were proving increasingly unworkable. Alvin Toffler

(1981) in *The Third Wave*, advanced the view that the challenges to governmental institutions was not a country-specific phenomenon but was a consequence of the transformation of industrial modes of production into post-industrial modes. In his view, the post-industrial mode transcended the limits of smoke-stack, assembly line, fossil-fuel, hierarchical division-of-labour type modes of production. Very dialectical and materialistic in his analysis, Toffler (1981, 413) argues that as the material transformations continue to become more fast-paced and complex, "all leaders become dependent on increasing numbers of people for help in making and implementing decisions". He argues that the "more powerful the tools at a leader's command – supersonic fighters, nuclear weapons, computers, telecommunications – the more, not less dependent the leader becomes". Arguing that "our institutions are reeling from a decisional implosion", he suggests that "too many decisions, too fast, about too many strange and unfamiliar problems – not some imagined 'lack of leadership' – explain the gross incompetence of political and governmental decisions today" (Toffler 1981, 420–21).

It is in a similar vein that Osborne and Gaebler (1993) regarded the bureaucratic inertia which they felt were characteristic features of both socialist and capitalist states at the end of the twentieth century. They argued that the

> kind of governments that developed during the industrial era, with their sluggish, centralised bureaucracies, their preoccupation with rules and regulations, and their hierarchical chains of command, no longer work very well. They accomplished great things in their time, but somewhere along the line they got away from us. They became bloated, wasteful, ineffective. And when the world began to change, they failed to change with it. Hierarchical, centralised bureaucracies designed in the 1930s and 1940s simply do not function well in the rapidly changing, information-rich, knowledge-intensive society and economy of the 1990s. They are like luxury ocean liners in an age of supersonic jets: big, cumbersome, expensive, and extremely difficult to turn around. Gradually, new kinds of public institutions are taking their place (Osborne and Gaebler 1993, 11–12).

It is significant that Osborne and Gaebler spoke of the changes in management techniques occurring in the United States, in the hyperbolic, but justifiable terms of an "American Perestroika". What it suggested was that the collapse of communism was not a problem inherent to socialist ideology and practice, but was a consequence of shifts in the material infrastructure of global production relations, which were also impacting upon western capitalist bureaucratic systems.

However, these acknowledgements of the need for transformation of the western capitalist state, gave rise to a deeper post-colonial challenge for Caribbean democracies. This is because, what emerged in the wake of the collapse of global communism, was not a further democratization of the state to greater levels of popular control and economic democratization. Instead, the ideology of neo-liberalism and free market capitalism emerged as the triumphant world view, and externally imposed the imperative of 'capitalist adjustment' on Caribbean states.

Thus, in the wake of the crisis of the collapse of communism during the period from the late 1990s to early 2000s, despite the evidence of corresponding crises in the capitalist economies, the Caribbean was confronted with a new and immediate crisis of neo-liberal adjustment. This neo-liberal adjustment was presented, not as a response to a crisis of capitalism, but as a 'corrective' to social-democratic state-centrism in the Caribbean. This was most clearly discerned in the emphasis on 'small government' and in the universal drive towards 'privatization', and in the attempts at limiting the role of the state in the economy and society. The implications of this development for Caribbean democracy and economic development were captured by C.Y. Thomas (1989) who pointed to the related danger of the embryonic recolonization of the Caribbean by market forces, under the guise of state failure. According to Thomas,

> in the period leading up to political independence... and indeed immediately thereafter, there was widespread acknowledgement of "market failure" under the previous colonial system. This gave

support to those views which saw development as impossible without the state becoming the leading force... Since then, the crisis has engendered among these classes the view that "political failure" of the state-led process is so complete that the only solution is the unconditional embrace of market forces. Development is only possible if there is a leading role for the private sector. Similar developments abroad in the U.S.A. and Britain in particular, and recently reinforced by popular interpretations which present "perestroika" as proof of state political failure in the developmental process, have given this outlook unprecedented legitimacy (Thomas 1989, 39–40).

This marked the beginning of the rise and hegemony of neo-liberal ideology in the Caribbean, and though it reflected, in a broad sense, the Jamesian expectation of the 'obsolescence' of the bureaucratic capitalist state form, neo-liberalism did not allow for the corresponding emergence of popular control and economic empowerment of workers in new production-related organized forms as James had anticipated. Instead, from the late 1980s into the early 2000s, neo-liberalism promoted the freedom of the market, and the freedom of the rich, to escape popular control and distribution of wealth and economic power. This has remained the defining feature of the politics of the English-speaking Caribbean, into the third and fourth decades of the twenty-first century.

The proliferation of this 'dominant outlook' of neo-liberalism on a global scale has been facilitated by the removal of the more autonomous and independent developmental alternatives, presented by the existence of a 'socialist bloc' which provided a certain degree of social and political space, within which weaker countries could pursue 'developmental' objectives.[1] The period following the emergence of the USA as a unipolar power, saw the interests of the US and other Western capitalist states vigorously pursued by organizations such as the IMF, the International Bank for Reconstruction and Development (World Bank), and the General Agreements on Tariffs and Trade (GATT), now the World Trade Organization (WTO). The standard prescription of these entities has imposed upon the Caribbean, after each adjustment, the "familiar package: deregulation (that is removal of price controls), subsidies, exchange controls and import licensing, devaluation of the currency; emphasis on the development of the private sector as a corrective to the 'inefficient' statist bias of the previous period; a reduced public sector; strict fiscal goals to be set in terms of the size of the government's deficit and the amount of borrowing permitted from the banking system; and wage controls" (C.Y. Thomas (1988, 225–26). Similarly, the main objectives of the GATT and WTO were designed to further entrench capitalist norms and values, and to secure the continued domination of the United States and other territories of the core over the periphery, prompting Raghavan (1990, 40), to describe these organizations as institutions of re-colonization.

In the third decade of the twenty-first century however, it can be safely asserted that the neo-liberal turn in the Caribbean has not been met with economic or political success. Indeed, if the decade of the 1990s marked the crisis of communism, it is safe to argue that the decade of the 2000s, particularly since the 2008 financial crisis, marked the beginning of the crisis of global neo-liberalism.

Following 2008, there was a definitive shift in the global narrative surrounding neo-liberalism. Sparked by a crisis in the financial sector arising out of the deregulation of banks and financial institutions which first manifested itself as a "sub-prime mortgage crisis" in the USA, the crisis resulted in the closure of a number of leading financial institutions and a near-collapse of the US financial system. Significantly, many of the ideologues who had been leading the chorus around the triumph of capitalism, following the collapse of communism, suddenly found themselves having to temper their earlier optimism.

A classic example of this rethinking of triumphant neo-liberalism can be seen in the work of Francis Fukuyama (1992), who, in his *End of History and the Last Man*, had celebrated the fall of communism with his over-optimistic assertion that western liberal democracy had represented the final stage of man's political evolution. He had claimed famously that as mankind was approaching the end of the millennium "the twin crises of authoritarianism and socialist central planning have left only one competitor standing in the ring as an ideology of potentially universal validity: liberal democracy, the doctrine of individual freedom and popular sovereignty" (Fukuyama 1992, 42). In celebrating the market freedoms associated with liberalism Fukuyama insisted that what was emerging as victorious was "not so much liberal practice, as the liberal idea" (45). Relatedly, he identified possibilities for global peace and prosperity, in what he perceived as the universalizing of liberal democratic practice. In his view, "liberal democracy replaces the irrational desire to be recognized as greater than others with a rational desire to be recognized as equal. A world made up of liberal democracies, then, should have much less incentive for war, since all nations would reciprocally recognize one another's legitimacy" (Fukuyama 1992, xx). (How quaint all of this sounds in the context of the Russia-Ukraine war of February 2022). Perhaps most euphoric of all was his assertion that the world was possibly witnessing "the end point of mankind's ideological evolution and the universalization of western liberal democracy as the final form of human government" (Fukuyama (2000, 162).

However, shocked by the scale and rapidity of the crisis which gripped the global capitalist economy following 2008, Fukuyama, dramatically reversed himself as reported in an article in the New Statesman of September 17, 2018 (in Woods 2018). In a more sober reflection on the failure of deregulation and neo-liberalism, he admitted that the period of neo-liberalism "which started with Reagan and Thatcher, in which a certain set of ideas about the benefits of unregulated markets took hold, in many ways had a disastrous effect". He recognized that the period "led to a weakening of labour unions, of the bargaining power of ordinary workers" and facilitated the "rise of an oligarchic class almost everywhere that then exerts undue political power" (in Woods 2018). In response to all of this, Woods (2018) reaches a conclusion on the future of capitalism, which, Fukuyama, despite his admission of error, studiously avoided. According to Woods, "the political and social ferment that is shaking the whole world to its foundations is only a symptom of a far deeper crisis: not the crisis of neoliberalism, which is only a particular form of capitalism, but a terminal crisis of the capitalist system itself". In his view the "crisis is destined to last for quite some time. On the basis of capitalism, there is no solution to it. Governments will rise and fall and the pendulums will swing from left to right, and from right to left, reflecting an increasingly desperate search of the masses to find a way out of the crisis".

Similarly, the crisis of neo-liberalism led Joseph Stiglitz (2019) to argue that "as we face a retreat from the rules-based, liberal global order, with autocratic rulers and demagogues leading countries that contain well over half the world's population, Fukuyama's idea seems quaint and naïve". He noted specifically the power of finance capital to subvert the sovereignty of weak states as one of the consequences of runaway neo-liberalism which Fukuyama had not taken into account. According to Stiglitz, "the effects of capital-market liberalization were particularly odious: if a leading presidential candidate in an emerging market lost favour with Wall Street, the banks would pull their money out of the country. Voters then faced a stark choice: give in to Wall Street or face a severe financial crisis. It was as if Wall Street had more political power than the country's citizens".

Likewise, the work of Samuel Huntington (1996), also provided indications of doubt in the confidence in the global liberal mission. In contrast to the expected "peace dividend" which Fukuyama had anticipated would result from the universal adoption of liberal ideology and practice, the emergence of Islamic religious fundamentalism as a political and military force capable of attacking the capitalist centre, meant that the post-Cold War world was more vulnerable to global instability than the period of the Cold War itself. Thus, instead of the homogenizing tendencies of economic rationality associated with liberal thinking, Huntington (2000, 3), by the end of the twentieth century was arguing that "the fundamental source of conflict in this new world will not be primarily ideological or primarily economic", but instead, "the great divisions among humankind and the dominating source of conflict will be cultural". In his view therefore, while nation states would remain the most powerful global actors, "the principal conflicts of global politics will occur between nations and groups of different civilizations. The clash of civilizations will dominate global politics. The fault lines between civilizations will be the battle lines of the future". Thus, the notion of a "clash of civilizations" represented a far more pessimistic rendering of the future of the capitalist world than the one imagined at the end of the 1980s.

Intersecting between periods of temporary recovery and decline, since 2008, the crisis of global neo-liberalism has reflected itself in internal political stresses within the major capitalist centres. As is typical when crises set in, one of the major symptoms, appears to be the collapse of elite consensus on the future response. In the third decade of the twenty-first century there is a glaring absence of a universal commitment among the ruling class to sustain and defend global neo-liberalism along singularly accepted ideological and practical lines.

In the USA, the tensions associated with the crisis of neo-liberalism have resulted largely in the return of right wing neo-fascist nationalism which came to a head with the election of Donald Trump as US President in 2016, and the rise in tensions over long-standing issues of racial discrimination. These contradictions resulted in the most overt domestic threat to the US political system, when hundreds of protestors stormed the Capitol building on January 6, 2021 to block the official certification by the Congress of the 2020 election which saw the defeat of Donald Trump by Joseph Biden. The uprising resulted in deaths, injury, and hundreds of arrests, and more importantly, exacerbated the divisions in American society and revealed clear evidence of the collapse of elite consensus around American democratic institutions and values. These protests were occurring in an atmosphere of BLM and other civil society protests over the killing of black persons, as well as a sharp slowing down in US economic activity arising out of a year-long COVID-19 global pandemic.

Of further significance, is the fact that the election of Donald Trump had promised to reverse post-war attempts at global economic integration, and multi-lateral neo-liberal institution building in which the US had played a leading role. In sharp contradistinction to the US's post-war global engagement, Trump signaled a return to American nationalism and domestic economic self-interest, proposing to undo decades of US institutional leadership in areas as diverse as military alliances in NATO, trade alliances in the Trans-Atlantic Trade and Investment Partnership, and global environmental cooperation (The Paris Accord). Taken together, these developments suggested that elite consensus around the pursuit of global neo-liberal values had collapsed. Despite the attempts by Biden to restore the US to its previous role of US global neo-liberal leadership, the events in the third decade of the twenty-first century suggests that the future global role of the US, and its internal liberal values remain contested issues among the governing elite.

This collapse of elite consensus in the capitalist North can also be seen in the renewed popularity of the idea of socialism in the advanced capitalist countries seen most vividly in the electoral campaigns of Senator Bernie Sanders of the United States and Jeremy Corbyn of the British Labour Party in the UK. While the electoral strategies of Sanders and Corbyn might have ended in failure with Bernie Sanders suspending his Presidential campaign "four days after Jeremy Corbyn's tenure as Labour Leader ended" (Jones 2020), the fact of their popular movements themselves, their large bases of support among the youthful population, and their ability to place at the centre of political discourse perspectives and approaches which had been viewed as "passe" after 1990, were important features of the new global environment influencing the possible expressions of future socialist alternatives, and providing further evidence of the collapse of elite consensus in the advanced capitalist countries on the future of global capitalism. As one writer has concluded in 2020,

> Yes, the British and US new left have failed to achieve a lasting political leadership in their own parties, let alone assume state power; their activists are currently demoralised and exhausted. Both found a mass reception for their ideas after the left had spent a generation in the wilderness, meaning they lacked personnel with political experience, all while being undermined by entrenched hostility from their own parties. But on neither side of the Atlantic is the left going anywhere (Jones 2020).

Similar evidence of reversal in the post-war global neo-liberal order and of collapse of elite consensus in the liberal future, was seen in Britain's withdrawal and exit from the European Union (BREXIT) following a referendum in 2016. Similar to developments in the USA, BREXIT was an indication that global neo-liberalism with its ideological claims to equality, levelness of the playing field, the universality of free market values, the end of the nation-state, all claims which had gained prominence with the collapse of European communism, had entered a period of uncertainty. The mobilization of a large section of the British public by organized right wing groups and sections of the conservative party in the UK, to undo a critical part of the UK's post-war reorganization of the world economy, was further evidence that the triumphant neo-liberalism of the 1990s, had been replaced by pessimism. Instead, tendencies towards economic nationalism, xenophobia, anti-immigration, and a shift to neo-fascism and racism, began to define the domestic politics of erstwhile liberals. All of these developments suggested that the global neo-liberal order which it was assumed would have characterized the post-communist era had not materialized. Indeed, the condition of global capitalism can be said to be one of continuous crisis and flux. In short, the ideological self-confidence and hegemonic certainty exhibited by neo-liberalism at the time of the collapse of communism, had waned considerably by the third decade of the twenty-first century.

Finally, in addition to the internal crisis of neo-liberalism, the twenty-first century has witnessed the global consolidation of the communist regimes which survived the collapse of European communism and the emergence of new socialist states as well. This consolidation of socialist states stands in stark contrast to the dismal prognostications on the future of socialism when words like "death", "failure" and "end" dominated academic literature and mass media pertaining to descriptions of the future of Marxism and socialism. In this regard therefore, the rise of China as an alternative pole to the traditional dominance of western capitalism, is one of the most important features of the global political economy in the first three to four decades of the twenty-first century. Despite the mainstream views which seek to deny China as a socialist experience, China is openly led by a communist party and organizes its political life around Marxist-Leninism and Maoism. The significance of China resides in the fact that it has achieved what the Soviet Union failed to sustain: world-power status as a communist country.

On June 30, 2021, the Communist Party of China celebrated the hundredth anniversary of its founding. In his remarks to mark the occasion, Chinese President Li Jing Ping issued a stern warning that China would not accept "sanctimonious preaching from those who feel they have the right to lecture us", and insisted that "China would never allow any foreign force to bully it". He further warned that anyone attempting to do so would "find themselves on a collision course with a great wall of steel forged by over 1.4 billion people." He reminded his audience that while a "century ago China was declining and withering away in the eyes of the world," he made it clear that in the twenty-first century "the image it presents to the world is one of a thriving nation, that is advancing with unstoppable momentum toward rejuvenation" (in Cheng 2021). It is significant too, that the centennial of the founding of the Chinese Communist Party was occurring against the backdrop of China's successful landing of a probe on the planet Mars, positioning itself at the cutting age of space exploration

(Xiong and Escobedo 2021). In contrast to the dominant narratives surrounding the collapse of the Soviet Union, the rise of China provides a compelling counter-narrative and stands as a strong empirical case of the continuing presence of twentieth-century inspired models of non-western modes of state-capitalist but ideologically Marxist-Leninist modes of development.

Similarly, Cuba's survival of over fifty years of capitalist counter-revolution, in addition to the Latin American pink-tide revolutions most spectacularly witnessed in the Hugo Chavez-inspired Bolivarian revolution in Venezuela, in Bolivia under Evo Morales (2006–19), in Brazil under Inácio Lula (2003–10), in Argentina under Cristina Kirchner (2007–15), and in Nicaragua under a re-elected Daniel Ortega (since 2007), provide clear indications that notions of the 'death of socialism' were premature. While these "pink tide" revolutions have faced significant challenges, their very existence provide a sharp contrast to the immediate post-USSR period when the likelihood of state-led socialist projects, independent of the existence of the Soviet-Union was largely seen as improbable.

Yet however, there is little doubt that the internal contradictions which saw the collapse of the Soviet Union (as distinct from 'external capitalist destabilization'), remain critical issues confronting Cuba, Venezuela and China in the twenty-first century. James's warning against state-capitalism remains a critical tool of analysis for examining the future of development trajectories of these states, and for offering guidelines on how internal, mass-based participatory democracy can be developed and strengthened, beyond its formal liberal-democratic expression. Perhaps, Venezuela, despite the harsh economic challenges which it had faced because of sustained and concerted attacks on its economy, but with its continual and ongoing efforts at constitutional reform, popular assemblies alongside formal democratic elections, provides the closest example of an ongoing experiment which seeks to balance state-socialism with institutions of popular democratic expression from below, existing alongside formal liberal-democratic institutions.

The Caribbean Dimension: Face to Face with the Future

These global transformations, from the collapse of communism in the late twentieth century to the crisis of neo-liberalism in the twenty-first century, to the continuing fluctuations in fortune within state capitalist projects, have had a profound impact on the politics of the Caribbean. Their impact has been mostly seen in the imposition of neo-liberal norms and practices on the Caribbean state, and in the consequent resistance by Caribbean populations to the imposition of free market capitalism.

In the immediate aftermath of the collapse of communism the dominant concern by leaders and thinkers revolved around the impact of globalization on Caribbean post-colonial development options and the consequent crisis of the Caribbean state. The globalization of production, the roles played by multilateral organizations in negating the state's regulatory function in the economy, as well as the growing inability of the Caribbean state to satisfy the basic and traditional post-colonial social-democratic expectations of the population, were key issues confronting the Caribbean towards the end of the twentieth century.

Bgoya and Hyden (1987, 7), though addressing specifically the situation in Africa in the age of globalization, raised several issues which were of direct relevance to the situation confronting the Caribbean state. In their estimation, the crisis confronting the post-colonial state centered on its "role as (1) actor in the international arena – the sovereignty dimension – (2) determinant of power relations in society – the accountability dimension – and (3) execution of policy – the delivery dimension". They concluded that the "problematic condition affecting the... state with regard to these three dimensions is that as actor in the international arena it is besieged, in its relation to society it is set apart and as the executor of policy it is overloaded".

Indeed, by the late 1980s into the early 2000s, the Caribbean state was finding it increasingly difficult to maintain its sovereignty in the context of an international system in which domestic social and economic space was being occupied by transnational corporations and the internal decision-making power of governments was being eroded by multilateral institutions. The very validity of the term 'sovereignty' itself was being questioned (see Joseph 2011; see Lewis 2015). From the perspective of the ordinary Caribbean citizen, the crisis of the Caribbean state was most directly evident in the "delivery dimension". C.Y. Thomas (1989, 23) observed that "co-incident with the economic downturn" and a "decline in the fiscal capacity of several of these states... slow growth...led to falling revenues from traditional sources, while on the other, these states continue to face great social pressures to deliver basic goods". He observed that "when linked to the 'retreat' of the state in its role as guarantor and provider of basic needs", this confirmed and "reinforced the 'besieged' and beleaguered" nature of the globalized Caribbean state (Thomas 1989, 23). It should be noted too, that much of the reason for the decline in revenue from traditional sources was the liberalization of trade and the loss of traditional preferential arrangements in the UK market, which had a severe impact on rum and banana dependent economies in the Caribbean, as Joseph (2011) has shown in the case of the political economy of St. Lucia.

Significantly, the crisis of the Caribbean state and the emergent notions of 'state failure' reinforced, rather than undermined the thrust towards neo-liberal adjustment. It was within the context of the failure of the Caribbean state to deliver basic goods and services to its citizens that an ideological context that facilitated the privatization of government-owned enterprises and a general process of the retreat of the state, became dominant. This development was widely interpreted as a defeat of the Caribbean left and as a setback for the workers' movement, given the prevailing view that an interventionist state was synonymous with a workers' state or a 'progressive' state.

However, the application of a Jamesian perspective provides an alternative view to the question of the retreat of the state, and its possibilities for worker emancipation. While the ideology and practice of privatization has certainly opened spaces for the return of private capital ownership in areas previously occupied by the state, it is also true that nationalization had been utilized by several states in the defence and expansion of capital, rather than in the empowerment of labour. Mészáros (1987, 84–85) has noted for example that, "a great variety of 'hybrid' combinations – all possible permutations of the mystifying 'mixed economy' – are thoroughly compatible with the continued survival (even temporary revitalization) of private capitalism". To illustrate his argument, he points to the common practice of "fairly large scale 'nationalisation' of bankrupt industries which we have experienced in capitalist countries – frequently followed by the profitable practice of denationalisation in due course, after the imposition, that is, of the necessary, and by fragmented private capital unachievable, political/economic changes (with regard to trade union power, for instance)". The post-2008 nationalization of the US auto-industry by Presidents George Bush and Barrack Obama, and their 'cash for clunkers' scheme to shore up a collapsed auto-industry during the 2008 financial crisis, only to return them to private ownership once they had been rescued by taxpayers' money, is a clear example of the symbiosis between nationalization and the survival of capital (see The White House, n.d.).[2]

The Jamesian notion of state capitalism provides the perfect analytical tool for comprehending such political developments. While the application of James to the experience of neo-liberalism in the twenty-first century Caribbean will be treated more fully in the final section of this chapter, it can be noted here that James (1986b, 48), in describing Stalinist Russia as state capitalism, had argued that the "rulers of Russia perform the same functions as are performed by Ford, General Motors, the coal operators and the huge bureaucratic staffs". He had always insisted that while "Stalinist sociology rests on the theory that the conversion of private property into state property is the conversion of capitalism into socialism", in his view, the real "basis of socialism is the emancipation of the proletariat from enslavement to capital, that is, soviet power, the state power in the hands of the proletariat in its own proletarian organizations. This, and this alone constitutes socialism, a new society, and a new state, or a transition to a new society" (James 1986b, 28).[3]

This perspective raises important normative questions about how progressive, anti-systemic intellectuals and movements should view the state-capitalist or state-led anti-Western capitalist projects like China, Cuba and Venezuela, particularly in the context where these states constitute the few remaining formal state alternatives to Western capitalist approaches. What is critical however, is for socialist thinkers to offer solutions to the internal authoritarian and anti-democratic tendencies within such states, and to recognize the manner in which new modes of technology, new modes of social organization and global connectivity, as well as transformations within global capitalism itself, can open spaces for previously inaccessible tools for democratic and economic participation by the mass of the populations in relation to their own states, while at the same time preserving their anti-Western capitalist character. The development of internal democratic practices, inclusive of and beyond liberal democratic forms in such states, would open up further spaces for the pursuit of post-Soviet socialist alternatives in the Caribbean by offering concrete examples of what is possible.

In addition to the major examples of state-led anti-western capitalist alternatives, the other major response to the crisis of the Caribbean state, in the context of its failure within the 'delivery dimension' has been a discourse and practice around 'civil society' as an instrument of democratic governance and as an alternative centre for delivering goods and services to Caribbean citizens in the late 1990s and beyond. Alongside, and in symbiosis with this development, has been the emergence of various 'survival strategies' by Caribbean persons who have generally accepted the limitations of the state in delivering basic goods and services, and have turned towards new modes of economic self-reliance.

A researcher on civil society organizations in the Caribbean has noted that "the resilience of Caribbean people and the somewhat unlikely viability of the states they occupy has been supported in no small part by myriad organizations that fill social, economic and political gaps that have been left vacant by formal politics and the state apparatus" (Hinds 2019, 1).

It should be noted however, that this development has served to further compound the crisis of the state since the legitimacy of the post-colonial Caribbean state was hinged upon its ability to provide basic goods and services necessary for social existence. While the burden of this expectation was never shouldered by the colonial state, for the post-colonial Caribbean state, however, a "basic pillar of state legitimation" has been its ability to "command a significant resource base which facilitates the patron-client distributive ethic" (Riviere 1990, 83–84).

The reduced capacity of the Caribbean state to shoulder the social burden, in addition to the high levels of support for NGOs and non-state actors by neo-liberal multilateral institutions, largely explains the rise in prominence of civil society bodies to fill the vacuum created by the retreat of the state in the 1990s Caribbean. At the time when this phenomenon was in its most overt phase of actualization, Ghai and Hewitt de Alcantara (1989, 36) had offered a very optimistic outlook for democratic development. In their view, the crisis of the state would "encourage changes in social organisation and political practice" which would in turn facilitate the emergence of "a more participatory society in nations where exclusion for many groups has long been the rule". They had also anticipated that the economic and social challenges associated with neo-liberal adjustment would "lend momentum to other kinds of family and neighborhood co-operation which go beyond simple 'survival strategies' and create centres of dialogue and mutual assistance within an inchoate civil society". They also celebrated the fact that while many community organizations tend to be affiliated to various political parties, "the majority seem to prefer political independence and to exhibit noteworthy skepticism toward the established political structure" (Ghai and Hewitt de Alcantara 1989, 37).

A similar view was held by Kathy McAfee (1991) in the wake of the structural adjustment programs which were being aggressively pursued in the late 1980s. In her work *Storm Signals*, she argued that Caribbean NGOs and popular organizations were "creating the basis for a form of democracy more meaningful and profound than that reflected in European and U.S.-style elections". Defining democracy as "the opportunity for individuals and the communities to have a significant degree of control over decisions that affect their lives particularly decisions about the allocation of resources", she suggests that such a form of "democracy depends upon the guarantee of civil liberties and of the freedom to form organisations without harassment, and to act in an organised manner to affect the political policies and change economic conditions" (McAfee 1991, 208). This is as precise a definition of C.L.R. James's 'free creative activity' as can be found.

However, later developments have given rise to more sober, and more pessimistic analyses of the impact of NGOS on Caribbean democracy. Far from being the door to a new age of popular democratic participation, there were clear indications that much of the supportive narrative for the rise of NGOs in the Caribbean, was being spurred by neo-liberals who wished to undermine the Caribbean state. In other words, the support for NGOs was seen, not so much as a means of supporting new forms of popular empowerment, but as a way of weakening the sovereignty of the state, to make Caribbean society more vulnerable to the control of external political and market forces. Indeed, the clearest case of this process of *NGOisation* was seen in Haiti, prior to and particularly following the devastating earthquake in 2010. One report claimed that, "estimates of the number of nongovernmental organizations (NGOs) operating in Haiti prior to the earthquake range from 3,000 to as many as 10,000" (Kristoff and Panarelli 2010). The situation in Haiti gave rise to several publications which suggested that NGOs represented a new form of neo-colonial control, as identified by Kristoff and Panarelli (2010) denying Haitian citizens control over decision making in their own lives, and effectively undermining the sovereign government.

It is significant to note that the earlier support for NGOs as models of democratic governance which were championed by the main global agencies of free market capitalism, was quickly reversed in a particular historical moment when civil society organizations rejected the efforts by the OECD and G7 countries to establish a Multilateral Agreement on Investments (MAI). Buoyed by the success of the WTO and the IMF and other multilateral agencies in facilitating the entrenchment of private capital norms in various national theatres, the OECD vigorously pursued the MAI between 1995 and 1998 with the goal of establishing a global rules-based system which would allow corporations the unconditional rights to engage in financial operations around the world, while removing the ability of sovereign states to constrain their activity through domestic economic policies and legislative regulations. It was following the successful opposition by civil society bodies to the MAI, that there appeared to be a shift in the discourse against NGOs, and the reassertion that "ultimate responsibility for concluding binding rules must rest with governments as the only legitimate and accountable representatives of their populations" (Muchlinski 2000, 1950). In short, in the eyes of the agents of private capital, NGOs are useful as 'democratic' institutions when they facilitate private capital, but they are impediments to democracy, when they do not. Despite abandoning the negotiations on the MAI in 1998, the G7 in 2021 was able to get agreement on a "global minimum tax rate" of 15 per cent on corporations, representing a direct form of global control into the taxation policies of sovereign states, and in particular, the ability of states to determine their own internal financial policy responses towards multinational corporations (see Rappeport 2021).

None of these tensions and transformations in the political superstructure, and their impact on Caribbean society and politics in the later twentieth and early twenty-first century, can be understood without considering the transformations occurring within the economic infrastructure. C.Y. Thomas (1989, 25) described the transformations occurring in the global political economy as a "second industrial revolution" and saw the crisis in the late twentieth century as being "fuelled by fundamental changes in the global division of labour". Significantly, from as early as the mid-1960s, activists associated with C.L.R. James, had been pointing to transformations in the production processes of capital and had been anticipating that these transformations would have had implications for human relations, democracy, and political society in the years to come. For example, James Boggs (1968, 46) (the husband of James's associate Grace Lee Boggs), in an analysis of the industrial transformations occurring in the United States in the 1960s, had argued that,

> many people in the U.S. are aware that, with automation, enough could be easily produced... so that there would be no need for the majority of Americans to work. But the right to live has always been so tied up with the necessity to produce that it is hard for the average person to visualise a workless society... Within a few years, man as a productive force will be as obsolete as the mule.

In the third decade of the twenty-first century, with a far greater use of technology in production than James had described, and with less reliance on humans for production given the rise of robotics and the "second machine age", (see Sprague and Sathi 2020, 50) there is even greater pressure for new modes of distribution which separate the right to live from the necessity of work. At the same time however, the moment has given rise to staggering new levels of worker exploitation as seen, for example, in the Amazon global distribution network (see Alimahomed-Wilson and Reese 2020).

Underlying and accompanying these developments are the irreversible material and organic transformations in the planet itself due to the over-exploitation of the earth's finite resources by capitalism. These developments have brought the question of climate change and the global environmental and health crises at the centre of global political discourse and have raised issues which are central to the future survival of capitalism, the necessity for a future socialist alternative, and indeed for the economic and physical survival of the Caribbean itself. These issues have raised new dimensions in Caribbean global and domestic politics in which new 'development questions' are now embroiled with questions of material survival and the limits to capitalist exploitation, and the balance that should be placed between protecting local patrimony, ensuring local access to Caribbean resources, local democratic control over livelihoods and traditionally accessible resources and practices, all enmeshed in the broader discourse on 'sustainable development'. Surviving hurricanes, earthquakes, floods and volcanic eruptions, and ensuring economic recovery and sustainable development in the face of these natural disasters now occupy the attention of Caribbean policy-makers at the level of their "international relations" (See C. Gonsalves 2019), but the domestic self-organised grass-roots intervention into these questions have only begun to take embryonic form in the Caribbean. The cases of the anti-DSH mass protests in St. Lucia during the Allen Chastanet prime ministership period, the anti-Sandals protests in Tobago, and the "save our beaches", access protests in Jamaica discussed earlier in this work, provide indications of the kinds of popular struggles which are likely to intensify and perhaps adopt new forms as the contradictions inherent in climate change and sustainable development become more entrenched and deeply rooted.

Similarly, in terms of the epoch-altering shifts in the material base of capitalism, perhaps the most directly impactful, has been the emergence of the COVID-19 pandemic of 2020 and 2021. COVID-19 moved from a public health challenge "into an unparalleled economic crisis, forcing governments around the world to take action to reduce the spread of the virus and its economic impacts" (Allen, Jenkins and Howard 2020). One of the main consequences of the crisis of COVID-19 was that it imposed the necessity of new modes and relations of work, with a greater burden being placed on workers to 'work from home' and to transfer much of the traditional costs of production from the employer to the worker. Equally significant is the fact that the crisis has re-opened important questions about the role of the state in the provision of social services like healthcare, education and labour protection. Relatedly, the COVID-19 pandemic has brought directly to the fore questions of the fragility of Caribbean democracy, given the emergence of authoritarian tendencies in the reflexive use of 'states of emergency', curfews, mandates, lock-downs and mandatory vaccinations as tourism-dependent governments sought to walk the shaky tightrope of 'balancing lives and livelihoods' and as they were caught between public health questions and ensuring the dominant capitalist class of continued access to profits.

The sheer scale of the impact of the coronavirus crisis in presenting an existential crisis for capitalism, cannot be overstated. Following closely upon the heels of the 2008 financial crisis, the COVID-19 crisis of 2019–22 has given rise to an extended period of harsh adjustment to capitalism's failures and underscores the permanent crisis-laden nature of capitalism following the highly optimistic prognostications on its future in the decade of the 1990s.

The observations of the editors of the *Journal of Global Faultlines* provide an adequate summation of the crisis of capitalism at the time of the COVID-19 crisis. Citing Lenin's famous observation that "there are decades where nothing happens, and there are weeks where decades happen", the editors observed that,

> at the start of 2020, according to all available data, more than ten years after the collapse of the Lehman Brothers sparked the greatest financial crisis and economic downturn since the Great Depression, none of the underlying contradictions of the world economy have been resolved. The false claim that governments have broken the back of the recession was running out of steam. Global imbalances and deep-rooted tensions have deepened even further. Although economic worries are mounting in the advanced world, the growth deceleration is likely to be more painful in many emerging economies, notably Southern Africa, several economies

in Latin America, and South and West Asia, including Turkey. Even before the recent trade tension, growth rates were slipping in parts of the emerging world because of falling capital inflows – following announcements of monetary tightening by leading central banks – which have in some cases already turned negative, compounded by falling commodities prices. These weaknesses are emerging in the context of a significant build-up of debt across the emerging world, much of it short-term and denominated in foreign currencies, with the biggest increases in the private sector... Then came the coronavirus, which has plunged the global economy into a new phase of uncertainty (Journal of Global Faultlines 2020, 3).

It is in such a context that the applicability of the thought of C.L.R. James to the politics of the Caribbean can be understood.

Capitalism's Crisis, Global Transformation and the Jamesian Analysis

The great value of C.L.R. James's political thought to transformations occurring in capitalism long after his death, remains its rigid identification of what constitutes the universal of the socialist and workers' movement. James was always able to draw a strict line between that *Universal* which is the ultimate end to which the movement is directed - the liberation of mankind from every basis of exploitation and domination - and the *Particular*, the specific tactical and organizational entities adopted by the movement towards the realization of the universal. This was the source of James's revolutionary optimism. Developments and occurrences which are normally considered as 'setbacks' or 'defeats', and which force other socialists to abandon Marxism, would be incorporated into James's general analysis as part of the broad process of mankind's march to self-liberation (James 1980a).

James insists that the abandonment of Marxism on the emergence of such setbacks comes about when revolutionaries mistake a *particular* for the *universal*. The particular is transformed from being a temporary measure into being an end in itself. This recurring error by revolutionary movements was one of the factors which guided Rosa Luxemburg (1961) in her critique of Lenin's vanguard party. Luxemburg (1961, 79) had warned against the danger of making "a virtue of necessity" and of freezing "into a complete theoretical system all the tactics forced upon them by... fatal circumstances" and of recommending "them to the international proletariat as a model of socialist tactics". She warned sternly against placing in "its storehouse as new discoveries all the distortions prescribed in Russia by necessity and compulsion". When the particular replaces the universal, distortions occur in determining the likelihood of socialism. The strength of socialism is then measured, not by the extent to which the liberation of the working class is nearing fruition, but by how firmly entrenched the particular remains.

The classic example of the manifestation of such an error was seen in the response by revolutionaries to the experiences of Stalinism, in the USSR. In James's view, even Trotsky, the most famous victim of Stalinism, failed to abandon his particular and create a new one more suited to the developments occurring in Russia. James (1980a, 33) writing in the 1940s addressed this phenomenon in the following way:

> An unreasoning obstinacy seems to take hold of them. They grasp their categories. They will not leave them. Not only Mensheviks, but all, every member of the old Bolshevik Central Committee stuck to the categories of the bourgeois revolution. And miracle of miracles, the Petrograd workers in the party had thrown it over. No, we are not going to run away from this. Not when we hear Trotsky say: "A workers' state equals nationalised property" and parks there for good. Twenty million workers in concentration camps. He does not budge. Budge? No sir. He will prefer to say that if within a reasonable time after the war the bureaucracy remains, then all of Marxism is wrong. Let the whole work of a hundred years perish rather than change my categories. I shall not say: Perhaps my concept of the workers' state is wrong. No Never.

It is for this reason that James's thought remains useful after the collapse of the Soviet Union. James's commitment to the *universal* and his willingness to re-examine his *particular* provides a firm basis for the analysis of the transformations occurring within the global political economy and facilitates a continued application of Marxist analysis to account for such transformations.

There are several theoretical parallels between the twenty-first century crisis of Marxism associated with the collapse of the Soviet Union (1990 to 2020s) and the crisis of Marxism associated with Stalinism in the 1930s to 1950s, where many committed Marxists abandoned Marxism and questioned the relevance of the Marxist world view. What is particularly relevant about James for overcoming the long crisis of Marxism, is his focus on the pertinent question of the relevance of such transformations to the workers' movement. Indeed, James was often accused of romanticism or mysticism by his contemporaries, such as Max Schachtman for exaggerating the imminence of socialist liberation (James 1980a, 19). When the USA was largely seen as the most politically backward, conservative and reactionary nation James, would, in contrast, be anticipating that "your culturally and politically backward America is going to produce a proletarian literature, a specific social expression, and a new proletarian social organization". Explaining that this expectation was based on the "law of historical compensation", James argued that "its importance is that in bringing up to date a delayed reaction, it projects into the future, and backwardness is transformed making its very backwardness the dynamic of transition into vanguardism, its opposite" (James 1980a, 136). In short, James was pointing to the US working class's potential for revolution, based on the objective material development of US society.

Similarly, Worcester (1992, 127) provides an equally vivid illustration of this revolutionary optimism in James's analysis of the May 1968 events in France. On reflecting on the 1968 student uprisings James had argued that the "very structure of modern society prepares the working class and sections of society to undertake immediately the creation of socialist institutions". He had also argued that the "the world revolution has entered in what could be a decisive and final stage". According to Worcester (1992, 127), "even by the standards of the time, this prediction seems rather extravagant".

Extravagance notwithstanding, the critical question remains James's methodology for understanding how transformations in the working-class movement occur due to changes in the material transformations in capitalism. In this regard, the lukewarm response to James's anticipated revolution can be explained by the inability of Marxists to shift their particulars beyond the familiar early-twentieth century expression of the workers' movement. To many Marxists, the particulars associated with socialism such as a large workers' party and vibrant and militant trade union activity were relatively weak or non-existent in the United States and from this perspective, 'socialism' stood very little chance of success there. To James, however, the development of industry, technology, communications, and aspects of the organic political culture such as the US citizens' inbred hostility to state power and central authority provided a more fundamental basis for the establishment of socialism in the United States. The presence of these objective and subjective factors, in the Jamesian perspective, is more important than the presence of a hierarchically organized conspiratorial 'vanguard' party and attendant features. While the global mass uprisings of the 1960s did not achieve widespread political success in terms of attaining political power, that these uprisings occurred independently of communist and socialist vanguard parties, James's analysis is better appreciated and understood.

It was James's firm belief that the basis of socialism lay in the appropriation and further development of the products of capitalism by the working class in the interest of the working class. Thus, material advances in capitalism were seen, not as impediments, but as providing the more advanced infrastructure upon which the future socialist society and economy would be established. It is for this reason that the concept of an "invading socialist society" – a gradual and barely perceptible, ongoing development – was a favorite conception of James in explaining the anticipated transition to socialism (James, Forest and Stone 1972). In this sense, despite the untold cost paid in human suffering, social dislocation, and environmental degradation in the establishment of a capitalist world market, the fact remains that it has laid the technological and material basis for the distribution of resources on a socialist basis to all of mankind (Luard 1979, 28).

Thus Wallerstein (1984, 24–25) observed, that "the capitalist development of the world economy itself moves towards the socialisation of the productive forces". He argued that "there is an organisational (as opposed to political) imperative, in which the full achievement of capitalist relations of production - through its emphasis on the increase of relative surplus value and the maximum efficiency (free flow) of the forces of production - pushes towards a fully planned single productive organisational network in the world economy". Further, Wallerstein saw the global adoption of the capitalist system as being part of the dialectical movement of the contradictions within capitalism manifesting themselves at the global level. In his view (Wallerstein 1984, 55),

> the full triumph of capitalist values is a sign, indeed, *the* sign of the crisis of capitalism as a system. Capitalism has never historically operated in the mode its ideology dictates, because it cannot...The universalisation of the law of value is precisely what will make it finally impossible to maintain the 'mystical veil' of commodities, what will complete the process of the 'destruction of the protecting strata'. This will happen because the contradictory processes of the current phase of the capitalist world-economy will have so thoroughly demystified the techniques of domination that they will render them politically untenable.

Building on this argument, George Belle (1994) has viewed the post-globalization developments in the capitalist world economy as a vindication of both Immanuel Wallerstein and C.L.R. James. Belle (1994, 106) observes that,

> we have seen with our own eyes the rise today indisputably of a global system of world capitalism. Soviet socialism has collapsed and Islam is 'under manners'. Wallerstein says this world-economy

has been there for five hundred years. Buttressing this system as presently formulated are economic integration movements on a continental scale. In these all the same lie... one of the contradictions of the new world order. Let us remember James. "Other of Stalinism"; "The Other of Stalinism is an international socialist economic order, embracing from the start whole continents".[4] How else should we get there but maybe through the present historical farce of a new world order, with its regional integration movements led by the European Economic Community, the I.M.F. and the World Bank?

In the third decade of the twenty-first century there are perhaps three ways in which the applicability and relevance of James's Marxist perspective to contemporary revolutionary politics can be most clearly seen: the crisis of the state, the crisis of the political party and the rise of spontaneous mass movements.

In most of the socialist revolutions of the twentieth century, beginning with Russia in 1917, it was generally assumed that the seizure of the formal organs of the state by a revolutionary movement was a sufficient condition for revolutionary change. After the October Revolution, it was generally felt that the control of state power would facilitate the establishment of socialism through the nationalization of the "commanding heights" of the economy, the establishment of a large coercive apparatus to defend the state against external "capitalist invasion" and internal "capitalist destabilization" (Luard 1979, 2). Writing in 1979, Luard (1979, 1) argued that "socialism now universally means state socialism".

Unsurprisingly therefore, much of the discourse around the "death of socialism" has emerged over the failures of the specific strategies associated with state socialism, in the era of neo-liberalism and hegemonic capitalism. However, James had always insisted that the seizure of state power, the nationalization of private property, the successful military and ideological defence of the state from 'capitalist infiltration' could not in themselves serve as evidence of the attainment of socialism. Under the experience of twentieth century state socialism, the state had not 'withered away', and government was not in the hands of workers, and there were no institutions which facilitated worker-based direct democracy. On the contrary, an even more brutal and efficient exploitation of the workers was instituted, facilitated by the involvement of the state apparatus in every facet of society, the non-existence of civil liberties, the control of trade union activity and other mechanisms.

It is for these reasons that the concept of state capitalism was adopted by James to account for the absence of ownership and control on the part of workers and the perpetuation of capitalist social relations. The failure of models of state socialism and the continued demand for new forms of social organization underscore the limits to state socialism whose transcendence James had been anticipating. It is significant that with the challenges of state socialism since the late twentieth century, many committed Marxists, (in contrast to those who have abandoned Marxism and the dialectic), have been working within perspectives which offer a re-evaluation of the role of the state in establishing socialism.

Immanuel Wallerstein (1984) for example, has presented a perspective of the capitalist world-economy in which the role of the state in revolution has been radically rethought. Given the constrained nature of the state in relation to global capital, Wallerstein (1984, 51) has argued that, "no state (not even that of a hegemonic power) can do quite as it wishes. Hence no group which gains power in a given state is free to transform processes within its boundaries as it sees fit". He suggests optimistically, but logically, that one of the consequences of the challenges of the twentieth century state socialist model, is that "after a century of detour, the emphasis may return to the importance of creating real world wide inter-movement links - one that would cut across North-South and East-West boundaries" (1984, 67). It should not escape notice that the movements discussed in chapter three – Occupy Wall Street, the Arab Spring, the Black Lives Matter Movement and many others – bear direct resemblance to

Wallerstein's 'real world wide inter-movement links'. Significantly, too, these inter-movement links are now facilitated by the objective material possibilities offered by communications and transportation technology.

Like the challenges to state power, the issues surrounding the political party represent a second area in which the relevance of C.L.R. James to radical politics in the twenty-first century can be assessed. James had insisted that the objective movement of the working class was toward the creation of new forms of organization such as workers' councils and soviets, which transcended the limits of bourgeois political institutions like the political party. The modern political party and trade union are both institutions whose existence is tied in a relation to state power. However, they both are under challenge because of shifts in the global political economy.

The trade union, faced with a new globalization of production, loss of membership due to the displacement of workers by technology, a weakened power of the state and local productive institutions in improving the economic situation of workers, has found its traditional modus operandi severely threatened (Marshall 1992). These developments have had profound impact on the operationalization of trade unionism in the Caribbean. The response of Caribbean trade unions and political parties strongly confirm C.L.R. James's analysis that trade union and political party representative bureaucracies serve to stifle, rather than to facilitate the development of the workers' movement. Under the conditions of an austerity programme in the 1990–94 period in Barbados, for example, the trade union movement was forced to reduce its labour-related demands, become reasonable and cooperative, and enter a social partnership with the private sector and government. This development has been largely presented as a 'model' for the Caribbean and has been hastened by the peculiar historical experience of Caribbean 'political unionism'. Under political unionism, the origin of trade unions was closely tied to the emergence of political parties, and trade union representatives often sat as members of parliament and as ministers of government. In this situation the interests of the state inevitably took precedence over the interests of workers (Hackshaw 1991). In the early decades of the twenty-first century, following several years of IMF structural adjustment, and following a series of economic crises from the 9/11 terrorist attacks in the USA, the 2008 sub-prime mortgage crisis, the 2019–22 COVID-19 crisis, and the sharp rises in global inflation as a result of the Russia-Ukraine war of 2022, it is now common place for Caribbean trade unions, particularly those whose leadership are inter-meshed with governing political parties, to be at the forefront of demanding restraint on the part of their membership, rather than as serving as the defenders of workers' economic interests.

It is as a response to the limits and anticipated obsolescence of the state, the trade unions, and the political party that C.L.R. James developed his concept of "free creative activity". In clarifying the significance of the concept within James's thought, Paget Henry (1992, 23) has noted that,

> a worker-based move is extremely important to James. It is necessary for overcoming the problems left unsolved by these... forms of social organisation, in particular, the problems created by increased bureaucratisation and delegation of decision-making power. This growth of economic and political bureaucracies suppresses the growth of participatory aspects of public life. As a consequence, the active life is drained of substance. Politics becomes professionalised on the model of the doctor-patient or lawyer-client relationship. Such models rest upon the assumption that clients cannot do for themselves, an assumption contrary to James' deepest beliefs.

The challenges faced by the Caribbean post-colonial state in meeting the expectations of the population, the growing loss of confidence in the political party, the weaknesses and shortcomings of representative politics, and the crises of the trade union, have all resulted in the previously discussed thrust towards James's idea of 'free-creative activity' not only in the Caribbean, but globally. Perestroika and glasnost in the late 1980s were precipitated by public disillusionment with governmental bureaucracy and centralized authority by the Russian populace, and a realization by the governing class of the need to concede to demands for greater levels of participatory democracy. The actions of Gorbachev were an attempt to redress these political imbalances. Gorbachev, like C.L.R. James before him, had realized that the only basis upon which a new participatory democracy could be established was through the supersession of representative democracy. He, like James, had seen the basis for such a participatory democracy as lying in the soviets, whose "rapid, even spontaneous spread throughout the country was in the fact that they made the decisions and implemented them on their own while being in the focus of the public eye, under open control of all those whom their moves might concern" (Gorbachev 1988, 97–98).

Nor have the capitalist centres been immune from the demands for democracy which manifested themselves in the Soviet Union. By the turn of the century, Europe, Asia and North America would be encountering a series of mass demonstrations starting with the anti-globalization riots such as in Seattle in 2000 and continuing into the later revolts associated with BLM and the public upheavals over voting and representation in the USA in the third decade of the twenty-first century. In short, the events following the collapse of the Soviet Union, far from signalling the end of revolutionary activity, have largely vindicated C.L.R. James's expectation that new forms of popular struggles would emerge, independent of the vanguard leadership of political parties, forcing the emergence of new types of democratic expression and practice which would challenge the existence of capitalism.

Meeting the Challenges: Effecting a Jamesian Solution in the Caribbean

In concluding this assessment of the relevance of C.L.R. James to Caribbean revolutionary politics in the twenty-first century, it is important to scan the landscape to identify the political moments, events and groupings no matter how scant, which consciously identify as 'Jamesian' or to which the label of 'Jamesianism' can be attached. This will assist in 'updating the story' on James and will point to the possibilities of Jamesian-type activity in the future.

In an earlier chapter, a lengthy account was provided of Walton Look Lai's (New Beginning Movement) analysis of the February 1970 revolution in Trinidad in which he highlighted the Jamesian features of the revolt. Perhaps the nearest political groupings in the Caribbean which approximate deliberate Jamesian formations were the New Beginning Movement (NBM) of Trinidad and Tobago, and the Antigua Caribbean Liberation Movement, led by Tim Hector. In writing specifically of the former, Matthew Quest (2017, 267–68) observed that,

> the New Beginning Movement (NBM) (1971–1978) in Trinidad functioned as a voice of direct democracy and workers' self-management through popular assemblies, and a global coordinating council of a Pan-Caribbean International with linkages across the region, in Britain, the United States and Canada... NBM aspired to interpret Afro-Trinidadians and Indo-Trinidadians equally, and on their own autonomous terms, toward self-directed emancipation. Led by Bukka Rennie, Wally Look Lai, and Franklyn Harvey, NBM was inspired by C.L.R. James's intellectual legacies. NBM members also included Darcus Howe, Earl Lovelace, Efebo Wilkinson, Brinsley Samaroo, Lloyd D'Aguilar, Pat Bynoe, Douglass Gregg, Annette Charles, Kenrick Rennie, Winston Rennie, Ken Reyes, and Roderick Thurton. Through publications such as New Beginning, Caribbean Dialogue, and The Vanguard, these partisans advocated labor's self-emancipation and critical perspectives on capitalism and state power, and exposed the limits of elite party politics and representative government.

Quest (2017, 268) observes however that, "there was no active conscious 'cell' trained by James for intervening in Trinidad politics", and notes further that, "James's own intermittent and individualistic interventions in Caribbean politics discouraged those sympathetic to his fuller radical vision". Beyond its functions as an intellectual centre and coordinating council and a news service therefore, there is little evidence of direct action or of an engaged and sustained moment of radical activism by the

NBM, although the key activists in the NBM, were involved in pre- and post-NBM radical activities in the Caribbean and elsewhere such as the 1970s Black power uprising in Trinidad and Tobago and the embryonic movements which preceded and predated the Grenada revolution (Quest 2017, 275–76).

In a similar way, it can be said that Tim Hector's ACLM, by the early 2000s, was heading towards formal absorption into electoral party competition. First with the accommodation between Hector and the leader of the Antigua Labour Party Lester Bird in the early 2000s and later following the death of Hector in 2002 and the later absorption of key former ACLM activists into mainstream electoral politics, it can be said that the role of the ACLM as a party inspired by the ideas of C.L.R. James had ceased to exist.

Despite the formal 'closure' of specifically Jamesian-inspired political groupings in the Caribbean, the utility of James can be more readily seen in the type of anti-systemic activities that have dotted the Caribbean landscape between the 1990s and the first decade of the twenty-first century.

Perhaps, amongst the earliest of these '1990s' revolts can be counted the mass strikes organized by the so-called Banana Salvation Committee (BSC) in St. Lucia between 1988 and 1992, and which culminated in the blocking of the main road arteries and the killing of two protesting banana farm workers by the police. These protests, essentially arose in the context of the liberalization of the European market and the removal of colonial-era preferential protections in the UK which in turn were threatening the livelihoods of St. Lucian and Windward Island banana producers. In short, what unfolded was an anti-globalisation movement but with localized concerns at the forefront of the minds of the protestors. While the impact of these developments was felt throughout the Windward Islands, it was in St. Lucia, owing largely to the militancy of the leadership of the BSC that the protests adopted insurrectionist features and resulted in the use of deadly force by the state. In providing a brief summary of the events associated with the protests Joseph (2019, 103) reports that from its first skirmish with the government in 1988, the entire period up to 1993, can be seen as a long period of struggle between the government and the banana community. A perusal of the newspaper headlines in St. Lucia between 1988 and 1993 provides a clear catalogue of conflict between the government and the Banana Salvation Committee in a context of the loss of preferential markets and the movement towards liberalized, globalized trade. The headlines in *The Voice* newspaper such as "1988 – Year of Intense Activity" (Dec. 10th 1988, pp. 9), "Banana Protest" (Oct. 26 1988, pp 1), "Politics Goes Bananas" (October 29, 1988, "Banana Strike Looms" (Sept. 21st 1993, 1;14)","Growers Threaten New Strikes" (Nov. 25th 1993, pp. 1;14), "SLBGA Board in Exile" (Nov. 25th 1993, pp. 1; 14), reveal a long and sustained moment of constant upheaval and revolt in the banana industry. The main tactic was the "no-cut strike", in which the power of the farmers as independent producers to starve the buyers of produce proved a critical weapon, and frightened government officials with the possibility of collapse of the economy. The "no-cut-strikes" were reinforced by the tactic of harassment of strike breakers and by the erection of road blocks to prevent the movement of trucks carrying produce to the various ports and collection centres. The peak of the banana revolts was a three day strike which ended on October 5th 1993, and culminated in the killing by the police of two unarmed strikers, Julius and Randy Joseph.

Among the specifically Jamesian features of the Banana Salvation Committee protests was the fact the St. Lucia Banana Growers Association (SLBGA), had from its formation in the late 1950s, possessed the features of a democratic producers' association in which small and large growers could vote on critical issues affecting the industry. Indeed, much of the struggle against the government in the late 1980s early 1990s revolved around the stealthy take over by the state of the SLBGA as the government sought to play a key role in adjusting the banana industry to the demands of global neo-liberalism. Other features such as the 'no-cut strike' revealed the creativity of the farmers, since they were able to counter the claim by the state that a striking farmer is striking against himself given his status as an independent producer. Finally, the tactics used to shut the main arteries of the country – the burning of tires and other debris and the felling of trees – affecting the transportation of tourists between the two main airport towns in the north and the south, revealed an embryonic militancy on the part of the workers and their creative insurrectionist instincts which James had always argued made them independent of vanguardist direction from above.

However, the anti-globalization banana struggles in St. Lucia and the Windward Islands were unable to create lasting institutional footprints of farmer militancy and organization as a counter to global neo-liberalism. Similarly, none of the features of regional coordination with other farmers groups in St. Vincent, Dominica and Grenada which had sprung up at the time when global trade liberalization was perceived as a common threat, have survived into the 2000s. This might be largely because the successful unfolding of trade liberalization has resulted in the end of the banana farmers as a political force due to the sharp declines in the industry (Joseph 2019, 106–107), but the broader lessons of worker resistance to largely external economic forces have not been replicated in other areas of political life in St. Lucia and the OECS. The lesson of the 1990–93 protests in St. Lucia from a Jamesian perspective, however, is the reminder of the innate capacity of the people to revolt.

These protests have continued in the new millennium. The earlier chapters of this work have provided accounts of large scale mass protests and other spontaneously organized activity in opposition to environmentally harmful tourism investments in Tobago and Carriacou, Grenada; in Barbados around demands for racial dignity and respect for black identity in the official iconography as seen in the "Tek Down Nelson" protests; in Jamaica around the right to access the beaches free of cost; and in St. Lucia in opposition to a neo-liberal Allen Chastanet administration's move to facilitate the possession of a large segment of lands in the south of the island by a foreign company Desert Star Holdings, at peppercorn rates. In addition to the specific episodes of spontaneous mass protests highlighted in the earlier chapters, have been movements around 'new issues' such as cannabis legalization, same sex marriage and sexual rights, and domestic violence and the protection of women and children. Many of these movements and protests, have occurred independently of political parties and trade unions and have found their institutional energy from the possibilities offered by the internet, social media and new communications technology.

In many instances, these demands from below have been impacting on government policy and have been affecting political outcomes. There is little doubt that a line can be traced between the global BLM protests, the demands to 'Tek Down Nelson' in Barbados, the eventual removal of the statue of Lord Nelson by the Barbadian state, and the move to republican status in 2021 and the promise of constitutional reform in 2022–23 by the Mia Mottley-led BLP administration, even while it is recognized that these demands had formed part of the 'left critique' of the post-colonial Westminster order from the 1960s. Similarly, the defeat of the Chastanet administration in St. Lucia in the 2021 general election by the St. Lucia Labour party cannot be separated from the mass opposition to the DSH investment, nor can the abandonment of the Sandals investment in Tobago be separated from the activities of the environmental protests in that island. It is safe to conclude, therefore, that in the English-speaking Caribbean, despite the absence of formally ideologically-parented "Jamesian" groupings, Jamesian type mass protest movements have been impacting upon Caribbean political life and have been influencing state policy, and have limited, in some instances, the capacity of capitalist development to affect the lives of segments of the Caribbean population. What has not been evident in the English-speaking Caribbean however, are broader demands for self-directed activity, for worker control of the workplace and for the full development of people's assemblies and people's parliaments, despite the fact that the current communications technology makes such possibilities more feasible than in the period of the February revolution in Trinidad and the Grenada revolution in the 1970s.

Perhaps however, the most politically significant of the Jamesian-type mass movements which has occurred in the Caribbean in the twenty-first century, emerged, not in the English-speaking Caribbean, but in French-colonized DOMs of Martinique and Guadeloupe, French Guiana (Cayenne) and Reunion, where between February and March 2009, a forty-four day mass general strike erupted over the "elevated and inequitable cost of living" in the DOMs relative to France (see Murdoch 2021, 1). Murdoch (2021, 2), provides a useful summary of these events from which their full scale and impact can be assessed:

> this rise in the cost of living was accompanied by huge demonstrations against the severe inequities of prevailing social and economic conditions, often involving as many as one hundred thousand people – one quarter of the population of these territories. By February 21, these strikes and demonstrations spread to Reunion. An agreement with the French government was eventually reached on March 4 on 165 demands including a €200 ($250) increase in the monthly minimum wage and reduced prices for public transportation, gasoline, food, housing and water. The strike was organized by a coalition of forty-eight organizations, including trade unions from a wide spectrum of industries (gasoline distribution, commerce, tourism, civil service, health care, education and agriculture, to name a few), as well as environmental groups, peasant organizations, political parties, pro-independence activists, consumer rights advocates, associations for disability rights, fair housing proponents, music and dance groups, and a wide range of other political, cultural and civic leaders. These diverse activists came together under the name Lyannag Kont Pwofitasyon (LKP), which can be loosely translated as the Alliance Against Profiteering.

In a related study, Murdoch, along with Paget Henry, have sought to show the Jamesian element in the DOM's revolt in the first decade of the twenty-first century (Henry and Murdoch 2021). One of their novel and important observations is the plausible relationship between the LKP cost of living protests in the French colonies in 2009 and the later emergence of the yellow vest's protests in France (Murdoch and Henry 2021, 183). In thinking about how James would have seen and understood the

LKP modes of organizing Murdoch and Henry (212–13) suggest that,

> we would be best advised to look at it comparatively and intextextually. How do the solutions dramatized in the forty-four days of collective action compare with those of earlier uprisings, and what do they tell us about the increasing formation or deformation of the collective self that authored those solutions? James would have been struck by its strategic actions taken, such as the blocking of ports and key arteries into the cities. These would have given LKP its distinct insurrectionary credentials. James would have been struck by the spontaneous creation of the alternative television station Télé Otonom in response to the established media's misreading of the carnivalesque modes through which workers dramatized their grievances.

However, as has been observed in the cases of the other mass protests in the current period, the movements have been unable to sustain themselves as genuine alternatives to the political and economic systems against which and within which they were struggling. In the case of the LPK struggle, Murdoch and Henry lament the fact that, despite the creativity witnessed in the protests themselves, in the final analysis they resolved themselves into being cost of living protests within the established context of the colonial relationship with France. In their view (213–14),

> Although the insurrection quite explicitly raised issues of racism, exploitation, and relations with France, these issues were addressed within the existing departmentalized framework, excluding the LKP insurrection from the category of a "lute de libération nationale" (struggle of national liberation). The increases in wages and changes in the tax structure, significant as they were, took place within the collapsing dirigisme economies of France, Guadeloupe, and Martinique... The setting up of more participatory media was another significant political statement by LKP, which echoed political demands from earlier Caribbean uprisings. But here too, the challenge of giving this idea a broader institutional expression were not met. Thus, after the uprising ended, we saw a return to preinsurrectionary economic and political practices, which gave rise to the ambivalent feelings and outcomes that we noted at the beginning of this chapter.

Yet, despite the failure of the LPK protests to undertake a more complete break with French colonialism, and despite the failure of the protests to sustain the institutions and frameworks of 'self-activity', Murdoch and Henry were nevertheless aware of the importance of the events for presenting the possibilities of revolutionary action not only for the French DOMs but for the English-speaking countries, sovereign and non-sovereign alike. In their view, "in spite of its strategic pragmatism, the uprising exposed and made clear for all to see the potentially revolutionary public self of workers in Guadeloupe and Martinique. It lifted the veils that kept this collective self hidden and revealed its specific creative responses to increased pressures coming from a declining neoliberal order" (214–15).

These movements, protests and uprisings suggest strongly that despite the absence of specifically Jamesian-inspired groupings like the ACLM and New Beginning, James's relevance to developments occurring by way of anti-systemic activity has not been diminished, nor has the urgency of normatively applying his methods and ideas to radical politics in the twenty-first century been reduced. It is useful therefore to conclude this analysis by normatively prescribing Jamesian solutions to specific challenges.

James provides key prescriptive guidelines which can assist in overcoming the specific organizational and tactical challenges faced by radical movements in the Caribbean. A vacuum has been created by the failure of the statist Marxist formula. A major symptom of the crisis resides in its continuing failure to reformulate and develop new organizational and tactical mechanisms better suited to the specific stage of development of global capitalism. It is in offering of alternatives, that James becomes particularly relevant.

The lesson from James is that a Caribbean Marxist response should strengthen and encourage the development of popular, community-based, non-governmental organizations, and civic groups, since these represent the nearest approximation of a worker-oriented, democratization of Caribbean politics. This would approximate a withering away of the state by placing greater emphasis on the empowerment of society. However, while the retreat of the Caribbean state presents immense possibilities for the pursuit and achievement of socialist objectives, this process of state-withdrawal also presents the very imminent challenge of the further entrenchment of capitalist social and economic relations and a possibility of the recolonization of the region (Raghavan 1990).

The dilemma for the workers' movement posed by the retreat of the left revolves around the contradictions posed by the Caribbean state in being both an instrument of social-democratic empowerment as well as of capitalist penetration. Despite Marxist concerns about the state being an instrument of bourgeois rule, it cannot be denied that the independent Caribbean state has pursued, over time, several progressive worker-oriented policies such as the provision of free health care, state-aided education and housing policies, the enforcement of minimum wage policies and in general, the provision of welfare policies to cushion Caribbean families from the harsh realities of the global capitalist economy. However, under the hegemony of neo-liberal capitalism since the 1990s, all Caribbean states have been forced to structurally adjust away from their traditional social democratic postures. Thus, policies of denationalization in key areas such as telecommunication, utilities, and transportation, as well as instituting of fees in areas such as tertiary education and health care and the pursuit of privatization of government-owned enterprises, have been key features of the public policy direction of Caribbean states since the 1990s.

While the process of privatization can be applauded from a Marxist perspective as representing a movement toward the withering away of the state, the manner in which the process is being undertaken has not resulted in worker empowerment. In a context of neo-liberal hegemony, key productive sectors of the Caribbean economy have been placed in the hands of the metropolitan bourgeoisie, through privatization. In contrast, the opportunities for economic democratization consequent upon the retreat of the state have not been capitalized upon. Instead of placing the commanding heights of the national economies in the hands of the metropolitan and traditional domestic bourgeoisie, opportunities might have been provided for ownership in the privatized enterprises by grassroots credit unions, youth and community groups on a collective basis. In the view of C.Y. Thomas, (1988, 361) "whether or not government intervenes per se is neither here nor there..., what is significant... is the purpose of the government intervention and what class and social interest it serves or seeks to serve. It is pure fantasy to believe that political freedom in the region can be reduced to, or is in some way, dependent on the operation of un-restrained market forces" (361).

A Jamesian response to the state-socialist crisis of the working-class movement lies in the adoption of new forms of organizational structures more appropriate to the present stage of capitalism. The achievement of this goal, will necessarily involve a struggle between rank-and-file workers and their representatives in both political parties and trade unions. It will also be reliant on new forms of technology, already in existence, which will revolutionize, communications, social relations, and management, indeed, every aspect of the work relationship, the nature of work and the 'workplace' itself. The new organizational structures would overcome the weaknesses created by the division-of-labour within the party and trade union, and the general shortcomings of representative politics, as well as address the distortions resulting from the separation of politics and economics, a reality furthered by the separate aims and functions of political parties and trade unions within Caribbean society.

C.L.R. James had identified the features of the workers' councils and soviets as being spontaneous responses to these problems. The development of popular community organizations in the Caribbean, though they represent only an embryonic stage in the development of soviet-like organizations, has to be strengthened and encouraged. Moreover, new organizational entities and tactical approaches which transcend the limitations of the political party and trade union should be fostered. Writing in the 1970s, Franklyn Harvey (1974, 39) had argued that

> the working-class not only gains its intellectual knowing and practical experience from the political party, but also from its economic organisation, the trade union. But as the political party becomes an instrument of social oppression so too does the trade union... Capitalist production, by the objective process of its development, forces the reunion of politics and economics. The working-class, realising that neither trade union or political party any longer serves their class interest, abandons both and reunites the political, economic, social and cultural struggle into one struggle with their new instrument - the organised social movement of the whole working masses.

Similarly, Errol Mcleod, President General of the Oil Workers Trade Union of Trinidad and Tobago, in the late 1980s, had offered some elements of the tactical approaches needed to effect the transcendence of union and party politics. He argued that,

> the solution is to create institutions of popular power in the work-places and in the communities. The people in the work-place can then plan and organise to improve production, monitor performances of managers, develop accountability and be vigilant against corruption. And in the communities, the people can identify and mobilise their resources to satisfy their own needs, according to the priorities they establish. So it is not left to some technocrat to decide what must be done to solve local problems in a village. Such institutions of power would then not be 'talk-shops' but would be localised centres of action (Mcleod 1988, 25).

In short, the new thrust of Caribbean working-class activism should aim at effecting a fundamental democratization of Caribbean society upon the basis of real ownership and control on the part of the masses of Caribbean people. Such ownership and control should be given a literal interpretation and should transcend the abstract and mythical 'ownership' which characterizes nationalization and state control. State property should be transformed into social property, not private property. Social property should be administered on the basis of mass participatory democracy, not centralised authoritarianism. Developmental priorities should be decided on the basis of human need, and not private profit. Developmental policies in the Caribbean, should have as their central focus the political and economic empowerment of the Caribbean masses. C.Y. Thomas (1988, 356) is clear as to what such socialist development should entail. He notes that,

> in direct contrast to what prevails, development requires a system of ownership, control and production oriented towards satisfying the basic needs of the masses...[D]evelopment also implies that work, politics and social organisation are based on democratising power in society and on the effective (as opposed to nominal) exercise of fundamental rights... The democratisation of power also implies the democratisation of all the decision making structures in the society, from the level of the workplace and community right through to central government. An equitable distribution of wealth and income, equitable access to the use and management of society's resources and equitable access to information are, of course, necessary requirements for achieving this objective.

The political thought of C.L.R. James provides the most lucid indication of the continued validity of the Marxist approach in the attainment of these goals. In the twenty-first century, with the rise of spontaneous global social movements like Occupy Wall Street and Black Lives Matter, with the advances in information, communications and production technology, with widespread increases in levels of education, and with the continuing crises of global capitalism, these objectives are far more realizable than when C.L.R. James presented their outlines in the middle of the twentieth century.

Notes

CHAPTER 1

1. The collection of papers of the CLR James institute are currently housed with Columbia University, serving as a special collections library. See Murray 2006 for an account of his role alongside other James associates, in establishing the institute.
2. A cursory perusal of any select bibliography of works by or about James reveals clearly the dominant position occupied by James's colleagues in writings on James (see for example James 1984a (291-9)). While not a weakness in itself, it has implications for the analytical conclusions reached in these works.
3. Dialectical logic suggests that thought cannot be divorced from the social context which gives birth to it. What is sought in this work, however, is the application of James's thought, rather than a mere chronicling of the social events which contributed to the evolution of that thought, as has been undertaken by La Guerre (1972) for example.
4. Indeed, most of the existing publications on Caribbean political thought have been pre-occupied with making a case for Caribbean thought. This can be seen in Dennis Benn (1987) and Paget Henry 2000. Bogues's work on James is therefore a continuation of this "extended debate with Europe" over the denial of Caribbean Philosophy (Henry 2000, 3).

CHAPTER 2

1. James's work provides one of the most articulate and deliberate presentations of the need to alter dialectical categories within the Marxist school. This task by itself is sufficient basis for the treatment of James as an independent and original authority within the Marxist tradition. It is this perspective, more than any

other which highlights the utility of James's thought to the present context.

2. Pierre Chaulieu was the nom de guerre of a young Greek associate of James, who shared his perspectives on the revolutionary potential of the technological transformations occurring within advanced capitalism and on the self-organisation of the proletariat. His real name is Cornelius Castoriadis, the author of a chapter in Cudjoe and Cain (1995) further clarifying the freshness of James's dialectical approach. I am thankful to Selwyn Cudjoe for his insights during a 1997 conversation at Cambridge University into the relationship between James and Castoriadis.

3. The work of Popper (1960; 1962, vol. 2) stands as the direct antithesis of the perspective presented by James. While James (1980a) insists that the real value of the dialectical outlook lies in its emphasis on the need to change analytical concepts in response to the transformations within the 'content' to which these concepts are applied, Popper (1960, 1962, vol. 2) sees any such reformulations as 'reinforced dogmatism' and as evidence of the unscientific nature of Marxism.

4. It is for a similar reason that Belle (1994, 94), in seeking to provide an explanation for the collapse of the Soviet system and its implications for the durability of capitalism, makes reference to Hegel's observation that "the higher maturity or stage which any Something can reach is that in which it begins to perish." Belle's observation is connected to the Gramscian hegemonic perspective in two ways. First, it seeks to highlight the absence of sound analysis in the frequent pronunciations of the 'highest stage' of capitalism having been reached. In a second and more obvious way, it seeks to challenge the perspectives which see the collapse of the Soviet system as representing the 'death of socialism'.

5. The final chapter of this work, closes with a broad statement of where the Caribbean social movement is today, in the early twenty-first century.

6. This perspective provides the basis for Luxembourg's critique of Lenin's vanguard party. To James, Lenin's vanguard party serves as the classic example of a particular transformed into a universal. Trotsky too, had seen the implications of the establishment of Lenin's vanguard party into a permanent structure and the possibility of its existence retarding the revolutionary process.

7. Alvin Toffler (1981, 64) has seen Lenin's vanguard party as having more in common with Western democracy than is widely acknowledged. Both systems place emphasis on the representation of individuals rather than on facilitating their participation in the political process (Lenin 1969, 108-9). From Toffler's perspective, therefore, the difference between Lenin and the 'democratic' parties of the West is a difference in degree rather than kind; a quantitative, as opposed to a qualitative, difference.

8. Where James errs is in his inability to explicitly link the democracy established by the ancient Greeks to the exclusion of women, slaves and metics (foreigners). However, James's view that a similar democracy in today's context can only be built on a more 'highly developed economic level' implies that he was cognizant of this reality.

CHAPTER 3

1. This is not to suggest that Marxist theory (as theory) has not always been hostile to the state. The inconsistencies on this issue have always manifested themselves in the realm of the actual practice.

2. A significant share of the responsibility for this continued fixation on the seizure of state power by twentieth century revolutions can be attributed to Stalin's Socialism in One Country (See James 1937). Wallerstein (1984) correctly observes that this emphasis on state power is a form of "false consciousness" among working class revolutionaries.

3. The validity of this argument can be better appreciated when it is considered that the emergence of the nation state was broadly coterminous with the emergence of capitalism. The economically dominant bourgeoisie replaced the administrative feudal structures of the formerly dominant aristocratic class primarily because the feudal structures did not, and could not, facilitate the realization of the economic aims of the rising bourgeoisie. It is for this reason that in its original manifestation, Marxism saw the disappearance of the state as evidence of the emergence of socialism and the disappearance of capitalism (Engels 1978, 338). The fact that the 'socialist' revolutions of the twentieth century did not smash the state, despite the limited success and possibilities of soviets and workers councils between 1905 and the mid-to-late

1920s,was proof of the continued rule of the bourgeoisie and the persistent marginalization of the proletariat. It is on this basis that James's conception of the Stalinist state as "state capitalism" was built.

4. Despite the obvious support of the Bolshevik Party for the soviets – ("All Power to the Soviets"), Arendt is pointing to a later tension which will emerge when state and party orientations find themselves unable to exist alongside the alternative political form presented by workers' councils, particularly after the bourgeoisie had been overthrown. It was therefore a tussle between two organizational nodes of class power, one established and facing its limits, and the other embryonic and newly emergent, yet uncertain and unable to fully manifest itself.

5. This broad anti-party perspective by James in the 1950s, must be weighed against his involvement in small movements like the Johnson-Forrest tendency, Correspondence, Facing Reality, the PNM in the 1960s, the Workers and Farmers Party (WFP) following his break with the PNM and his later acknowledgement of the role of the party in Caribbean post-colonial development. However, the essential point being made by James was that the elitist, exclusionary, bureaucratic form of political organization, what Toffler (1981) later described as 'first industrial revolution' organizations needed to be transcended.

6. This observation is very important, since it was made in reference to the Caribbean political party. While many have sought to separate James's Caribbean discussions from his application in the "more advanced" capitalist countries, later discussion will show that the two theatres are not easily separated analytically in James's mind.

7. These observations on the organizational questions of the Obama campaign are not diminished by the failures of Obama in addressing racism or in offering a radical alternative to capitalist development. The critical questions raised here are intended to show how the shift in the material base of society has given birth to new organizational forms which have implications for radical politics as a confirmation of the Jamesian perspective.

8. The demand to take down the statue of Horatio Nelson was a long-standing demand of the Barbadian pan-African movement. However, it was the global energy of the Black Lives Matter

movement, adopted by Barbadian young people, which provided the impetus and created a context for the eventual removal of Nelson's statue in 2020.

9. As an illustration and contextualization of the moment in which the Cahill protests were occurring, it should be noted that the ruling DLP would later lose the 2018 election, losing all seats in the thirty-seat parliament – the most lopsided electoral outcome in independent Barbados.

CHAPTER 4

1. Although Emmanuel (1992, 8) suggests several factors can influence the level of voter turnout, he suggests that reports on the 1954 and 1957 general elections in St. Lucia "both pointedly referred to the existence of illiteracy and apathy among the electorate". In St. Lucia, the level of voter turn-out remained below sixty percent for every election prior to 1974 (Emmanuel 1992, 13).

2. As illustrations: the situation obtained in Antigua during the 1976 elections where the Progressive Labour Movement (PLM) won 49.6% of the national vote and gained only five seats while the Antigua Labour Party (ALP) won 49.0% of the national vote and gained eleven seats; and in St. Vincent in the 1966 general election where the St. Vincent Labour Party (SVLP) won 50.9% of the national vote gaining four seats while the Peoples' Political Party (PPP) won 49.0% of the national vote and gained five seats (Emmanuel 1992, 21–22; 44).

3. The case of Jamaica in 1983 was due to the decision by the main opposition party the PNP to boycott the elections (Patterson 2019).

4. The occurrence of this phenomenon in a historically democratically even-handed society like Barbados, suggests the levels to which the democratic landscape may be eroding under the impact of a shifting global political-economy in the decades leading into the twenty-first century.

5. This year has been chosen to include the mass protest activities organized by the broad coalition grouped under the NJM.

CHAPTER 5

1. This is important since it is a common practice of thinkers who are blind to the racism in mainstream Western ideas, but are quick to attack Marxism for its racism and Eurocentrism.
2. Tapia refers to the organization with which Lloyd Best was associated – the Tapia House Group.

CHAPTER 6

1. A measure of clarification is required here. While from a Jamesian perspective, the existence of the Soviet Union largely limited and determined the nature of Caribbean socialism, it is also true that the existence of a socialist bloc, from the perspective of international relations and the global political economy, in the context of a cold-war global reality, provided a source of support to those territories willing to embark upon a course of development, independent of, and opposed to that prescribed by the United States of America.
2. Indeed, an official Obama White House (n.d) website openly boasted that, "when President Obama took office, the American auto industry was shedding jobs by the hundreds of thousands and GM and Chrysler faced the possibility of liquidation.... The President made the tough choice to help provide the auto industry the temporary support it needed to grow and prosper. Two years later, GM, Ford, and Chrysler are all adding jobs, generating profit, and investing in their U.S. facilities. The industry is once again leading the world and is stronger because the President demanded it retool and build more fuel-efficient cars in exchange for aid."
3. See also Gilligan and Niles (2022, 220–22) for a discussion of how Raya Dunayevskaya had arrived at a similar notion of 'state-capitalism' independently of CLR James, leading to her later fruitful collaboration with James, along with Grace Lee-Boggs in the Johnson-Forrest Tendency
4. James's "Other of Stalinism" referred to here, was posited as the antithesis of Stalin's "Socialism in One Country". The global developments towards the establishment of regional integration movements have vindicated James and correspondingly invalidated Stalin's perspective.

References

Albert, Michael and Robin Hahnel. 1978. *Unorthodox Marxism: An Essay on Capitalism, Socialism and Revolution.* Boston: South End Press.

Allen, Juliet, Daniella Jenkins and Marilyn Howard. 2020. "Crises Collide: Capitalism, Care, and COVID-19." *Feminist Studies* 46, no. 3: 583–95. URL: https://www.jstor.org/stable/10.15767/feministstudies.46.3.0583

Alleyne, Barry. 2022. "Hope for Stronger Ties." In *Daily Nation*, March 7, 3.

Alimahomed-Wilson, Jake and Ellen Reese, eds. 2000. *The Cost of Free Shipping: Amazon in the Global Economy.* London: Pluto Press.

Ambursely, Fitzroy. 1983. "Grenada and the New Jewel Revolution." In *Crisis in the Caribbean*, edited by Fitroy Ambursely and Robin Cohen, 199–222. London: Educational Books.

Amin, Samir. 1990. "The Future of Socialism." *Monthly Review* 42, no 3: 10–29.

Anderson, Kevin. 2010. *Marx at the Margins: On Nationalism, Ethnicity and Non-Western Societies.* Chicago: University of Chicago Press.

Arendt, Hannah. 1963. *On Revolution.* London: Faber and Faber.

Austin, David, ed. 2009. *You Don't Play with Revolution: The Montreal Lectures of C.L.R. James* (California: AK Press).

———, ed. 2018. *Moving Against the System: The 1968 Congress of Black Writers and the Making of Global Consciousness.* London: Pluto Press.

———. 2018. "Introduction: The Dialect of Liberation – The Congress of Black Writers at 50 and Beyond." In *Moving Against the System: The 1968 Congress of Black Writers and the Making of Global Consciousness,* edited by David Austin, 1–76. London: Pluto Press. Kindle.

Bajan Reporter. 2015. "Opposition Leader Demands for Cahill WTE Plant's MOU Be Tabled Before Parliament." In *Bajan Reporter*. September 1, 2015. https://www.bajanreporter.com/2015/09/opposition-leader-demands-for-cahill-wte-plants-mou-be-tabled-before-parliament/

Barbados Government Information Service. 2020. "Black Lives Matter Resolution Passed in Parliament". July 3, 2020. https://gisbarbados.gov.bb/blog/black-lives-matter-resolution-passed-in-parliament.

Barbados Underground. 2015. "Proposed Cahill Waste to Energy Plant Generating More Questions than Answers", July 29, 2015. https://barbadosunderground.net/2015/07/29/proposed-cahill-waste-to-energy-plant-generating-more-questions-than-answers.

Barber, Benjamin. 1984. *Strong Democracy: Participatory Politics for a New Age*. London: University of California Press.

Barrow-Giles, Cynthia. 2017. *The National Integrity System and Governance in the Commonwealth Caribbean*. Christ Church, Barbados: Carib Research and Publications.

Barrow-Giles, Cynthia and Tennyson Joseph. 2006. *General Elections and Voting in the English-Speaking Caribbean, 1992–2005*. Kingston: Ian Randle Publishers.

Baudrillard, Jean. 1996. "Symbolic Exchange and Death." In *From Modernism to Post-Modernism: An Anthology*, edited by Lawrence Cahoone, 437–60. Oxford: Blackwell Publishers.

Beard, Charles. [1913] 1965. *An Economic Interpretation of the Constitution of the United States*. Reprint. New York: The Free Press.

Beckford, George. 1972. *Persistent Poverty: Underdevelopment in Plantation Economies of the Third World*. New York: Oxford University Press.

Beckles, Hilary. 1989. *Corporate Power in Barbados – the Mutual Affair: Economic Injustice in a Political Democracy*. Bridgetown: Lighthouse Communications.

——. 1991. "Columbus Still Sails'". Lecture delivered at the University of the West Indies School of Continuing Studies at Roseau, Dominica July 16. St. John's: Caribbean Conference of Churches.

———. 1992. "Independence and the Social Crisis of Nationalism in Barbados." *Bulletin of Eastern Caribbean Affairs* 17, no. 3 (July-September): 1–18.

———. 2013. *Britain's Black Debt: Reparations for Caribbean Slavery and Native Genocide.* Kingston: University of the West Indies Press.

Belle, George. 1977. 'The Politics of Development: A Study in the Political-economy of Barbados', Manchester: PhD Dissertation, University of Manchester

———. 1988. "The Struggle for Political Democracy: The 1937 Riots." In *Emancipation III: Aspects of the Post Slavery Experience in Barbados*, edited by Woodville K. Marshall, 56–91. Bridgetown: Department of History, University of the West Indies and Barbados National Cultural Foundation.

———. 1994. "The Collapse of the Soviet System: Implications for the Caribbean Left." In *Crossroads of Empire: The Europe-Caribbean Connection 1492–1992*, edited by Alan Cobley, 94–110. Bridgetown: Department of History, University of the West Indies.

Benn, Denis. 1987. *Ideology and Political Development: The Growth and Development of Political Ideas in the Caribbean 1774–1983.* Kingston: Institute of Social and Economic Research, University of the West Indies.

Bernal, Martin. 1987. *Black Athena: The Afro-Asiatic Roots of Classical Civilization.* Vol. 1, *The Fabrication of Ancient Greece 1785–1985.* New Brunswick: Rutgers University Press.

Best, Lloyd. 1968. "Outline of a Model of Pure Plantation Economy." *Social and Economic Studies* 17, no. 3: 283–326.

———. 1971. "Constitutional Reform - Tapia's Proposals: Government and Politics in the West Indies, Trinidad and Tobago." *Tapia Pamphlets*, nos.4 and 5, Tunapuna: Tapia House Group.

Bgoya, Walter. and Goran Hyden. 1987. 'The State and the Crisis in Africa: In Search of a Second Liberation." *Development Dialogue*, Issue 2: 5–29.

Bluhm, William. 1978. *Theories of the Political System: Classics of Thought and Modern Political Analysis*, 3rd ed. Englewood Cliffs: Prentice Hall.

Boggs, James. 1968. *The American Revolution: Pages From a Negro Worker's Notebook.* New York: Modern Reader Paperbacks.

Bogues, Anthony. 1997. *Caliban's Freedom: The Early Political Thought of C.L.R. James*. London: Pluto Press.

Bracey, John. 1981. "Nello." *Urgent Tasks: Journal of the Revolutionary Left* 12 (Summer): 125.

Breckman, Warren. 1998. "Cornelius Castoriadis contra Postmodernism: Beyond the 'French Ideology'." In *French Politics and Society* 16 no. 2 (Spring): 30–42

Braun, Aurel and Richard Day.1990. "Gorbachevian contradictions." *Problems of Communism* 39 (May- June): 36–49.

Bruce, Deveron. 2019. "Mitigating the Democratic Deficit in Westminster: Prospects and Challenges of Techno-Democracy in the Commonwealth Caribbean." MPhil Thesis, University of the West Indies.

Buhle, Paul, ed., 1986a. *C.L.R. James: His Life and Work*. London: Allison and Busby.

———. 1986b. "Marxism in the U.S.A." In *C.L.R. James: His Life and Work*, edited by Paul Buhle, 81-194. London: Allison and Busby

———. 1988. *C.L.R. James: The Artist as Revolutionary*. London: Verso.

Cabral, Amilcar. 1969. *Revolution in Guinea: An African People's Struggle. Selected Texts*. London: Stage 1.

Cambridge, Alrick. 1992. "C.L.R. James: Freedom, Through History and Dialectics." In *Intellectuals in the Twentieth century Caribbean*. Vol. 1, *Spectre of the New Class: The Commonwealth Caribbean*, edited by Alistair Hennessy, 163–78. London: Macmillan Education.

Campbell, Horace. 1985. *Rasta and Resistance: From Marcus Garvey to Walter Rodney*. London: Hansib Publishing.

———. 1995. "C.L.R. James, Walter Rodney, and the Caribbean Intellectual". In *C.L.R. James: His Intellectual Legacies*, edited by Selwyn Cudjoe and William Cain, 405–31. Amherst: University of Massachusetts Press.

———. 2010. *Barrack Obama and Twenty-first century Politics: A Revolutionary Moment in the USA*. New York: Pluto Press.

CARICOM 2014. "CARICOM Ten Point Plan for Reparatory Justice." https://caricom.org/caricom-ten-point-plan-for-reparatory-justice/.

———. 2021. "Caricom African Leaders Identify Areas of Co-operation at Historic First Summit." https://caricom.org/caricom-african-leaders-identify-areas-of-co-operation-at-historic-first-summit/

Carmichael, Trevor and Justin Robinson. 1985. *The Essential Owen: Speeches and Statements of Professor The Hon. Owen S. Arthur.* Bridgetown: Miller Publishing Company.

Castoriadis, Cornelius. 1995. "C.L.R. James and the Fate of Humanity." In *C.L.R. James: His Intellectual Legacies*, edited by Selwyn Cudjoe and William Cain, 277–97. Amherst: University of Massachusetts Press.

Cheng, Evelyn. 2021. "Xi at Communist Party Anniversary: China won't Accept 'Sanctimonious Preaching' from Others." *CNBC*, July 1, 2017. https://www.cnbc.com/2021/07/01/china-ccp-anniversary-xi-speaks-at-100th-anniversary-of-communist-party.html

Chrome, Keith and James Williams. 2006. *The Lyotard Reader and Guide.* New York: Columbia University Press.

Coard, Bernard. 2018. *Forward Ever: Journey to a New Grenada: The Grenada Revolution* Vol. 2. Kingston: McDermott Publishing.

Cooper, Carolyn. 2018. "Winning the Fight for Public Beaches." *The Gleaner,* September 28, 2018. https://web5.jamaica-gleaner.com/article/commentary/20180930/carolyn-cooper-winning-fight-public-beaches.

———. 2021. "Managing Hellshire Beach Withdrawal Symptoms." *The Gleaner,* January 17, 2021. https://jamiaca-gleaner.com/article/commentary/20200117/carolyn-cooper-managong-hellshire-beach-withdrawal-symptoms.

Cornforth, Maurice. 1968. *The Open Philosophy and the Open Society: A Reply to Dr. Karl Popper's Refutations of Marxism.* London: Lawrence and Wishart.

———. 1971. *Dialectical Materialism: An Introduction.* 3 vols. New York: International Publishers.

Cripps, Louise. 1997. *C. L.R. James Memories and Commentaries.* New York: Cornwall Books.

Cudjoe, Selwyn. 1992. "The Audacity of it All: C.L.R. James's Trinidadian Background." In *C.L.R. James's Caribbean*, edited by Paget Henry and Paul Buhle, 39–55. London: MacMillan Caribbean.

———. 1997. "C.L.R. James and the Trinidad and Tobago Intellectual Tradition, Or Not Learning Shakespeare Under a Mango Tree". *The C.L.R. James Journal*, 5, no.1 (Winter): 4–43.

———. and William Cain, eds. 1995. *C.L.R. James: His Intellectual Legacies.* Amherst: University of Massachusetts Press.

Cummins, Ian. 1980. *Marx, Engels and National Movements*. London: Croom Helm..

De Tocqueville, Alexis. [1945] 1989. *Democracy in America*. Vol. 1. Reprint. New York: Alfred A. Knopf.

Dhondy, Farrukh. 2001. *C.L.R. James: A life*. New York: Pantheon Books..

Digital Business. 2020a. "The Black Lives Matter Movement Effect in the Caribbean – As Seen Online. (Jamaica Part 1), June 22, 2020. https://www.siliconcaribe.com/2020/06/22/the-black-lives-matter-movement-effect-in-the-caribbean-as-seen-online-pt-1/

Digital Business. 2020b. 'The Black Lives Matter Movement Effect in the Caribbean – As Seen Online. (Trinidad Part 2)", June 23, 2020. https://www.siliconcaribe.com/2020/06/23/the-black-lives-matter-movement-effect-in-the-caribbean-as-seen-online-trinidad-pt-2/

Diop, Cheikh.1974. *The African Origin of Civilization: Myth or Reality*. New York: Lawrence Hill Books.

——. 1981. "Origin of the Ancient Egyptians." In *General History of Africa*. Vol. 2, *Ancient Civilizations of Africa*, edited by G.K. Mokhtar, 27–51. Berkeley: UNESCO/Heinemann Educational Books Ltd.

——. 1987. *Precolonial Black Africa: A Comparative Study of the Political and Social Systems of Europe and Black Africa from Antiquity to the Formation of Modern States*. Westport: Lawrence Hill Books.

——. 1991. *Civilization or Barbarism: An Authentic Anthropology*. New York: Lawrence Hill Books.

Domínguez, Jorge, I. 1993. 'The Caribbean Question: Why has Liberal Democracy (Surprisingly) Flourished?', in Domínguez, Pastor and Worrell eds., *Democracy in the Caribbean: Political, Economic and Social Perspectives*, Baltimore: Johns Hopkins University Press, 1–25.

Douglas, Rachel. 2019. *Making the Black Jacobins: C.L.R. James and the Drama of History*. Durham: Duke University Press.

Drucker, Peter. 1969. *The Age of Discontinuity: Guidelines to Our Changing Society*. London: Heinemann.

Du Bois, W.E.B. 1965. *The World and Africa: An Inquiry into the Part Which Africa has Played in World History*. New York: International Publishers.

Duncan, Neville. 1989. "Foreword." In *Corporate Power in Barbados – the Mutual Affair: Economic Injustice in a Political Democracy*, by Hilary Beckles, xiv–xvi. Bridgetown: Lighthouse Communications

Duverger, Maurice. 1964. *Political Parties: Their Organization and Activity in the Modern State*. 3rd ed. rev. London: Methuen.

Eckhardt, Wolfgang. 2016. *The First Socialist Schism: Bakunin VS Marx in the International Workingmen's Association*. Translated by Robert M. Homsi, Jesse Cohn, Cian Lawless, Nestor McNab, and Bas Moreel. Oakland: PM Press.

Edie, Carlene. 1991. *Democracy by Default: Dependency and Clientelism in Jamaica*. Boulder: Lynne Rienner Publishers; Kingston: Ian Randle Publishers.

Emmanuel, Patrick. 1983. "Revolutionary Theory and Political Reality in the Eastern Caribbean", in *Journal of Inter-American Studies and World Affairs* 25, No. 2: 193–227.

———. 1992. *Elections and Party Systems in the Commonwealth Caribbean, 1944-1991*. St. Michael, Barbados: Caribbean Development Research Services.

Engels, Friedrich. 1978. *Anti-Duhring: Herr Eugen Duhring's Revolution in Science*. Moscow: Progress Publishers.

Fanon, Frantz. [1967] 1983. *The Wretched of the Earth*. Reprint, with preface by Jean-Paul Sartre. Middlesex: Penguin Books.

Farred, Grant, ed. 1996. *Rethinking C.L.R. James*. Cambridge, Mass: Blackwell Publishers.

Featherstone, David, Christopher Gair, Christian Høgsbjerg, and Andrew Smith, eds. 2018. *Marxism, Colonialism, and Cricket*. Durham: The C. L. R. James Archives /Duke University Press. Kindle Edition.

Featherstone, David, Christian Høgsbjerg, and Alan Rice, eds. 2022. *Revolutionary Lives of the Red and Black Atlantic Since 1917*. Manchester: Manchester University Press.

Finocchiaro, Maurice. 1988. *Gramsci and the History of Dialectical Thought*. New York: Cambridge University Press.

Foucault, Michel. 2002. *The Archeology of Knowledge*. Translated by A.M. Sheridan Smith. London: Routledge.

———. 2005. *The Order of Things: An Archeology of the Human Sciences*. 1st Published 1969. London: Routledge Classics.

Forsdick, Charles and Christian Høgsbjerg, eds. 2017. *The Black Jacobins Reader*, Durham: Duke University Press.

Fukuyama, Francis. 1992. *The End of History and the Last Man.* New York: Free Press.

———. 2000. "The End of History?" In *Globalization and the Challenges of a New Century: A Reader*, edited by Patrick O'Meara, Howard Mehlinger and Matthew Krain, 161–80. Bloomington: Indiana University Press.

Gair, Christopher, ed. 2006. *Beyond Boundaries: C.L.R. James and Post-Colonial Studies.* London: Pluto Press.

Garvey, Marcus. 1969. *Philosophy and Opinions of Marcus Garvey*, edited by Amy Jacques Garvey. New York: Atheneum.

Ghai, Dharam and C. Hewitt de Alcantara. 1989. "The Crisis of the 1980s in Africa, Latin America and the Caribbean: Economic Impact, Social Change and Political Implications." Paper presented at symposium, *Economic Crisis and Third World Countries: Impact and Response.* Kingston: ISER/UNRISD.

Gilligan, Chris and Niles, Nigel. 2022. "Raya Dunayaveskaya: the embodiment of the Red/Black Atlantic in Theory and Practice". In *Revolutionary Lives of the Red and Black Atlantic Since 1917*, edited by David Featherstone, Christian Høgsbjerg and Alan Rice, 217–34. Manchester: Manchester University Press.

Gittens, Thomas.1983. "Political Parties, Electoral Politics and Democracy in Post-colonial Societies: The Demobilization of Mass Mobilization." *Transition* 7: 14–30.

Glaberman, Martin. 1992. "The Marxism of C.L.R. James." *C.L.R. James Journal* 3, no. 1: 45–56.

Gonsalves, Camillo. 2019. *Globalised. Climatised. Stigmatised.* Kingstown: Strategy Forum, Inc.

Gonsalves, Ralph. 1980. "Some Theoretical Considerations on the Non-capitalist Path of Development: Africa and the Caribbean." Unpublished Paper Presented at Conference on Development and Under-development in the Black World, May 8–10. New York: Queen's College, City University of New York.

Gorbachev, Mikhail. 1988. *Perestroika: New thinking For Our Country and the World.* New York: Harper and Row.

Gould, Carol. 1988. *Rethinking Democracy: Freedom and Social Co-operation in Politics, Economy and Society.* Cambridge: Cambridge University Press.

Government of Saint Lucia. 2016. "Supplementary Agreement Between the Government of St. Lucia and DSH/Caribbean Star Ltd.". November 10, 2016.

Grenade, Wendy. 2010. "Retrospect: A view from Richmond Hill Prison: An interview with Bernard Coard." *Journal of Eastern Caribbean Studies* 35, nos. 3 and 4: 145–83.

———. 2015. "A Retrospective View from Richmond Hill: An Interview with Bernard Coard." In *The Grenada Revolution: Reflections and Lessons*, edited by Wendy Grenade, 59–86. Jackson: University Press of Mississippi.

Grimshaw, Anna.1991. *Popular Democracy and the Creative Imagination: The Writings of C.L.R. James 1950–1963.* New York: The C.L.R. James Institute and Cultural Correspondence.

———. 1992. "C.L.R. James: A Revolutionary Vision for the Twentieth Century." In *The C.L.R. James Reader*, edited by Anna Grimshaw, 1–22. Oxford: Blackwell Publishers.

———. and Keith Hart, eds. 1991. *C.L.R. James and the Struggle for Happiness.* New York: The C.L.R. James Institute and Cultural Correspondence.

Hackshaw, John. 1991. *Trade Union and Politics.* San Fernando: Vanguard.

Hart, Richard. 1989. *Rise and Organise: The Birth of the Workers and National Movements in Jamaica (1936–1939).* London: Karia Press.

Harvey, Franklyn. 1974. *The Rise and Fall of Party Politics in Trinidad and Tobago.* Toronto: New Beginning Movement..

Hector, Tim. 2000. "C.L.R. James and the Twenty-first Century." *C.L.R. James Journal* 8, no. 1: 126–33.

Henry, Paget.1992. "C.L.R. James and the Antiguan Left." *C.L.R. James's Caribbean*, edited by Paget Henry and Paul Buhle, 225–70. Durham: Duke University Press.

———. 2000. *Caliban's Reason: Introducing Afro-Caribbean Philosophy.* New York: Routledge.

Henry, Paget and Paul Buhle, eds. 1992. *C.L.R. James's Caribbean.* Durham: Duke University Press.

Hinds, Kristina. 2019. *Civil Society Organizations, Governance and the Caribbean Community.* Cham: Palgrave/Macmillan.

Hobbes, Thomas. 1914. *Leviathan.* London: J.M. Dent and Sons.

Hobsbawm, Eric. 1964. "Introduction." In *Precapitalist Economic Formations*, edited by Eric. J. Hobsbawm, 1–64. London: Lawrence and Wishart.

Hodge, Merle and Chris Searle. 1981. *Is Freedom We Making: The New Democracy in Grenada.* St. George's: Government Information Service.

Høgsbjerg, Christian. 2014. *C.L.R. James in Imperial Britain.* Durham and London: Duke University Press.

———. 2021. "C.L.R. James, the Mass Strike of 1919 in Colonial Trinidad, and the Case for West Indian Self-Government". In *The Global Challenge of Peace: 1919 as a Contested Threshold to a New World Order* (Studies in Labour History, no. 17), edited by Matt Perry, 91–106. Liverpool: Liverpool University Press.

Huntington, Samuel. 1996. *The Clash of Civilizations and the Remaking of World Order.* New York: Simon and Schuster.

———. 2000. "The Clash of Civilizations?" In *Globalization and the Challenges of a New Century: A Reader*, edited by Patrick O'Meara, Howard D. Mehlinger and Matthew Krain, 3–22. Bloomington: Indiana University Press.

Hunziker, Robert. 2018. "The Yellow Vest Insurgency – What's Next?" *Counterpunch*, December 14, 2018. https://www.counterpunch.org/2018/12/14/the-yellow-vest-insurgency-whats-next/.

International Marxist Tendency. 2018. "Marxism vs Identity Politics." *In Defence of Marxism*, September 28, 2018. Downloaded at: January 12, 2021. https://www.marxist.com/marxist-theory-and-the-struggle-against-alien-class-ideas.htm.

Jacobs, Richard and Ian Jacobs. 1979. *Grenada: The Route to Revolution.* Havana: Casa de Las Americas.

Jamadar, Peter. 1989. *The Mechanics of Democracy: Proportional Representation vs First-Past-the-Post.* Port-of-Spain: Inprint Caribbean.

James, C.L.R. 1937. *World Revolution 1917-1936: The Rise and Fall of the Communist International.* London: Martin Secker and Warburg.

———. 1940. "Marcus Garvey." *Labor Action* 4, no. 11, June 24: 3. Download from Marxists.org: J.R. Johnson: Marcus Garvey (June 1940) (marxists.org).

———. 1953. *Mariners, Renegades and Castaways: The Story of Herman Melville and the World We Live In.* New York: C.L.R. James.

———. 1960. *Modern Politics.* Port-of-Spain: PNM Publishing.

———. 1964. *Lenin, Trotsky and the Vanguard Party: A Contemporary View.* Detroit: Facing Reality.

———. 1966a. *The Making of the Caribbean Peoples*. Lecture Delivered at the Second Conference on West Indian Affairs, Montreal. Detroit: Facing Reality.

———. 1966b. *Perspectives and Proposals*. Detroit: Facing Reality.

———. 1969. *A History of Pan-African Revolt*. 2nd ed., rev. London: Drum and Spear Press.

———. 1971. "From Toussaint L'Ouverture to Fidel Castro." In *Black Society in the New World*, edited by Richard Frucht, 324–44. New York: Random House.

———. 1977a. *The Future in the Present. Selected Writings*. London: Allison and Busby.

———. 1977b. *Nkrumah and the Ghana Revolution*. London: Allison and Busby.

———. 1977c. "Towards the seventh: The Pan-Africanist Congress - Past, Present and Future." Address delivered at first congress of all African writers, Dakar, Senegal, January 8 1976. In *Not for Sale*, by Michael Manley. San Francisco: Editorial Consultants.

———. 1980a. *Notes on Dialectics: Hegel. Lenin. Marx*. New ed. London: Allison and Busby.

———. 1980b. *Spheres of Existence. Selected Writings*. London: Allison and Busby.

———. 1981. "The Birth of a Nation." In *Contemporary Caribbean: A Sociological Reader*, vol. 1, edited by Susan Craig, 3–35. Maracas: Susan Craig/The College Press.

———. 1982. "Walter Rodney and the Question of Power." In *Walter Rodney: Revolutionary and Scholar*, edited by Edward Alpers and Pierre Michel-Fontaine, 133–46. Los Angeles: Center for Afro-American Studies and African Studies Center, University of California.

———. 1984a. *At the Rendezvous of Victory. Selected Writings*. London: Allison and Busby.

———. 1984b. *C.L.R. James: 80th Birthday Lectures*, edited by Margaret Busby and Darcus. Howe. London: Race Today Publications.

———. 1985. "C.L.R. James Views Grenada: From Self-Defense to Self-Destruction". In *Intercontinental Press*, February 4, 61,

———. 1984c. *Party Politics in the West Indies*. San Juan: Inprint Caribbean.

———. 1986a. *Every Cook Can Govern and What is Happening Every Day*, edited by Jan Hillegas. Jackson: New Mississippi.

————. 1986b. *State Capitalism and World Revolution*. Written in Collaboration with Raya Dunayevskaya and Grace-Lee. Chicago: Charles H. Kerr Publishing Company.

————. 1989. *The Black Jacobins: Toussaint L'Ouverture and the San Domingo revolution*. 2nd ed. rev. New York: Random House.

————. 1992a. "Black Power." In *The C.L.R. James Reader*, edited by Anna Grimshaw, 362–74. Oxford: Blackwell Publishers.

————. 1992b. "The Class Struggle." In *The C.L.R. James Reader*, edited by Anna Grimshaw, 190–201. Oxford: Blackwell Publishers.

————. 1992c. "C.L.R. James: A Revolutionary Vision for the Twentieth Century". In *The C.L.R. James Reader*, edited by Anna Grimshaw, 1–22. Oxford: Blackwell Publishers.

————. 1992d. "Dialectical Materialism and the Fate of Humanity." In *The C.L.R. James Reader*, edited by Anna Grimshaw, 153–81. Oxford: Blackwell Publishers.

————. 1992e. "Letters on Politics." In *The C.L.R. James Reader*, edited by Anna Grimshaw, 263–80. Oxford: Blackwell Publishers.

————. 1992f "The Revolutionary Answer to the Negro problem in the U.S.A." In *The C.L.R. James Reader*, edited by Anna Grimshaw, 182–89. Oxford: Blackwell Publishers.

————. 1993. *Beyond A Boundary*, Durham: Duke University Press.

————. 2014. *The Life of Captain Cipriani: An Account of British Government in the West Indies (With the Pamphlet the Case for West Indian Self-Government)*, Durham: Duke University Press.

————. [1937] 2017. *World Revolution: 1917–1936: The Rise and Fall of the Communist International (*Edited and Introduced by Christian Høgsbjerg*)*, Durham: Duke University Press.

James, C.L.R., Freddie Forest, and Ria Stone.1972. *The Invading Socialist Society*. 2nd ed. Detroit: Bewick Editions.

James, C.L.R., Grace Lee, and Pierre Chaulieu. (1958) 1974. *Facing Reality*. Reprint. Detroit: Bewick Editions.

James, George. [1954] 1988. *Stolen Legacy: The Greeks Were Not the Authors of Greek Philosophy but the People of North Africa, Commonly Called the Egyptians*. Reprint. San Francisco: Julian Richardson Associates.

Joll, James. 1977. *Gramsci*. London: Fontana/Collins.

Jones, Owen, 2020. "Corbyn and Sanders May Have Gone, But They Have Radically Altered Our Politics". In *The Guardian* (Online), April 16. (Downloaded on June 6, 2022) https://

www.theguardian.com/commentisfree/2020/apr/16/corbyn-sanders-politics-radical-young-people

Joseph, Tennyson. 2011. *Decolonization in St. Lucia: Politics and Global Neo-liberalism 1945-2010*, Jackson: University of Mississippi Press.

——. 2014. "Book Review" of *We Move Tonight: The Making of the Grenada Revolution* by Joseph Ewart Layne. *Round Table: The Commonwealth Journal of International Affairs* 103, Issue 6 (December): 605–11.

——. 2015a. " 'An Extended Debate with Europe?', G.K. Lewis, Denis Benn, Paget Henry, and the Epistemological Challenge in the Writing of Caribbean Political Thought". In *Freedom, Power and Sovereignty: The Thought of Gordon. K. Lewis,* edited by Brian Meeks and Jermaine McCalpin, 46–68. Kingston: Ian Randle Publishers.

——. 2015b. "C.L.R. James and the Grenada Revolution: Lessons Learned and Future possibilities." In *The Grenada Revolution: Reflections and Lessons*, edited by Wendy Grenade, 152–79. Jackson: University Press of Mississippi.

——. 2019. "Peasant Revolts and Political Change in St. Lucia: The Rise and Fall of Peasant Movements, 1952–1957 and 1992–1997." In *Contemporary Left-wing Activism Vol 1. Demicracy, Participation and Dissent in a Global Context*, edited by John Michael Roberts and Joseph Ibrahim, 89–108. London: Routledge.

——. 2020. *Defending Caribbean Freedom: Press Articles 2010-2016*. (With Foreword by George Lamming). Christ Church, Barbados: Carib Research and Publications Inc

——. 2022. " 'European Marxist or Black Intellectual?': C.L.R. James and the Advancement of Marxism Beyond its Leninist-Russian Expression." In *Revolutionary Lives of the Red and Black Atlantic Since 1917,* edited by David Featherstone, Christian Høgsbjerg and Alan Rice, 235–54. Manchester: Manchester University Press.

Journal of Global Faultlines. 2020. "Editorial: Neoliberal Economic Model and Austerity Have Made Us Helpless in the Face of the COVID-19 Crisis." *Journal of Global Faultlines* 7, no.1, (June-August): 3–6.

King, Nicole. 2001. *C.L.R. James and Creolization: Circles of Influence.* Jackson: University Press of Mississippi.

King, Richard. 2006. "The Odd Couple: C.L.R. James, Hannah Arendt and the Return of Politics in the Cold War". In *Beyond Boundaries: C.L.R. James and Post-Colonial Studies*, edited by Christopher Gair, 89-107. London: Pluto Press.

———. 2011. "Hannah Arendt and the Concept of Revolution in the 1960s." *New Formations* 71, no. 1: 30–45.

Kiss, Arthur. 1982. *Marxism and Democracy: A Contribution to The Problems of the Marxist Interpretation of Democracy.* Budapest: Akademiai Kiado.

Korsch, Karl. 1937. "The Passing of Marxian Orthodoxy: Bernstein-Kautsky-Luxemburg-Lenin", *in International Council Correspondence* 3, Nos. 11 and 12. Downloaded from Marxists.org.
https://www.marxists.org/archive/korsch/1937/marxian-orthodoxy.htm

Krapivin, Vassily. 1985. *What is Dialectical Materialism?* Moscow: Progress Publishers.

Kristoff, Madeline. and Liz Panarelli. 2010. "Haiti: A Republic of NGOs?", in *United States Institute of Peace,* Peace Brief No. 23, April 26, 2010.
*PB 23 Haiti a Republic of NGOs.pdf (usip.org)

La Guerre, John. 1968. "Colonial Intellectuals in Politics: A Case Study of C.L.R. James." MSc Thesis, University of the West Indies.

Lai, Walton.1974. *The Present Stage of the Trinidad Revolution.* Tunapuna: New Beginning Movement.

———. 1992. "Trinidadian nationalism." In *C.L.R. James's Caribbean*, edited by Paget Henry and Paul Buhle, 174–209. Durham: Duke University Press.

Lane, Richard. 2009. *Jean Baudrillard.* London: Routledge.

Lalljie, Robert. 1990. "C.L.R. James: His Life Achievement and Thoughts." Transcripts of World Exclusive Radio Programme, Guyana Broadcasting Corporation, September 12–16, 1988.

Latin American Bureau. 1984. *Guyana: The Fraudulent Revolution.* London: Latin American Bureau.

Lawrence, Ken. 1981. "Interview with Darcus Howe in October 1980." *Urgent Tasks: Journal of The Revolutionary Left* 12, (Summer): 69–75.

Lenin, Vladimir. I. 1917. "Can the Bolsheviks Retain State Power?". In *Lenin's Collected Works* Volume 26 1972 (87–136). Moscow: Progress Publishers (Retrieved Online).

https://www.marxists.org/archive/lenin/works/1917/oct/01.htm

———. 1943. *State and Revolution.* New York: International Publishers.

———. 1969. *What is to be Done?: Burning Questions of Our Movement.* New York: International Publishers.

———. 1977. *Selected Works.* Volume 1. Moscow: Progress Publishers.

Lewis, Linden. 1990. "The Politics of Race in Barbados." *Bulletin of Eastern Caribbean Affairs* 15, No. 6: 32–45.

———, ed. 2015. *Caribbean Sovereignty, Development and Democracy in an Age of Globalization.* New York: Routledge.

Liebman, Marcel. 1975. *Leninism Under Lenin.* London: Merlin Press.

Lindahl, Folke. 2001. "Caribbean Diversity and Ideological Conformism: The Crisis of Marxism in the English-speaking Caribbean." In *New Caribbean Thought*, edited by Brian Meeks and Folke Lindahl, 309–24. Mona: University of the West Indies Press.

Lindsay, Louis. 1975. *The Myth of Independence: Middle Class Politics and Non-Mobilization in Jamaica.* Working Paper No. 6. Mona, Jamaica: Institute of Social and Economic Research, University of the West Indies.

Locke, John.1924. *Of Civil Government: Two Treatises.* London: J.M. Dent and Sons.

Luard, Evan. 1979. *Socialism Without the State.* London: The Macmillan Press.

Luxemburg, Rosa.1961. *The Russian Revolution and Leninism or Marxism?* Ann Arbor: University of Michigan Press.

———. 1971. *Selected Political Writings.* Edited and Introduced by Dick Howard. New York: Monthly Review Press.

Lyotard, Jean-François. 1996. "The Post-modern Condition: A Report on Knowledge." In *From Modernism to Post-Modernism: An Anthology*, edited by Lawrence Cahoone, 481–513. Oxford: Blackwell Publishers.

Magee, Bryan. 1975. *Popper.* London: Fontana/Collins.

Maingot, Anthony. 2012. "Discovering One's Own C.L.R. James." Review of *C.L.R. James and the Study of Culture*, by Andrew Smith and *You Don't Play With Revolution: The Montreal Lectures of C.L.R. James*, by David Austin. *New West Indian Guide* 86, no. 3–4: 291–97 https://brill.com/view/journals/nwig/86/3-4/nwig.86.issue-3-4.xml.

Mandel, Ernest. 1975. "Liebman and Leninism". In *Marxist's Internet Archive* (From *The Socialist Register* 1975, 95–114) (Downloaded on June 13, 2022). https://www.marxists.org/archive/mandel/1975/xx/liebman.html

Marable, Manning.1987. *African and Caribbean Politics: From Kwame Nkrumah to Maurice Bishop*. London: Verso.

MARHO - The Radical Historians Organisation.1983. *Visions of History*. Manchester: Manchester University Press.

Mars, Perry. 1998. *Ideology and Change: The Transformation of the Caribbean Left*. Kingston and Detroit: The Press UWI and Wayne State University Press.

Marshall, Don.1992. "The Trade Union Dilemma in a Changing World Economy." In *Bulletin of Eastern Caribbean Affairs* 17, no. 4: 6–13.

Martin, Tony.1984. "C.L.R. James and the Race/Class Question." In *The Pan-African Connection: From Slavery to Garvey and Beyond*. Dover, Massachusetts: The Majority Press.

——. [1976] 1986. *Race First: The Ideological and Organizational Struggles of Marcus Garvey and the Universal Negro Improvement Association*. Reprint, 1st edition. Dover, Massachusetts: The Majority Press.

Marx, Karl. 1906. *Capital: A Critique of Political Economy*. New York: The Modern Library, Random House.

——. 1964. *Precapitalist Economic Formations*. With Introduction by Eric.J. Hobsbawm. London: Lawrence and Wishart.

——. 1970. *A Contribution to the Critique of Political Economy*, edited by Maurice Dobb. Moscow: Progress Publishers.

——. and Friedrich Engels. 1968. *The Communist Manifesto*. New York: Monthly Review Press.

Marx, Karl and Friedrich Engels. 1974. *The German Ideology*, edited C.J. Arthur. London: Lawrence and Wishart.

Mazrui, Ali.1991. '*The World with One Superpower: Is It a More Dangerous Place*?. Bridgetown: Central Bank of Barbados.

McAfee, Kathy. 1991. *Storm Signals: Structural Adjustment and Development in the Caribbean*. London: Zed Books.

McComie, Val.1993. "It's About Time We Had True Democracy." *Sunday Sun*, July 11, 1993: 10A.

McLemee, Scott. and P. LeBlanc, eds. 1994. *C.L.R. James and Revolutionary Marxism: Selected Writings of C.L.R. James 1934–1949*. New York: Humanity Books.

McLeod, Errol.1988. *Towards a New Peoples' Order:* San Fernando: Vanguard Publishing.

Meeks, Brian. 1994. "Re-reading the Black Jacobins: James, the Dialectic, and the Revolutionary Conjuncture." *Social and Economic Studies* 43, no. 3: 75–103.

———. 2001. "Arguments Within What's Left of the Left: James, Watson and the Question of Method." *C.L.R. James Journal* 8, no. 2, (Fall): 152–77.

Meeks, Brian and Folke Lindhal, eds. 2001. *New Caribbean Thought.* Mona: The University of the West Indies Press.

———. and Kate Quinn, eds. 2018. *Beyond Westminster In The Caribbean.* Kingston: Ian Randle.

Melotti, Umberto. 1977. *Marx and the Third World.* London: The Macmillan Press.

Merquior, Jose. G. 1991. *Foucault.* London, Fontana Press.

Mészáros, Istvan. 1987. "The Division of Labour and the Post-capitalist State." *Monthly Review* 39, no. 3: 80–108.

Michels, Robert. 1962. *Political Parties: A Sociological Study of the Oligarchical Tendencies of Modern Democracy.* New York: Collier Macmillan Publishers.

Miliband, Ralph.1982. *Capitalist Democracy in Britain.* London: Oxford University Press.

———. 1983. *Class Power and State Power.* London: Verso.

———. 1991a. "Socialism in Question." *Monthly Review* 42, no. 10: 16–26.

———. 1991b. "What Comes After Communist Regimes?." In *The Socialist Register: Communist Regimes - the Aftermath*, edited by Ralph Miliband and Leo Panitch, 375–89. London: The Merlin Press.

Mill, John S.1975. *Three Essays: On Liberty; Representative Government; The Subjection of Women*, London: Oxford University Press.

Millette, James.1974. "Socialism: Theory and Practice." Paper Presented at Seminars on Contemporary Issues, no. 4, April 20, 1974. St. Augustine, Trinidad. Faculty of Social Sciences, University of the West Indies.

———. 1995. "C.L.R. James and the Politics of Trinidad and Tobago, 1938-1970." In *C.L.R. James: His Intellectual Legacies*, edited by Selwyn Cudjoe and William Cain, 328–47. Amherst: University of Massachusetts Press.

Mills, Charles. 1991. "Marxism and Caribbean Development: A Contribution to Rethinking." In *Rethinking Development*, edited by Judith Wedderburn, 14–35. Mona: Consortium Graduate School, University of the West Indies.

———. 1998. *Blackness Visible: Essays on Philosophy and Race*. Ithaca and London: Cornell University Press.

Milne, Anthony. 1982. "The Caribbean – A Very Special Place: Final Part of Anthony Milne's Chat With C.L.R. James". *Express Sunday*, December 12, 1982: 7–9.

Muchlinski, Peter. 2000. "The Rise and Fall of the Multilateral Agreement on Investment: Where Now?." *The International Lawyer* 34, no. 3 (Fall): 1033–53.

Munroe, Trevor. 1972. *The Politics of Constitutional Decolonization: Jamaica 1944–62*. Mona: Institute of Social and Economic Research, University of the West Indies.

———. 1990. *Jamaican Politics: A Marxist Perspective in Transition*. Kingston: Heinemann Publishers Caribbean.

Murdoch, Adlai 2021. "Introduction: Non-Sovereignty and the Neo-Liberal Challenge: Contesting Economic Exploitation in the Eastern Caribbean." In *The Struggle of Non-Sovereign Caribbean Territories: Neo-Liberalism Since the French Antillean Antillean Uprising of 2009*, (Kindle Version) edited by Alai Murdoch, 1–49. New Brunswick: Rutgers University Press.

———. and Paget Henry. 2021. "Neo-Liberalism and Caribbean Economies: Martinique, Guadeloupe and the Exploitative Strategies of Metropolitan Capital." In *The Struggle of Non-Sovereign Caribbean Territories: Neo-Liberalism Since the French Antillean Antillean Uprising of 2009*, (Kindle Version) edited by Alai Murdoch, 182–216. New Brunswick: Rutgers University Press.

Murray, Jim. 1999. "The C.L.R. James Institute and Me." *International Journal of Post-colonial Studies* 1, no. 3: 389–96.

Nangwaya, Ajamu. 2017. "Caribbean Reparations Movement Must Put Capitalism on Trial." *Black Agenda Report* April 19, 2017.

National Integrity Action. 2021. "Professor Trevor Munroe - National Integrity Action." niajamaica.org.

New Jewel Movement. 1973. *New Jewel Movement Manifesto of 1973*. St. Georges: New Jewel Movement.

Nielson, Aldon. 1997. *C.L.R. James: A Critical Introduction* Jackson: University of Mississippi Press.

Now Grenada. 2020. "Protest Rally Against Racist Police Violence," *Now Grenada*, June 8, 2020. https://www.nowgrenada.com/2020/06/protest-rally-against-racist-police-violence/

Nwafor, Azinna. 1973. 'The Revolutionary as Historian: Padmore and Pan-Africanism - A critical Introduction." In *Pan-Africanism or Communism* by George Padmore, xxvi–xxlii. New York: Doubleday.

Ohiorhenuan, John F. 1979. "Dependence and Non-capitalist Development in the Caribbean: Historical Necessity and Degrees of Freedom." *Science and Society* 43, no. 4: 386–408.

Ollman, Bertell. 1986. "The Meaning of Dialectics." *Monthly Review* 38, no. 6: 42–55

Osborne, David and Ted Gaebler. 1993. *Reinventing Government: How the Entrepreneurial Spirit is Transforming the Public Sector.* New York: Plume Penguin Group.

Oxaal, Ivar. 1968. *Black Intellectuals Come to Power: The Rise of Creole Nationalism in Trinidad and Tobago* . International Studies in Political and Social Change Series. Edited by Wendel Bell. Cambridge, Massachusetts: Schenkman Publishing Company, Inc.

———. 1982. *Black Intellectuals and the Dilemmas of Race and Class in Trinidad.* Cambridge, Massachusetts: Schenkman Books.

Padmore, George. 1972. *Pan-Africanism or Communism*. New York: Doubleday.

Parris, Carl. 1983. "Resource Ownership and the Prospects for Democracy." In *The Newer Caribbean: Decolonization, Democracy and Development*, edited by Paget Henry and Carl Stone, 313–26. Pennsylvania: Institute for study of Human Issues.

Patterson, Percival. 2019. *My Political Journey: Jamaica's Sixth Prime Minister.* Kingston: The University of the West Indies Press.

Popper, Karl. 1960. *The Poverty of Historicism.* London: Routledge and Kegan Paul.

———. 1962. *The Open Society and Its Enemies.* Vol. 2, *The High tide of Prophecy: Hegel and Marx.* London: Routledge and Kegan Paul.

Post, Ken. 1978. *Arise Ye Starvelings: The Jamaican Labour* Rebellion of 1938 and Its Aftermath. The Hague: Martinus Hijhoff.

Plys, Kristin. 2015. "Book Review: Workers; Self-Management in the Caribbean – The Writings of Joseph Edwards." In *International Journal of Comparative Sociology* 46, Issue 3–4: 299–301.

Quest, Matthew. 2017. "New Beginning Movement: Coordinating Council of Revolutionary Alternatives for Trinidad and the Caribbean." *C.L.R. James Journal* 23, nos. 1–2 (Fall): 297–305.

———. 2017b. "On Both Sides of the Haitian Revolution? Rethinking Direct Democracy and National Liberation in the Black Jacobins." In *The Black Jacobins Reader*, edited by Charles Forsdick and Christian Høgsbjerg, 235–55. (Kindle Version) Durham: Duke University Press.

Raghavan, Charkarvati. 1990. *Recolonisation: GATT, the Uruguay Round and the Third World*. London: Zed Books.

Rappeport, Alan. 2021. "Finance Leaders Reach Global Tax Deal Aimed at Ending Profit Sharing." *The New York Times,* June 5, 2021. (Downloaded on June 13, 2022). https://www.nytimes.com/2021/06/05/us/politics/g7-global-minimum-tax.html.

Rennie, Bukka. 2017. *Remembering and Understanding C.L.R. James*. Mayaro: Sene Press.

Renton, Dave. 2007. *C.L.R. James: Cricket's Philosopher King*. London: Haus Publishing.

Richards, Glen. 1992. *C.L.R. James and the Question of Black Self-determination in the United States*. Paper presented at 17th Annual Third World Conference, April 4–6, 1992. Detroit: Third World Conference Foundation.

Riviere, Bill.1990. *State Systems in the Eastern Caribbean: Historical and Contemporary Features*. Kingston: Institute of Social and Economic Research, University of the West Indies.

Robinson, Cedric.1983. *Black Marxism: The Making of the Black Radical Tradition*. London: Zed Books.

———. 1992. "C.L.R. James and the World System.", *C.L.R. James Journal* 3, no. 1: 57–73.

Robinson, Tracy. 2006. "Law, Freedom and Politics: The Praxis of Political Citizenship." In *Enjoying Power: Eugenia Charles and Political Leadership in the Commonwealth Caribbean*, edited by Eudine Barriteau and Alan Cobley, 31–69. Mona: University of the West Indies Press.

Roderick, Rick. 1995. "Further Adventures of the Dialectic." In *C.L.R. James: His Intellectual Legacies*, edited by Selwyn

Cudjoe and William E. Cain, 205–11. Amherst: University of Massachusetts Press.

Rodney, Walter. 1969. *The Groundings with My Brothers*, London: Bogle-L'Ouverture Publications.

———. 1981. *Marx in the Liberation of Africa*. Georgetown: Working Peoples' Alliance.

———. 1986. 'The African Revolution." In *C.L.R. James: His Life and Work*, edited by Paul Buhle, 30–48. London: Allison and Busby.

———. 2018. *The Russian Revolution: A View from the Third World*. Edited and Introduced by Robin D.G. Kelley with Foreword by Vijay Prashad. London and New York: Verso.

Rosengarten, Frank. 2008. *Urbane Revolutionary: C.L.R. James and the Struggle for a New Society*. Jackson: University Press of Mississippi.

Roux, Edward. 1964. *Time Longer Than Rope: The Black Man's Struggle for Freedom in South Africa*. 2nd ed. London: The University of Wisconsin Press.

Ryan, Selwyn. 1989. *The Disillusioned Electorate: The Politics of Succession in Trinidad and Tobago*. Port-of-Spain: Inprint Caribbean.

Sabine, George H. and Thomas L. Thorson. 1973. *A History of Political Theory*. 4th ed., rev. Orlando: Holt, Rinehart and Winston.

Saint Lucia Labour Party. 1997. *Election Manifesto. New Visions, New Directions for a New Century*. Castries: St. Lucia Labour Party.

Saint Lucia Times 2016. "Protest outside parliament against DSH deal", December 20, 2016. https://stluciatimes.com/2016/12/20/protest-outside-parliament-dsh-deal.

Saturday Sun. 2022. "Dame Sandra, Kenyatta in Bilateral Talks". In *Saturday Sun*, June 11, 5.

Silfry, Michael. 2015. *Wikileaks and the Age of Transparency*. With a Foreword by Andrew Rasiej. New York: OR Books.

Singh, Paul G. 1972. *Local Democracy in the Commonwealth Caribbean: A Study of Adaptation and Growth*. Port-of-Spain: Longman Caribbean.

Singham, Archie W. 1970. "C.L.R. James on the Black Jacobin Revolution in San Domingo: Towards a Theory of Black Politics." *Savacou* 1: 82–96.

Slovo, Joe. 1990. "Has Socialism Failed?" *African Communist: Journal of The South African Communist Party* 121 (2nd Quarter): 25–51.

Sprague, Jeb and Sreerekha Sathi. 2020. 'Transnational Amazon: Labor Exploitation and the Rise of E-commerce in South Asia." In *The Cost of Free Shipping: Amazon in the Global Economy*, edited by Jake Alimahomed and Ellen Reese, 50–65. London: Pluto Press.

Stanton, Fred, ed. 1980. *Fighting Racism in World War II. C.L.R. James, George Brietman, Edgar Keemar and Others.* New York: Monad Press.

Stiglitz, Joseph. 2019. "The End of Neo-liberalism and the Rebirth of History." *Social Europe,* Vol. 26 (November) (online). https://www.socialeurope.eu/the-end-of-neoliberalism-and-the-rebirth-of-history.

Stocker, Barry. 2006. *Derrida on Deconstruction.* Routledge Philosophy Guidebooks Series. London: Routledge.

Surtees, Joshua. 2019. "Sun, Sea, Sex and No Sandals - Trinidad and Tobago." *Newsday,* January 22, 2019. https://newsday.co.tt/2019/01/22/sun-sea-sex-and-no-sandals

Teelucksingh, Jerome. 2010. "Beyond Blackness: C.L.R. James the Working Class Messiah." *The C.L.R. James Journal* 16, no.1 (Spring): 67–82.

The White House. n.d. 'Rescuing the American Auto Industry." *The White House (President Barrack Obama) Briefing Room.* Rescuing the American Auto Industry | The White House (archives.gov)

Thomas, Clive Y. 1978. "'The Non-capitalist Path' As Theory and Practice of Decolonization and Socialist Transformation." *Latin American Perspectives* 5, no. 2: 10–28.

———. 1983. "State Capitalism in Guyana: An assessment of Burnham's Co-operative Socialist Republic." In *Crisis in the Caribbean*, edited by Fitzroy Ambursely and Robin Cohen, 27–48. London: Educational Books.

———. 1988. *The Poor and the Powerless: Economic Policy and Change in the Caribbean.* London: Latin American Bureau.

———. 1989. "Economic Crisis and the Commonwealth Caribbean: Impact and Response." *Caribbean Affairs* 2, no. 4: 21–48.

Trotman, Althea. 1993. "A C.L.R. James/Gramsci Conversation in Hegemony." *C.L.R. James Journal* 4, no. 1 (Winter): 44–69.

Trotsky, Leon. [1932] 1965. *The History of the Russian Revolution.* London: Victor Gollancz.

———. [1937] 1972. *The Revolution Betrayed: What is the Soviet Union and Where is it Going?* New York: Pathfinder Press.

Toffler, Alvin. [1970] 1990. *Future Shock.* Reprint. New York: Bantam Books.

———. 1981. *The Third Wave.* London: Pan Books.

———. 1991. *Power Shift: Knowledge, Wealth and Violence at the Edge of the Twentieth Century.* New York: Bantam Books.

Ulyanovsky, R. 1974. *Socialism and the Newly Independent Nations.* Moscow: Progress Publishers.

Wallerstein, Immanuel. 1984. *The Politics of the World Economy. The States, the Movements and the Civilisations. Essays By Immanuel Wallerstein.* London: Cambridge University Press.

Watson, Hilbourne. 1990a. "Recent Attempts at Industrial Restructuring in Barbados." In *Latin American Perspectives* 17, no. 1: 10–32.

———. 1990b. "The Question of the Black Middle Class in Barbados." *Bulletin of Eastern Caribbean Affairs* 15, no. 6: 16–31.

———. 2001. "Themes in Liberalism, Modernity, Marxism, Postmodernism and Beyond." In *New Caribbean Thought*, edited by Brian Meeks and Folke Lindahl, 355–94. Mona: University of the West Indies Press.

Williams, Eric. 1966. *Capitalism and Slavery.* New York: Capricorn Books.

Wilson, Basil. 1986. "The Caribbean Revolution." In *C.L.R. James: His life and Work*, edited by Paul Buhle, 22–29. London: Allison and Busby.

Woods, Alan. 2018. "Fukuyama's Second Thoughts: 'Socialism Ought to Come Back'." *In Defence of Marxism*, October 24, 2018. https://www.marxist.com/fukuyama-s-second-thoughts-socialism-ought-to-come-back.htm

Worcester, Kent. 1983. *C.L.R. James and the American Century: 1938-1953.* San German: Caribbean Institute and Study Centre of Latin America.

———. 1992. "'A Victorian with a Rebel Seed'": C.L.R. James and the Politics of Intellectual Engagement." In *Intellectuals in the Twentieth Century Caribbean.* Vol. 1, *Spectre of the New Class: The Commonwealth Caribbean*, edited by Alistair Hennessy, 115–30. London: Macmillan Education.

———. 1996. *C.L.R. James: A Political Biography.* Albany: State University of New York Press.

Worrell, Rodney. 2020. *George Padmore's Black Internationalism.* Kingston: The University of the West Indies Press.

Xiong, Yong and Tricia Escobedo. 2021. "China has Successfully Landed a Rover on Mars, State Media Says." *CNN,* May 15, 2021. https://edition.cnn.com/2021/05/14/world/china-mars-rover-landing-scn/index.html.

Public and Personal Correspondences

James, C.L.R. 1982. C.L.R. James to Michael Manley, May 10, 1982 (C.L.R. James Archives, Alma Jordan Library, St. Augustine, UWI, Trinidad).

James, C.L.R. 1983. C.L.R. James to Political Bureau of NJM, October 17,1982 (C.L.R. James Archives, Alma Jordan Library, St. Augustine, UWI, Trinidad).

Index

www.ingramcontent.com/pod-product-compliance
Lightning Source LLC
Chambersburg PA
CBHW032343280326
41935CB00008B/435